Fighting for the Soul of

BRAZIL

Fighting for the Soul of

BRAZIL

Edited by Kevin Danaher and Michael Shellenberger

Monthly Review Press
New York, NY

Text design and page layout by Kevin Danaher

Library of Congress Cataloging-in-Publication Data

Fighting for the Soul of Brazil/edited by Kevin Danaher and Michael
  Shellenberger
      p.cm.
    Includes bibliographical references and index.
    ISBN 0-85345-923-1. — ISBN 0-85345-924-X (pbk.)
    1. Brazil—Social conditions—1985- 2. Brazil—Economic
conditions—1985- 3. Brazil—Politics and government—1985-
4. Political corruption—Brazil.
I. Danaher, Kevin, 1950-. II. Shellenberger, Michael.
HN283.5.F45 1995
306'.0981—dc20   95-5139

Monthly Review Press
122 West 27th Street
New York, NY 10001

Manufactured in the United States of America

10 9 8 7 6 5 4 3 2 1

Table of Contents

Acknowledgments   ix

Introduction Michael Shellenberger and Kevin Danaher   1

Section I: International Capital, Local Economies and Popular Resistance

1. **Who Benefits and Who Bears the Damage Under World Bank/IMF-Led Policies** Maria Clara Couto Soares   8

2. **The Eternal Conquest** Stephen G. Bunker   17

3. **Capital Flight** Carlos Ravelo   33

4. **Forced Labor Revisited** Maryknoll Newsnotes   36

5. **The Labor Movement in Brazil** Stan Gacek   39

6. **Labor's Development Critique** Multinational Monitor   47

7. **New Directions for the Union Struggle** Paulino Montejo   51

8. **Brazilian Guns Flood the Market** Rodney Mello   56

9. **Hunger and Democracy Don't Mix: An Interview with Herbert 'Betinho' de Souza** Michael Shellenberger   58

Section II: The Politics of Corruption and the Corruption of Democracy

10. **The 1994 Brazilian Elections and US-Brazil Relations** Ken Silverstein   64

11. **Their Bright Shining Knight in Brazil** Ken Silverstein and Alexander Cockburn   70

12. **Brazil's Controlled Purge: The Impeachment of President Collor** Theotonio dos Santos   75

13. **"Don't Kidnap Me, I'm a Professor"** Marshall Berman   84

14. **Beware the Tanks** Carlos Ravelo   93

15. **The Black Hole** Rodney Mello   98

Section III: Destruction and Its Alternatives in the Amazon

16. **Jungle of Myths** New Internationalist   101

17. **What Future for Amazonia?** Ignacy Sachs   103

18. **The Rubber Tappers Under Fire Again** Linda Perney   109

19. **Prostitution Comes to the Indigenous Amazon**   113
    Gilberto Dimenstein

20. **Popular Struggle and the Preservation of the Amazon**   116
    Pastoral Land Commission

21. **Extractive Reserves: Economic and Social Alternatiaves**   123
    for the Tropical Rainforest Marcus La Tour

22. **Clowns Up the River** Charles Johnson   130

Section IV: Streetchildren and the Struggle for Justice

23. **Kids Out of Place** Nancy Scheper-Hughes and   139
    Daniel Hoffman

24. **Toil for Tots** Carlos Ravelo   152

25. **Targeted for Death** Paul Jeffrey   154

Section V: The View from the Grassroots

26. **In Brazil, Sterilizing Women is the Method of Choice**   163
    Jon Christensen

27. **In Live-and-Let-Live Land, Gay People are Slain**   168
    James Brooke

28. Brazil's Women-run Police Stations Fight the Odds   172
Thais Corrall

29. Brazil's Black Consciousness Movement   John Burdick   174

30. Pastoral Agents Movement Raises Black Awarenes   184
Ken Serbin

31. The Role of Liberation Theology   James S. Torrens   189

32. Activists Take on AIDS   Elizabeth Station   197

Section VI: The Workers Party and the Popular Alternative

33. Fighting for the Soul of Brazil   John Powers   204

34. Interview with Lula   James Bruce   223

35. Brazil's Workers Party: Socialism as Radical Democracy   232
Margaret Keck

36. Black, Female and *Favelada*: Benedita Speaks   244
Michael Shellenberger

37. The Rise of the Workers Party: An Interview with   249
Marco Aurélio Garcia   Michael Shellenberger

38. The Need for International Solidarity: An Interview   255
with Aloisio Mercadante   Michael Shellenberger

Conclusion   Michael Shellenberger and Kevin Danaher   257

Resources   261

Contributors   263

Index   266

About Global Exchange

Brazil

International boundary
Regional Division boundary
State/Territory boundary

Miles 0   200   400   600   800   1000
Kms 0   400   800   1200   1600

VENEZUELA

GUYANA
SURINAM
FRENCH GUIANA

COLOMBIA

TERRITORIO DE RORAIMA

TERRITORIO DO AMAPA

NORTH EAST

Belem

RIO GRANDE DO NORTE

Manaus

AMAZONAS   **NORTH**   PARA   MARANHAO   CEARA

PARAIBA
PERNAMBUCO

PIAUI

ACRE

ALAGOAS
SERGIPE

PERU

RONDONIA

São Felix de Araguaia

GOIAS

BAHIA

MATO GROSSO

Barra do Garças   Brasília

CENTRE WEST

Goiânia   MINAS GERAIS

MATO GROSSO DO SUL

BOLIVIA

Ribeirão Bonito

SAO PAULO

Belo Horizonte   ESPIRITO SANTO

São Paulo   RIO DE JANEIRO

Rio de Janeiro

PARAGUAY

PARANA   **SOUTH EAST**

CHILE

SOUTH

SANTA CATARINA

PACIFIC OCEAN

RIO GRANDE DO SUL

ATLANTIC OCEAN

ARGENTINA

URUGUAY

Acknowledgments

This book is dedicated to the many Brazilians who are building a new society without fear of being happy.

The editors would like to express our sincerest thanks to the following people who helped with various aspects of researching, editing and producing this book: Monica Barini, Amy Bohme, Johnna Bossout, Kerry Danaher, Ann Gallick, Amy Harter, Tracey Ann McLachlan and Maureen Vickers. Special thanks to Douglas Watson for the many hours and insights he put into this book.

Many thanks and *abraços* to those in Brazil who, in the midst of their busy schedules, took time out to be interviewed for this book. *Mil beijos* for Maria Luisa Mendonça who travelled with Michael in Brazil during the making of her film on the Workers Party: she is a wonderful filmmaker and *companheira*. Paulo Vannuchi at PT headquarters in São Paulo laid the groundwork for their visit and Dulce Maria Pereira was their delightful *guia* through the storm of the 1994 campaign. Thanks to Hercília de Camargo and Pedro Dalcero at the Brazilian Institute for Social and Economic Affairs (IBASE), for scheduling interviews with IBASE's bright researchers. Thanks to Marcia Meireles and Fernanda Pompeu in São Paulo, Suely Mendonça in Rio, and Eduardo Borges in São Luis for sharing their homes, their wit and their wisdom.

Our deepest gratitude to the many activists of the Brazil Action Solidarity Exchange (BASE) who are bridging popular movements in the U.S. and Brazil, and to the Brazil Information Committee (BIC) for raising awareness about the Workers Party. Caius Brandão and Jocelyn Weiss provided BIC with its spirited activism. Eric Leenson of EarthTrade deserves special mention for his commitment to BIC and the Landless Workers Movement (MST) in Brazil.

Special thanks to our many colleagues at Global Exchange who prove that fighting the good fight can be rewarding and fun.

We would like to thank the following publications and organizations for permission to reprint the chapters listed: *America* (Chapter 31), *Audubon* (Chapter 18), *CounterPunch* (Chapter 11), *Dissent* (Chapter 13), Latin American Information Agency (Chapter 7), *Maryknoll Newsnotes* (Chapter 4), *Ms.* magazine (Chapter 28), *Multinational Monitor* (Chapter 6), *National Catholic Reporter* (Chapter 30), *New Internationalist* (Chapter 16), *News from Brazil* (Chapters 3, 8, 14, 15, 24), *The New York Times* (Chapter 27), North American Congress on Latin America, *Report on the Americas* (Chapters 2, 12, 19, 23, 29, 32, 35), *North South* (Chapter 34), Pastoral Land Commission (Chapter 20), *The Progressive* (Chapter 26), Rainforest Action Network (Chapter 21), UNESCO Courier (Chapter 17), *Whole Earth Review* (Chapter 22).

Introduction

Michael Shellenberger
and Kevin Danaher

Perhaps more than any other country in the global south, Brazil epitomizes the conflict between two competing visions of development. The dominant vision is defined by the World Bank, the International Monetary Fund (IMF) and transnational corporations. It is a model that emphasizes free markets and keeping governments focused on assisting capital and keeping the working class in line. It is a model that has dominated Brazilian life for decades. And it is a model that has burdened Brazil—despite that country's fantastic natural wealth—with some of the most disgraceful inequality and human suffering in modern history.

There is a competing, people-centered model of development that is being constructed in every corner of the globe by community groups, peasant associations, trade unions, women's organizations and environmental groups. These forces are relatively weak in terms of money and military power but they possess a moral authority from their ability to embrace democracy in its true meaning from the Greek roots *demos* (people) and *kratos* (rule). They promote a model of development that seeks to democratize not only government structures but investment decision-making as well.

Vast Wealth and Vast Inequality

Brazil is abundantly endowed with natural and human wealth. Its gross national product (GNP) is several times greater than other

wealthy countries of the Third World such as Saudi Arabia and
South Africa. Its economy is nearly twice the size of India's. Its
area of cropland ranks second in the western hemisphere, behind
the United States. Brazil out-produces the United States in cattle,
horses, sheep and goats. Its farm output exceeds that of agricultural powerhouses such as France. Brazil is a major world producer of coffee, soybeans, corn, cocoa, sugar, orange juice, animal
products and wood.

Brazil's area of natural forest (more than 1.2 billion acres) is
greater than that of Canada and the United States combined. Yet
Brazil destroys more acreage of forest per year (nearly 5 million
acres) than any other country on earth.

Despite Brazil's fantastic agricultural abundance, it has millions
of people going hungry. As Herbert 'Betinho' de Souza points outs
in Chapter 9, there are agricultural storehouses that must be guarded
round-the-clock because the food they store is destined for export
and might be seized by the hungry people who live in the vicinity.

Of course, not all of Brazil's wealth leaves the country; the Brazilian elite get their 'cut' of the take as well. Brazil is well-known
for being one of the most unequal societies on earth. Even India, a
textbook example of a national class-system, is a far less divided
society. While India's richest 20 percent of the population controls
five times the wealth of the poorest 20 percent, Brazil's richest 20
percent holds *26* times the wealth of the poorest 20 percent. Brazil's
rich children are educated at private schools in Europe. Brazil's
poor children are educated on the streets of Brazil.

While elites spend awesome amounts of money on grand villas
and foreign vacations, nearly half the population of 155 million
experiences hunger on a regular basis. According to the Brazilian
government's own statistics, the richest one percent of the population receives as much of the national income as the poorest 50
percent. There are an estimated 7 million to 10 million Brazilian
children who have been abandoned to fend for themselves on the
streets. Some 1,000 children die in an average day due to the lack
of basic requirements such as food and clean water.

These horrifying statistics are linked to inequality in land ownership. Between 1967 and 1987, 24 million of Brazil's peasant farmers were pushed off their land and into the cities. Today, the wealthiest nine percent of landholders owns 44 percent of the land while the poorest 53 percent holds just 2.7 percent of the land. Roughly half of the land owned by the large land owners is unproductive, possessed solely for speculative purposes.

This extreme inequality is the legacy of decades of military dictatorship and neoliberal economic policies written at the Washington headquarters of the World Bank and the International Monetary Fund. Brazil is the classic case of the well-endowed third world country exporting its wealth to make payments on foreign debt—debt that never benefited much of the population in the first place.

Maintaining the Political Order

On the positive side, Brazil has spawned an alternative, grassroots vision of development. In the last decade, Brazilian trade unions and popular movements have mobilized under the umbrella organization of the Workers Party (PT), the largest and most powerful left-wing party in the Western Hemisphere. In June 1994, just four months before the congressional and presidential elections, the PT's candidate for the presidency, Luís Inácio Lula da Silva, reached 45 percent in opinion polls—far ahead of his nearest rival. As Chapter 34 reveals, Lula's dynamic style of grassroots campaigning was getting him out to every corner of the country. Lula appeared set to become the first socialist president of the western hemisphere's second-largest country.

Brazilian government officials grew increasingly concerned that even the combined force of the state and the mass media would not be sufficient to beat Lula in the October 1994 presidential elections. This threat prompted them to take on one of the country's most vexing problems: an extremely high rate of inflation that made it difficult for individuals and businesses to plan their futures. On July 1 the government launched an economic stabilization program called the *Plano Real* (*Real* Plan), named after a new currency called the *Real*. The new plan ended hyper-inflation virtually overnight, thus boosting the popularity of the plan's author, former Finance Minister and presidential candidate Fernando Henrique Cardoso. On October 3, 1994, Cardoso was elected president with 54 percent of the vote.

The 1994 elections provided a unique insight into the complex political and social forces at work in Brazil today. Grassroots movements and unions had lined up against big business, banks and the mass media. Lula's campaign had pressed for the redistribution of wealth and the reorientation of production to meet the demands of Brazil's poor majority. Cardoso's campaign had advocated free trade and increased foreign investment to achieve economic growth.

But the ideas of the two candidates were pushed into the background during the campaign as Cardoso benefited from the total support of the government and the mass media to capitalize on the *Real* Plan. The government's support for Cardoso was so overwhelming that in the course of the campaign, two government ministers were forced to resign. The first, Mining and Energy Minister Alexis Stepaneko, conspicuously unveiled a number of public works to help the campaign of Cardoso, whom he referred to as "our candidate" in a memo to then-President Itamar Franco.

The second, Finance Minister Rubens Ricupero, was at the heart of an explosive, if brief, political scandal. On September 1, Ricupero told a TV reporter that he was using his political office, and the *Real* Plan, to help Cardoso's campaign. "I don't have scruples," Ricupero said. "We exaggerate the good and hide the bad." Ricupero indicated that TV Globo, the private network with over 80 percent of the country's viewing audience, was working to sabotage Lula's campaign. Unfortunately for Ricupero, even though the official broadcast was over, the conversation was still being transmitted by satellite. The PT distributed numerous copies of the video tape but the public reaction to Ricupero's inadvertent confession was not strong enough to change the outcome of the election.

The mass media's full backing of Cardoso, and all-out criticism of Lula, was a constant throughout the campaign. During the month of July, the first month of the *Real* Plan, of all the articles in the country's seven largest newspapers, 66 percent of the stories about Lula could be characterized as negative while just nine percent were positive. For Cardoso, 20 percent were negative, and 40 percent positive. On television news, 61 percent of Lula's coverage had a negative slant while 37 percent was favorable. For Cardoso, 18 percent was negative, and 78 percent was positive.

Cardoso's Appeal

As one of the country's most prominent intellectuals and neoliberal politicians, Cardoso had strong appeal for Brazil's elite. Having been forced into political exile for several years by the military dictatorship which ruled Brazil from 1964 to 1985, and having been an early advocate of direct presidential elections, Cardoso could claim a history of democratic activism. His writings, including his classic "Dependency and Development in Latin America," were Marxist-influenced analyses of the Brazilian state and economy.

After the impeachment of President Collor in 1992, President Itamar Franco named Cardoso as his Foreign Minister and later, Finance Minister. With the encouragement of the U.S. government, the World Bank and the IMF, in the fall of 1993 Cardoso drafted the new economic program, the *Real* Plan. Cardoso resigned his position as Finance Minister in the spring of 1994 to run for the presidency. The new anti-inflation plan was implemented in July. Few political analysts expected the Brazilian electorate to react so favorably to the reduction of inflation. The failure of eight previous government-sponsored economic plans in the last decade and five Finance Ministers in the last four years convinced the PT that inflation would return in time for Lula to win the October elections. It was the PT's most serious miscalculation.

On July 1, salaries were frozen, inflation was halted, and the Plan started to grow in popularity. By eliminating inflation, the government made many Brazilians feel that it was no longer necessary to vote for radical change. As one Rio de Janeiro waiter told us: "People are worried that the PT is too radical and that it will do away with the *Real*. The PT has to realize that people simply like the *Real*." At the time of the October elections, 70 percent of those polled favored the Plan, and credited Cardoso with its success.

Nonetheless, others—including many Cardoso voters—were skeptical. One woman told us, "The plan was *eleitoreiro*, put in place just to get Cardoso elected. If not, then why didn't Cardoso implement the plan eight months ago when he was still the Finance Minister?"

Indeed, the success of the *Real* Plan was not due to any monetary magic, as many voters and journalists seemed to believe. Rather, the elimination of inflation was the result of a concerted effort on the part of business and banking elites to guarantee short-term stability before the elections. During the first week of September, the Federation of Businesses and Industries of São Paulo (FIESP), the most powerful voice of big business in the country, announced that they would hold down prices until the end of the year. FIESP did not hide its motives: in statements to the press, the Federation made it clear that they were keeping inflation down to support the *Real* Plan.

The combined forces of business, the media and Cardoso's political cronies were enough to win the election. The PT's pledges to stimulate production, encourage more equitable development and reduce dependence on exports by creating a mass internal market lost out to the government's actual halting of inflation.

The Need for This Book
The book you are holding seeks to explain how the horrible contrast of wealth and suffering in Brazil has been constructed and maintained. It also seeks to illuminate one of the best examples of an alternative path—the one embodied by the Workers Party of Brazil and its affiliated grassroots organizations.

We have tried to present the non-specialist reader with a broad overview of the most pressing issues confronting Brazilians today. We have chosen essays that are insightful yet accessible, scholarly yet non-academic.

The editors are not Polyannas: we understand the serious obstacles that confront progressive forces in Brazil. Nor are we cheer-leaders for the PT: we know—as do members of the PT—that the Party will need to reformulate its strategy and redouble its efforts if it is to ever win state power and get a chance to implement its alternative vision for Brazil.

We end the book with an entire section on the PT because the PT has much to teach the international left about how to develop a political organization that is broad enough and sophisticated enough to include electoral struggles and local, issue-based struggles. As we have seen in many countries, political change based on libera-tion movements that lack extensive organizational structure at the base can be toppled rather easily. By institutionalizing itself across the spectrum of Brazilian society, the PT is steadily building a broad power base for a different kind of class rule. And given the size and diversity of the Brazilian economy, it will be difficult for Wash-ington or any other outside power to destabilize a future PT gov-ernment.

No matter what new clothes the elites wrap around their poli-cies, no matter how many 'development' schemes they put for-ward, the PT will not go away. Whether or not it holds the presi-dency, the PT will remain a major force in Brazilian society be-cause of its 'people's power' at the grassroots.

1

Who Benefits and Who Bears the Damage Under World Bank/IMF-Led Policies

Maria Clara Couto Soares

Since the early 1980s, Brazil, which has one of the largest foreign debts among developing countries, has been applying stabilization and adjustment programs devised by the World Bank and the International Monetary Fund (IMF). In 1981, it signed the first agreement with the IMF, and in subsequent years signed financing contracts with the World Bank, meeting several of the required conditionalities. Back then, the conditionalities imposed by those agencies related mainly to the equilibrium of the balance of payments and inflation reduction. Following orthodox economic prescriptions, they stressed policies to reduce domestic demand and stimulate the generation of a trade surplus in order to guarantee payments on the foreign debt.

The Brazilian government carried out a sharp devaluation of the exchange rate and simultaneously adopted a recessionary economic policy in order to generate a high trade surplus and meet the debt payment requirements. In the 1981-1983 period alone, Brazil's GDP decreased 7.2 percent. On the other hand, there was a sharp increase in exports, while imports were drastically restricted, Brazil went from a $2.8 billion trade deficit in 1980 to a $13 billion surplus in 1984.

What were the consequences of these policies? First of all, the recession provoked an abrupt decline in living and employment conditions. Second, the trade surplus that might have been used to foster investment and resume economic growth in Brazil was absorbed by foreign debt payments. During the 1980-1985 period, Brazil paid $91 billion in foreign debt service. However, this did not solve Brazil's problem of foreign indebtedness, which, on the contrary, was aggravated. The foreign debt, which was $64 billion in 1980, reached $105 billion in 1985, an increase of 64 percent. Third, these high remittances abroad started an extremely perverse process for the Brazilian economy: the growth of public debt.

Ninety percent of Brazil's foreign debt was made by the public sector, which in the 1970s was forced to seek loans abroad, in addition to having absorbed most of the debt contracted by the private sector. Yet most hard currency is generated by the private sector, and this raised the problem of transferring hard currency from the exporters to the government. Those transfers were accomplished by the issuance of government bonds and by the expansion of the monetary base. This caused an accelerated growth of the government's domestic debt and introduced a speculative and destabilizing amount of inflation into the Brazilian economy.

So although the adopted policies increased exports, the effects were opposite than those projected by the World Bank and the IMF in terms of stabilizing the economy. In fact, the policies to adjust Brazil's balance of payments had an effect contrary to the objectives of domestic stabilization. The clearest reflection of this is shown by the annual inflation rate which rose from 105 percent in 1981 to 2,938 percent in 1990.

In sum, we can assert that the economic and financial imbalances in the public sector, the erosion of its capacity to finance projects, inflationary pressures, and the inhibition of private investment—compounded by the recession—resulted in dire social and economic consequences. Economic and social indicators of the late 1980s show some of the serious consequences of the adopted policies:

• the annual GDP growth rate fell from 8.6 percent in the 1970s to 1.7 percent in the 1980s, and became negative in the early 1990s;

• the 1990 per capita GDP was less than in 1979; between 1981 and 1990, it declined 5.3 percent;

• between 1980 and 1989, the real investment rate declined 5.3 percent, a reduction in the country's potential growth;

• foreign debt—despite massive payments—increased from $64 billion to $115 billion in the 1980-1989 period;

• income concentration increased: the poorest 10 percent of the population, which had 0.9 percent of the national income in 1981, had just 0.7 percent in 1989; the share of the poorest 50 percent of the population shrunk from 14.5 percent of national income to 11.2 percent;

• the percentage of Brazilians living below the poverty line went from 24 percent in 1980 to 39 percent in 1988;

• the real minimum wage plummeted 40 percent between 1980 and 1989.

It is easy to see who benefited from these policies. The ones who gained the most were the international creditors, who received $155 billion in interest and debt payments during the 1980s. Also, Brazil's large exporters and the national financial sector made profits. The latter gained from speculation and the crisis; in just ten years the financial sector increased its share of Brazil's GDP from 9 percent to 20 percent. The great losers were the workers and the low-income population, hit by increasing recession, unemployment and inflation.

In the early 1990s, the Brazilian government, in accordance with changes in the multilateral agencies' policies, adopted the main guidelines of the new doctrine of structural adjustment, also known as the Washington Consensus. This new doctrine was born from the realization by the World Bank, IMF and the other managers of the international order that the problems of economic instability, unmanageable foreign debts, and decline of growth rates continued even though the government had implemented the structural adjustment proposals. Instead of acknowledging the inconsistency of the adopted programs, the multilateral lenders merely considered them as insufficient. Complementary policies were formulated, geared above all to deregulating and liberalizing the economy.

These policies directly link adjustment to the implementation of a free-market economy, entrusting the market with the optimum allocation of resources and the definition of development itself.

The main focus of this new Washington Consensus is based on five main aspects: balanced budget, trade liberalization, privatization of state-owned enterprises, liberalization of foreign investments, and domestic market deregulation. According to the World Bank, these measures would now be capable of placing the countries on the road to economic growth, making it possible to reduce the public deficit, resume foreign investments, stabilize the balance of payments and return to economic stability. The implementation of these measures became a basic condition for access to funds from the international financial system.

How were these policies implemented in Brazil in the 1990s and what were their consequences?

Regarding economic liberalization, the Brazilian government deepened the process of tariff reduction initiated in the 1980s, ended the so-called "market reserve" for computers, changed the patent legislation extending intellectual property rights to pharmaceutical, food and biotechnology products, initiated a broad program to privatize public corporations and also made more flexible the legislation that regulates foreign capital. At the same time, the Brazilian government negotiated a new agreement with the IMF, applied heavy cutbacks to the public budget, rescheduled its foreign debt with the Paris Club, and reached a preliminary agreement to reschedule its debt with private banks.

Nevertheless, contrary to the multilateral agencies' predictions, these adjustment and liberalization initiatives placed Brazil's economy on a higher level of external vulnerability and also aggravated the domestic crisis. The rescheduling of the foreign debt, carried out to stimulate foreign investment, actually augmented the short-term outward flow of resources and at the same time kept the debt problem unaltered because its service continued to use up a great part of the government budget. This reduced the likelihood of stabilization and resumption of growth for the Brazilian economy.

The new flexibility for foreign capital stimulated the influx of short-term capital of a highly speculative character, which brought about serious monetary problems. The free market policies also stimulated the rapid increase of the public deficit, raising domestic interest and inflation rates without contributing to the growth of productive investments.

The nonselective free-trade policy, carried out in the midst of a recession and in the absence of restructuring programs, has harmed several economic sectors. The privatization program has been implemented without being grounded on a strategic policy, the assets of the privatized companies have been underestimated, and they have been sold in exchange for the so-called "rotten currencies" (virtually worthless government debt certificates). Therefore, privatizations have failed to generate new resources capable of promoting public investments in essential areas. The high-interest policy continues to stimulate financial speculation and inflation, bankruptcies are on the rise, the employment level keeps falling, real salaries remain extremely low and income concentration has reached peak levels.

In sum, the adjustment policies defined by the World Bank and the IMF have made us pay dearly for adjustments that do not open new roads for Brazilian society because they do not attack the root problems. Brazil's crisis goes beyond the debt crisis. It is linked to the exhaustion of the development pattern of industrialization through import substitution that prevailed until the 1970s, and it is also due to profound global economic and geopolitical changes.

Brazil faces huge challenges. We must put forward a new development strategy, redefine our international role, and overcome the authoritarian and exclusionary tradition that has been the hallmark of Brazil's development. Structural adjustment programs have been totally inadequate and incapable of facing these challenges.

Instead of fomenting investment in the industry's technological modernization, the interest rate has been raised to a level that precludes new investment, stimulates financial speculation, dismantles the state apparatus, disintegrates the public schools and the capacity for innovation—all beneath the argument that market liberalization will be capable of modernizing our economy. Instead of promoting a reform of the state, so it could resume its fundamental role in a developing economy such as Brazil's, privatizations without criteria are carried out, state financing capacity is eroded, regulatory instruments are discarded as if the sole reduction of its size would be enough to resolve the structural crisis of the Brazilian state. Instead of promoting income distribution and restructuring the land tenure pattern—factors that clearly stifle Brazil's development both economically and politically—neoliberal policies have increased poverty and marginalization in both urban and rural areas.

Although no one can deny the need for structural change in Brazil, it is good to recall that the nature of the adjustment process through which objectives are attained affects the productive sector. While neoliberal adjustment policies have proven utterly incapable of offering a new base for Brazilian development, the continuity of the crisis is compromising the productive structure, the technological capability and the institutional structure of Brazil.

Even more serious than the deterioration of possibilities for a new development pattern are the ways in which these policies endanger the democratic process. Although Brazil has always been a country with a very high income concentration, the adjustment policies have aggravated the poverty and caused the deterioration of the living conditions of most Brazilians and this has substantially increased social and urban violence.

According to the United Nations Development Program, Brazil has the world's highest degree of income concentration. Today, 32 million people face hunger on a daily basis, in a country that is one of the world's leading grain exporters. The official unemployment rate hit 15 percent by 1993, and the percentage of Brazilians living below the poverty line increased over 15 percent since 1980.

The World Bank recently included in its project portfolio a credit line geared to alleviating poverty. These compensatory programs, now incorporated by other multilateral agencies, have the objective of attenuating the growing criticism of adjustment policies for making poverty worse. However, the efficacy of those programs is extremely low. Not only because the allocated funds are relatively modest, but mainly because the adjustment programs go on unaltered, promoting poverty on such a scale as not to be reversed by the mere application of a compensatory policy.

The rationale used by the World Bank to deal with the "statistics of poverty" is the same it has utilized to change its image as the great funding agency of environmental degradation. In recent years, it has become impossible for the World Bank to escape the evidence of the perverse consequences for the environment of Southern countries due to the large projects it has financed, particularly in the agricultural, transportation, and energy sectors. In Brazil, for example, huge dams and roads were funded by the World Bank, like the Carajás Project, where they destroyed unique ecosystems, displaced thousands of people and stripped them of their only means for survival while the so-called agricultural modernization promoted by the Bank forced millions of small farmers into the cities.

The bank also funded the intensive use of pesticides and chemical fertilizers which are extremely harmful to the environment. In the case of the Itaparica dam, which displaced 40,000 people, the Bank itself acknowledged consequences such as "prolonged idleness, incidents of intra-communal violence, alcohol abuse, family disintegration, and low morale." However, this evidence did not lead the Bank to reevaluate its global funding policies. It merely introduced certain "environmental conditionalities" into the funded projects and created a new credit line geared toward environmental projects.

Today, criticism of the World Bank's policies are on the rise. Even many conservatives agree that the mere deregulation and reinforcement of the free market are insufficient to promote development. Recently, Japan's foreign aid agency, the Overseas Economic Cooperation Fund (OECF), issued a very strong criticism of the World Bank, arguing that the developing countries' indiscriminate open-door policy in foreign trade and foreign investments may not lead to industrial development and sustainable growth.

Other voices are joining the long-standing criticisms from NGOs. The World Bank itself was forced to acknowledge, in a

1991 internal report, that 38 percent of its projects were failures. In Brazil's case, the failure rate reached 44 percent. These figures would put any private bank into a very sensitive situation via-a-vis its shareholders. That same internal report pointed to causes of the high failure rate: the fact that the World Bank ignores "local inputs," assumes a "negotiating position, not a consulting one" and is more responsive to "pressures to lend than a desire for successful project implementation." (*Wapenhans Report*, 1991)

The World Bank and the IMF are public institutions. Their resources have their origins in budgetary allocations from member countries, i.e., money collected by national governments through taxes and levies, which are paid to those institutions in the form of participation quotas. Therefore, both the World Bank and the IMF should have their policies submitted to public decision-making, and have the necessary transparency to be evaluated and monitored by citizens. Nevertheless, one remarkable characteristic of these institutions is their insusceptibility to popular influence and their hostility towards democracy. It falls to us, citizens of the whole world, to take on the responsibility of applying pressure so the World Bank will review its policies. The World Bank has a $140 billion portfolio and the use of these resources must be transparent and geared to promoting development on a sustainable basis. This requires democratizing its management and making it accountable to society.

The extremely discriminatory character of World Bank/IMF policies toward developing countries clearly reflects the interests of big capital represented by the G-7. The vote on any decision of the World Bank or IMF is proportional to the participation quota, i.e., the governments of the wealthy countries, particularly the Group of Seven, define the policies of those institutions. While these agencies have imposed liberalization and deregulation in developing countries, they have kept silent in the face of increasing protectionism and the policy of high agricultural subsidies in industrial countries. The poor countries are forced into an extremely painful adjustment, while the United States maintains a very high public deficit, absorbing around five percent of world savings, with direct impact on international interest rates, as well the on the growth rate of indebted countries. Regarding the policies of deregulation and state reduction, it is well known that in most industrialized nations the state has a strong presence. In addition, these countries protect their sensitive and strategic sectors.

The most direct consequence of these discriminatory policies and of the changes in the world economy in recent decades is the remarkable increase of power and wealth concentrated in the hands of the elites in rich countries. Investment flows, trade, technology and the productive structure are converging toward the wealthy countries. The free market policies of the multilateral agencies have widened the North-South gap and have promoted social exclusion and poverty at all levels, including in the rich countries.

According to UNDP data, the richest 20 percent of the world population holds 82.7 percent of the GNP, 81.2 percent of the world trade, 94.6 percent of the commercial lending, 80.6 of the domestic savings and 80.5 percent of the domestic investments. Today, just in the OECD countries, there are about 35 million unemployed people, and the trend towards "flexibility" and reduction of workers' rights is occurring almost everywhere. The large corporations and transnational banks gain, while the rest of the world faces continuing poverty. Even World Bank data demonstrates that over a billion people around the world survive on less than one dollar a day, and the number of poor people increases daily.

We cannot remain silent in the face of this situation. Today's world requires profound adjustments that cannot continue to be borne by only part of the world's population. The road to change passes through an urgent and ongoing restructuring of international relations. It falls to us, citizens of each country and of the whole world, not only to denounce the current policies, but also to take on full responsibility for changes capable of reducing social exclusion and of laying the foundation, at the global level, for fair, equitable and sustainable development.

2

Eternal Conquest

Stephen G. Bunker

In February 1985, the first load of manganese and iron—11,500 tons in 160 railroad cars—left Carajás, a series of rugged hills in the southeast of the Brazilian Amazon. Discovered 17 years earlier by an affiliate of U.S. Steel in what had then been a heavily forested and little explored wilderness, Carajás turned out to contain one of the world's largest mineral deposits with 18 billion tons of high grade iron and smaller but significant amounts of manganese, bauxite, copper, nickel, gold and silver. Exploiting these minerals required the construction of an 890 kilometer railroad to the port of São Luis, at a cost of $2.4 billion, the construction at the port of the largest iron loading complex in the world and the building of numerous roads into the jungle. Total investment amounted to over $5 billion, undertaken by the *Companhia do Vale do Rio Doce* (CVRD), a state mining enterprise that bought U.S. Steel's shares in the project.

These infrastructure projects opened up previously inaccessible lands and created the lure of employment. Peasants, prospectors, ranchers and lumber companies led the rush for land, and an even greater assortment of people came looking for work. Small towns grew from a few thousand inhabitants to cities of over a hundred thousand; and towns sprang up where two or three years earlier there were no houses at all.

Under Brazilian law, in order to claim these untitled lands, hold them against other claimants or sell them, ranchers and peasants had to clear half the area they claimed. By 1985, when the first load of minerals was shipped out, much of what had been dense jungle between Carajás and Marabá—the nearest town, 163 kilometers to the east—had disappeared, leaving only the scorched trunks and branches of the largest trees standing. Lumber merchants hurried in to set up sawmills, buying cheaply the big trees that remained after the smaller trees had been burned.

Gold prospectors also rushed into the area. They set up ramshackle settlements, blasted the banks of streams with strong jets of water, and pumped mud through sluices to separate out the precious dust and the occasional nugget. Individual ranchers struggled to prevent prospecting on their lands, but could seldom resist the large numbers who arrived.

At the top of the hill across from the mine, the CVRD mining company built a carefully planned town for miners and administrators, with electricity, communications and other social service infrastructure. The company built a smaller town just outside its land claim to support its rail operations. The town near the mine remained a protected enclave but the second community was quickly engulfed by a spontaneous agglomeration of laborers, merchants and prostitutes, growing from three homes in 1980 to over 20,000 inhabitants in 1989. Its precarious water, drainage, sanitation, health and education services could not have served well a fifth of that number.

The filth, disorder and dangers of this unplanned city and the chaotic landscape around it are as much a product of Brazil's development policies as the planned community which spawned it. No matter how much care is taken to minimize the environmental impact of megaprojects in the jungle, the very existence of a large project sets off massive immigration and forest clearing that is difficult, if not impossible, to control. The mining company proclaims its concerns for the environment around the mine, but pays little attention to the chaos and violence beyond it.

Until two decades ago, the economy of this region was in many ways primitive and exploitative. Fishing, tapping rubber and gathering Brazil nuts did not sustain high living standards, nor could they sustain their contributions to Brazil's trade with the rest of the world. They did, however, allow the jungle's flora and fauna to reproduce themselves. Now the 900,000 square kilometers around the mine—nearly a fifth of the Amazon's total area—is the focus of government strategy for the entire region. The mines have stimulated road building, brought in new social services, and opened up new agricultural lands.

The company and the government argue convincingly that the labor and living conditions of these new enterprises are vastly superior to the socially repressive but environmentally more sound extractive economies of the past, though relatively few enjoy the benefits. The tension between the progress symbolized by large loans and big machines, on the one hand, and the preservation of the forest under exploitative labor regimes on the other, puts progressive regional politicians and environmentalists at a disadvantage in their campaigns to protect the fragile jungle ecosystem.

The devastation at Carajás is the latest chapter in the long saga of natural resource exploitation in the Amazon. The commodities extracted have varied considerably but they have all reduced the chances for subsequent development by damaging the environment and by instituting exploitative labor relations and unstable human settlements. Planners, politicians and academics often equate high levels of natural resource endowment with the capacity for economic development, assuming a natural progression from dependence on the export of raw materials to a diversified economy.[1] In fact, economies based on resource extraction tend to remain isolated enclaves supplying foreign markets and enriching absentee owners. When the resource is depleted, extractive regions are left socially impoverished and environmentally degraded.

The growing indebtedness of many countries that attempted to industrialize during the 1950s and 1960s has pushed them back toward dependence on raw materials exports. Raw materials prices, always unstable, have been particularly soft during most of the past decade, in part because of the same global economic downturn which worsened the debt position of the developing countries. Low prices have narrowed profit margins in extractive enterprises and have enhanced the pressures to exploit cheaply, with minimal environmental safeguards. The Brazilian Amazon has been severely affected by these pressures, and is particularly susceptible to being treated as a panacea for debt and deficit in the rest of the nation, as its ecological fragility and economic history have left it politically and economically weak.[2]

The Amazon basin contains the world's largest rainforest and largest river system. Carrying water and soils east from the Andes, it starts its journey to the Atlantic less than 100 miles from the Pacific coast. The Andean waters, rich in sediments, are joined by more sterile waters flowing from plateaus north and south of the main river, where the soil is old and weathered. The most fertile areas of the basin are therefore those where the annual floods drop the Andean soils. Both because of the added fertility along the river and because the rivers allow for easy movement, people have tended to cluster near the waterways. In the uplands, dense vegetation of highly diverse and often interdependent species provides a cover whose exuberance and depth disguises the poverty of the underlying nutrient base in the soil.[3]

Early European chronicles related that large indigenous settlements along the rivers maintained stores of maize, manioc, sweet potatoes, dried fish, live turtles and fowl, together with plantations of pineapples, avocados, guavas, and other fruits. One account claims that a single society, the Tapajó, was capable of fielding an army of 60,000 men. Food supplies were sufficiently large to sustain the inhabitants and a Spanish expedition of 900 men for over a month in a single village. These riverine societies could maintain dense populations and complex social organization by coordinating hunting, fishing and agriculture with the yearly rise and fall in the river's height.[4]

Indigenous societies exploited a wide range of natural resources at rates which allowed for their regeneration. The colonial economy, in contrast, exploited a few, highly marketable resources to exhaustion. Portuguese attempts to extend sugar cultivation into the Amazon, along with strong European markets for native spices, created extensive demand for Indian slaves, fostering raids and wars between different groups, and causing drastic depopulation. Certain tribes, including the Tapajó, were held to ransom in exchange for slaves from other tribes. Others fled from the fertile river banks which exposed them to attack. The decimation of native populations accelerated as the colonial economy declined. Amazonian sugar could not compete with sugar from Bahia in either quality or price. Depletion of native spices near colonial settlements obliged collection to expand further inland and upstream. Slaving expeditions became more and more wasteful of Indian life. As early as 1693 there were complaints from slavers that it was necessary to go up river as far as the present boundaries of Peru to find slaves; numerous captured Indians died from malnutrition on the home-bound trip.[5]

European demand for animal oils eliminated natural resources crucial to the subsistence of dense populations. Turtle-egg oil and turtle meat were sold as a delicacy on local and international markets. The manatee, a large aquatic mammal, was intensely hunted both for local consumption and to supply oil and meat for ships involved in the West Indies sugar trade.[6] The massive exploitation of turtles and manatees disrupted critical links in the riverine ecosystem and thus reduced the other resources, such as fish, on which human populations depended.

During two centuries, Portuguese colonists devastated the resources they extracted and sold. By the end of the 18th century, the twin assaults on native populations and natural resources had created a demographic and economic vacuum, broken only by a few small and impoverished cities. Europeans had conquered the Amazon, using those portions of it which had commercial value (indigenous labor, turtle and manatee oils and meat, wild spices, and grass for cattle) for their own short-term profit in ways which precluded sustained economic exploitation. The Amazon's economy stagnated until the mid-1800s, when technological changes in the industrial world started a new round of extractive exports.

Goodyear discovered rubber vulcanization in 1839. Subsequent technological refinements made vulcanized rubber sufficiently heat resistant for use in internal combustion motors. These events coincided with a major new development in industrial capitalism—the production of machines for general consumer purchase and use.

Rubber could be found in various forms throughout the humid tropics, but only the Amazon basin offered the quantity and quality necessary for industrial use. Rubber trees grow widely dispersed through vast areas of jungle. They yield latex in slow drippings which must be collected daily. The distance between trees—up to 100 meters—and the need for constant attention made rubber collection extremely labor-intensive.

Peasants and laborers near or within the few established urban centers provided labor for the early rubber markets, as did the surviving native groups in a few areas of *terra firme* (uplands). The *seringalistas* (owners or lessees of rubber forests) soon had to import labor from outside Amazônia.[7] A long, severe drought in the 1870s caused famine in the Northeast and drove many peasants to seek work elsewhere. It was only then—due to the abundant 'cheap' labor—that the *seringalistas* could keep up with world demand.

Persistent labor shortages led many *seringalistas* to prohibit tappers from growing food so that they could dedicate themselves exclusively to tapping and processing latex. The tappers were obliged to pay heavily inflated prices for their transport, food and tools. The low prices set for their rubber output kept most of them in perpetual debt, bound to their masters by the threat of violence.

The *seringalistas* traded rubber for provisions within the closed vertical system of *aviamento* houses. These houses traded goods down through a series of intermediaries (*aviadores*) who advanced goods against eventual repayment in the rubber which would be traded up through the same sequence. *Aviadores* at each level in this chain maintained control through the indebtedness of those at the next level down. The prices of goods the tappers received were inflated at each of the multiple intermediary levels, as was the price of the rubber exported.

The rising costs of extraction and exchange in this system were more than compensated for by the rise in prices. It was the steady rise in prices, however, and a growing appreciation in Europe of long-term industrial demand for rubber which inspired the long, costly, and uncertain process of developing a plantation-cropped variety.[8] When the English succeeded at this in Asia in the early 1900s, the high costs of the Amazon system priced its rubber off the market. In less than a decade, Amazonian rubber fell from supplying nearly 100 percent of the world market to only 20 percent.

As it had after the exhaustion of its first round of extractive exports, the Amazon's economy sank into a profound depression. The rubber tappers who remained turned to a mix of agriculture, hunting and fishing. Minor extractive economies sustained isolated households, particularly during the 1950s when national and international demand for skins of jaguars and caimans provided export opportunities. These animals were depleted just as the manatee and turtle before them. Once again the reduction of fauna had profound effects on other parts of the ecosystem and further impoverished human communities.[9]

During this period, the economy of the Marabá and Carajás region—later the site of the iron mines—revolved around the extraction and sale of Brazil nuts from huge groves covering over one million hectares.[10] The few families that bought them and shipped them down river for export controlled the region's politics, rotating in and out of office and monopolizing the rental of the Brazil-nut groves from the state of Pará.

As with rubber, the rest of the local population lived in direct dependence on these families. The local merchants would advance the tools and provisions necessary for an extended stay in the groves at the beginning of the rainy season when the nuts started to fall from the trees, and then discount the price of these goods from the price of the nuts gathered, setting the price for each. Most gatherers ended the season with debt to carry over into the next.

The booms and busts of resource extraction left the Amazon isolated and impoverished until the 1960s. Since then, a series of government initiatives has aimed to use the Amazon as a solution for the political and economic problems caused by Brazil's attempts to industrialize. The Amazon is seen as a reserve of natural resources which can diminish a swelling national debt, and a reserve of land that can resolve growing tensions between classes.

Through mining, lumbering and ranching concessions granted to large transnational and Brazilian corporations, the government hoped to stimulate exports to pay off its debt.[11] By opening Amazonian land to colonization, it hoped that increasing political tensions and demand for land reform—caused by the mechanization of agriculture in the South and recurrent droughts in the Northeast—would be alleviated. As the idea of an Amazon rich in natural resources was incorporated into national economic policy, the old fear that other nations might wish to control those resources was resuscitated.

The completion of the Belém-Brasilia highway in 1959 stimulated a massive immigration by dispossessed peasants from other regions, especially the Northeast. An influx of large ranching and lumbering enterprises soon followed the peasant migrants. Using their greater political and economic power, and frequently force, they were able to take control of the land which the peasants had cleared and then to take advantage of the labor reserve which their expulsion had created.

The establishment of an authoritarian and centralist military regime in 1964 created the conditions for further disruptions of land tenure guarantees,[12] leaving peasants extremely vulnerable to repeated expulsion.[13]

The large ranching and lumbering concerns used various tactics to assert legal claim to lands which peasants had settled: purchasing old or lapsed titles, forging and fraudulently registering deeds, buying state lands, or simply occupying the land. They usually offered small sums, and then, in collusion with local police and military, employed violence to remove those who would not leave.

In 1970, the Brazilian government embarked on a new development effort, the Program for National Integration (PIN). PIN stressed road-building and colonization with a strong emphasis on small farms, agricultural extension and integrated rural development.[14] The enormous public relations campaign which accompanied it made migration to the Amazon seem like a real option for millions of landless peasants. A few Brazilian critics pointed out that the PIN roads supposedly built for colonization and communication appeared to connect the major mineral deposits discovered in the 1960s. As it turned out, they were right. In 1974 the government announced a new development strategy, *POLAMAZÔNIA*, aimed to promote mining, lumbering, ranching, fishing, agriculture and hydroelectric energy.[15] During the following decade, most subsidies were applied in three "growth poles" centered around large mineral deposits. The zone of the huge Carajás iron ore deposits received the greatest share.

Where PIN distributed access to resources in order to encourage domestic markets, *POLAMAZÔNIA* concentrated resources in order to accelerate exports to the rest of Brazil and overseas. The language used to promote the strategy alternated between lyrically rhapsodic and coldly economic but the central idea underlying the plan was expressed quite boldly:

The time has come to take advantage of the potential which the Amazon region represents, principally to obtain a significant contribution for the growth of the Gross National Product.[16]

The Amazon was thus declared a resource reserve whose purpose was to finance Brazilian industrial development. The region was directly subordinated to the nation and to the national debt.

POLAMAZÔNIA's greatest impact was in two new extractive frontiers. In the first, the Brazilian government promoted small- and medium-scale colonization in Rondônia, an area of relatively fertile soils which had been accessible only by river transport. Against the advice of some of its own officers and consultants, the World Bank financed asphalting of the road. This accelerated migration into the area and resulted in significant disruptions of indigenous societies and massive deforestation, with very little of the agricultural development which had been the project's justification.[17]

The second project, in southern Pará, was a massive undertaking to develop the largest iron ore deposit in the world at Carajás. Migrants began flowing into the area around Carajás about 1971, encouraged by the prospect of jobs and by the certainty that the roads and railroads would open up new lands for settlement. This migration intensified land conflicts already underway at the edge of the old Brazil-nut groves.

During this period the military regime experimented with greater political openness as it moved toward a return to civilian rule. The need to placate domestic opposition and to satisfy foreign banks who voiced concerns about environmental destruction and indigenous rights stimulated ambitious statements about how the "minerals pole" would contribute to national development.

In 1980 the Minister of Planning inaugurated the Greater Carajás Program (PGC) to "promote the most efficient domestic use of the benefits [from mining] in the region."[18] In glossy brochures with extensive photos and maps, the program's objective was put forth as "the harmonious growth of the country's diverse regions, industrial decentralization, redirection of migratory flows by generating new jobs, and payment of the external debt." Mineral extraction would go hand in hand with the opening of new agricultural and forest lands, the brochures claimed, as the PGC was inspired by the "government's concern to ... achieve inter-sectoral integration." National income would be enhanced by legislation requiring minerals to be at least minimally processed before export.

Nothing in the plan took account of the isolation, capital intensiveness and technological dependency of economies based on mining. The government's planners simply asserted that the program, together with the material and infrastructural resources that mineral extraction made available, would induce private investment.

In practice, the only industrial projects proposed or approved have been for technologically simple, environmentally destructive basic minerals processing, primarily of iron ore into pig iron. Companies have benefited from fiscal incentives and tax holidays, and they use the abundance of native woods to make charcoal for smelting the pig iron. The technology required to make charcoal is simple and can be subcontracted to local entrepreneurs and peasants. Initial and probably conservative estimates are that 33,000 hectares of native forest will be consumed each year for charcoal.[19] By 1987, the three pig iron plants nearing completion had already stimulated the construction of at least 200 charcoal ovens, and engendered a new series of conflicts over access to forest resources.

Contrary to its claims, the PGC's fiscal incentives will likely reduce much of the area along the railroad line to a smoky wasteland of depleted forests, impoverished soils, and fouled waters, a degradation that will only exacerbate the mounting problems of unemployment, landlessness, and violent conflict over land, which resulted from massive migration to the region.[20]

The iron mines, however, were only part of the revolution which turned Pará into a mineral-exporting province. Not only had manganese been found there by Union Carbide in 1966, but in 1963 and again in 1967 large reserves of bauxite were discovered on the Trombetas River, which flows into the Amazon 500 miles west of Belém. By 1973 a consortium of Japanese aluminum companies called NAAC (Nippon Amazon Aluminum Company) had started negotiations with CVRD, the state mining company, to set up an aluminum plant where the Tocantins River flows into the bay of Guamá near the city of Belém. The Japanese idea, strongly supported by the Brazilian Government, was to build a huge hydroelectric dam on the Tocantins River about halfway between Marabá and Belém and generate electricity to turn bauxite and the alumina derived from it into aluminum for export.

Plans for the dam were announced in 1974. The following year the Japanese made it clear they would not invest in either the dam or the equally necessary port facilities. By this time, the Brazilian government was so committed that it went ahead with these huge and very expensive projects by itself. In 1976, NAAC and CVRD set up a joint venture to build the Albras aluminum processing plant at Maranhão. The Japanese held 49 percent of the capital and the Brazilians the rest. Work on the Tucuruí Dam started a year later. Despite a series of delays, the dam was finished in 1984 and started to back up water in a 200-kilometer long lake whose upper end almost reached Marabá, the center of the old Brazil-nut groves and site of fierce disputes over land. The construction of the dam attracted huge armies of workers; its completion dislocated both indigenous and peasant communities and left the recent migrants unemployed. Many of the dispossessed and the unemployed gravitated toward Marabá.

Another mineral with an extraordinary impact on the region was gold. In 1980, a discovery was made at Serra Pelada about 20 miles west of Marabá. Up to 40,000 prospectors flooded the area. Since Serra Pelada was worked manually as an open pit, it was subject to slow-downs during the rainy season—when mudslides would kill many—and to occasional closing when the walls became too steep for safety and the top of the pit had to be widened. During the slow periods, miners tended to spread out to prospect in the surrounding hills.

Both CVRD and the ranchers found these activities threatening and disruptive. The use of mercury to extract gold dust from alluvial deposits poisoned water and diminished the fish catch, an important source of protein for both rural and urban poor along the Tocantins and its tributaries. Even more than Carajás, Serra Pelada spawned a large demand for prostitution; quarrels over shares of gold spilled over into the towns where miners went for amusement, supplies and banking. The state of Pará and the municipality of Marabá, both already very poor, received little additional revenue to provide for the health, education and security of this rapidly growing and often violent population.

Thus, on that morning in 1985 when the first trainload of iron and manganese left the Carajás mountains, it crossed a landscape where the vegetation had been substantially altered, where patterns of ownership, commerce and transport had been transformed, and where the economy and topography of the rivers, the towns and the land itself had changed dramatically. The city of Marabá, into which the train pulled 163 kilometers down the line, had more than 200,000 inhabitants, over 12 times what its population had been when the iron ore was first discovered in 1967. The Tocantins river was no longer the only means of transport to Belém and to world markets beyond. It had been supplanted by road and rail, and cut in two by the Tucuruí Dam. The old Brazil-nut economy was in rapid decline as agriculture, ranching, and lumbering took over the land and polluted the air which had supported the old groves.

Shortly beyond Marabá, and across the 2.5 kilometer bridge over the Tocantins, the train entered the Mãe Maria Indian Reserve, home of the Gavião people and the site of another set of problems created by the development of the region. The name Mãe Maria comes from the huge Brazil-nut grove exploited by a single family since 1923 but partially ceded to the Indians who were resettled there from further east in 1947. The installation of power lines from Tucuruí and then the opening of the railroad stimulated massive invasion by peasant migrants and engendered a three-way conflict, between the large landowner, the new peasants and the native people. To assure safe passage of the railroad line through Gavião territory at Mãe Maria, the mining company supported the Indians' claims and looked to the official Indian agency (FUNAI) and the military's land agency (GETAT) to remove the invaders and resettle them elsewhere.

The only available areas for resettlement around Marabá were Brazil-nut groves. GETAT was not particularly concerned with the legislation protecting those trees, but the Brazil-nut groves were also the only lands around Marabá still under the state of Pará's jurisdiction. Governor Jader Barbalho, a populist committed to reclaiming state control over unused lands, used environmental arguments to dissuade GETAT from expropriating the Brazil-nut groves to resettle the invaders. The Brazil-nut oligarchy, still using coerced indebted labor, found it convenient to ally themselves with the governor, creating a very awkward alliance for a government publicly committed to land reform and dependent on support from left-wing labor.

Environmentalists nominally sympathetic to the territorial claims of indigenous groups were put in the position of denying the peasants on Gavião land access to the Brazil-nut groves, thus subordinating both peasants' and Indians' needs to the protection of the forest. GETAT and the Gavião simply wanted an expeditious solution, as did CVRD, especially when the Gavião threatened to block the railroad tracks in 1986.

This battle highlighted the inherent conflict between two different modes of extracting natural resources from the same environment. Brazil-nut extraction was older, depended on a self-regenerating plant, required far less capital investment, and had engendered a social organization of labor and distribution of access to resources which epitomized the most backward and reprehensible aspects of underdevelopment or of a "traditional" economy. In these ways, the Brazil-nut groves represented everything that a self-consciously modernizing society seeks to overcome. At the same time, the exploitation of Brazil nuts required very little foreign capital; it was protective of the natural environment; it depended on a beautiful and noble tree, which symbolized for many the ideal of a self-sustaining relationship between humans and nature; and it was locally controlled. The iron mine and the railroad stood for modernity, for high technology, for rational labor organization based on bureaucratic position, technical qualifications, and regulated wages, and for connection to the rest of the world.

As these two modes of extraction were so located that they affected and used the same space, their differences brought them into direct conflict, both as symbols and as physical operations. In 1987, GETAT managed to expropriate enough old Brazil-nut groves to resettle the invaders of the Gavião reserve at Mãe Maria.

It is difficult for environmentalists operating at a distance to judge the effects of supporting or opposing particular political groups in Brazil, as these have learned to use environmental rhetoric for their own purposes. It is all too easy to do things *para o inglês ver,* "for the English to see," in the cynical old Brazilian expression. One of CVRD's projects to conserve native fauna, for example, is an extravagant zoo which embarrasses even the company's environmentalists. Brazil-nut grove owners can invoke the ecological integrity of their traditional ways to marshal outside support, even when they themselves are transforming the groves into pasture and charcoal. At the same time, landowning and corporate interests have managed to present the concerns of foreign environmentalists and indigenous rights advocates as cynically disguised incursions against Brazil's sovereignty, using this to discredit Brazilian environmentalists.

Current development doctrine and the large-scale enterprises it promotes promise to repeat the history of previous conquests of the Amazon. Each new form of resource extraction, from the reduction of river animals to the transformation of vast areas of forest into pasture, has severely limited the potential for subsequent human settlement and economic use of the forest. Each extractive cycle has intensified the devastation and—seduced by the lure of world markets—limited local opposition. Extraction organized in response to technologically driven market changes and to politically determined economic decisions is not only a short-term disaster; it places permanent limits on the Amazon's potential for sustained autonomous development.

Footnotes

1. This notion reflects the nineteenth century experience of the United States and Canada, two of the more impressive cases of late industrial development. Yet closer examination of U.S. and Canadian cases shows that luck, timing, and location were all crucial. Only when the discovery of raw materials coincided with strong international markets, and the materials themselves were located in places that offered advantages to other enterprises, did raw materials extraction foster further development. Raw materials exports in the twentieth century are admittedly more problematic, as the complexity of technologies and the scale of capital investment needed to be competitive in most sectors restrict opportunities for transforming naturally produced exports into socially constructive enterprises.
2. Stephen G. Bunker, *Underdeveloping the Amazon: Extraction, Unequal Exchange, and the Failure of the Modern State* (Chicago: Univ. of Chicago, 1988).
3. Ibid.
4. John Hemming, *Red Gold: The Conquest of the Brazilian Indians* (Cambridge: Harvard University Press, 1979).
5. Infectious diseases brought in by the Europeans may have reduced native populations even more than slavery did. The dense riverine populations would have been enormously susceptible to the rapid transmission of new diseases, even ahead of direct contact with Europeans. The combination of crowding, excessive

work and poor nutrition made urban slaves vulnerable to disease. Belém suffered a series of devastating epidemics which ravaged the Indian populations. Trade with the missions also spread epidemics. See David Sweet, *A Rich Realm of Nature Destroyed* (Ph.D. diss. University of Wisconsin-Madison, 1974).

6. Nigel J.H. Smith, "Destructive Exploitation of the South American River Turtle," *Association of Pacific Coast Geographers*, Vol. 36 (1974), pp. 85-101.

7. This account relies on Barbara Weinstein, "Capital Penetration and Problems of Labor Control in the Amazon Rubber Trade," *Radical History Review*, No. 27 (1982), pp. 121-140; and *The Amazon Rubber Boom, 1850-1920* (Stanford: Stanford University Press, 1983) by the same author.

8. Lucile H. Brockway, *Science and Colonial Expansion: The Role of the British Royal Botanical Gardens* (New York: Academic Press, 1979) describes the ways industrial capital captured wild rubber and other Latin American plants, turning them from extracted to plantation-cultivated commodities.

9. Bunker, *Underdeveloping the Amazon*.

10. Roberto Santos, *História da Amazônia, 1800-1920* (São Paulo: TAO, 1980). Otávio Guilherme Velho, *Frentes de Expansão e Estructura Agrária* (Rio de Janeiro: Zahar Editores, 1972).

11. Dennis J. Mahar, *Frontier Development Policy in Brazil: A Study of Amazonia* (New York: Praeger Publishers, 1979).

12. Ibid. In 1968, the central government extended its program of fiscal incentives to large ranching enterprises in the Amazon. The government agency involved was not obliged to consider the validity of titles for the land on which its enormous subsidies were to be applied. The effect was to aggravate the already severe land tenure crisis.

13. Joe Foweraker, *The Struggle for Land* (New York: Cambridge University Press, 1981). This book explains the close connections between violence and the extension of capitalist investment into the Amazon.

14. Charles Wood and Marianne Schmink, "Blaming the Victim: Small Farmer Production in an Amazon Colonization Project," *Studies in Third World Societies*, No. 7 (1979), pp. 77-93.

15. SUDAM, *II Plano Nacional de Desenvolvimento: Programa de Ação do Governo para a Amazônia, 1975-1979*, (Belém: SUDAM).

16. Conselho Nacional de Desenvolvimento, *POLAMAZÔNIA: Exposição de Motivos Interministerial*, No. 015 (Brasília: CDE, 1974).

17. Dennis J. Mahar, *Government Policies and Deforestation in Brazil's Amazon Region*, (Washington: The World Bank, 1989). The Bank, already under pressure to protect indigenous groups and fragile ecosystems in its projects, achieved only partial success in its negotiations with the Brazilian government. It went ahead with the loan despite the weakness of the controls agreed to.

18. *Projeto Grande Carajás, "Programa Grande Carajás: Análise a Situação Atual e Novas Diretrizes,"* (Brasília: mimeo, 1985).

19. Government propaganda and plans call for reforestation and the eventual use of plantation fuel but, at least around Marabá, the first experiments with eucalyptus groves failed. It is unlikely there will be much reforestation as long as cheaper sources of vegetable charcoal remain available in the native forest.

20. Stephen G. Bunker, "Extração e Tributação: Problemas de Carajás," *Pará Desenvolvimento*, No. 19 (1986), pp 11-13.

3

Capital Flight

Carlos Ravelo

What do Uruguay, Switzerland, Miami, the Cayman Islands and the British Virgin Islands have in common? Brazilian money, of course! In Brasilia, the 1994 Parliamentary Inquiry Committee (CPI) on the Budget uncovered a scandal that has opened a Pandora's box of unfathomable proportions in which billions of dollars have been funneled into safely guarded foreign bank accounts, which are the final stops for "dirty" or "laundered" money originating from many sources.

Brazilian firms and individuals have stashed more than $60 billion overseas during the last 15 years alone. Each and every year, more than one billion dollars are lost by the government through purchases and sales transactions carried out overseas, mostly involving foreign currency. Much of this money originates from trafficking in drugs or weapons from *bicheiro* (number runner) operations within the slums of Brazil's larger urban centers, and from corruption or skimming of funds from political campaign coffers.

Another portion comes from legitimate business deals, twisted into profitable little side schemes, which border on the very fringes of illegality. Federal sources in Brasilia calculate that close to 35 percent of the more than $85 billion deposited in Uruguay's banks belongs to Brazilians. Billions of *Cruzeiros* [the currency which preceded the *Real*, introduced in July 1994] are "legally" tendered in the parallel market and transferred out, eventually winding up in such far away places as Tortola (British Virgin Islands), Grand Cayman, Panama, Lichtenstein and Switzerland or invested into some of the 150,000 apartments or homes owned by Brazilians in south Florida.

According to U.S. officials, in the United States alone, Brazilians have deposited over $20 billion. Recent reports also indicate that within a recent three-year period, an average of three billion dollars from Brazilian sources has found its way into South Florida's booming housing investment market.

Talk No Evil

Taking quick advantage and control of the situation created by the Budget Committees' investigations into the P.C. Farias scandal [see Chapter 12], the federal government used the ongoing process as a means to uncover all sorts of illegal operations involving foreign currency transactions. Due to the extreme secrecy under which most mega-dollar transactions take place, and also in part due to the reluctant and at times arrogant attitude exhibited by many foreign and local banking institutions, the government has ultimately become the beneficiary of the scores of ongoing investigations.

Let's take a look into some of these schemes. For example, in just one investigation executed under a so-called CC-5 Account from the Brazilian Central Bank, an illegal transaction which totaled more than $200 million was unexpectedly discovered because the client-bank secrecy clause was breached. Recently, 14 foreign firms, nine of them headquartered in "fiscal paradises," were under such an investigation. They fell into the net only after the P.C. Farias affair came out into the open. Furthermore, over 500 other separate investigations have been conducted so far, most of them directly due to the P.C. Farias scandal's fallout.

Wash, American Style

Laundering money can be a clean and simple transaction. Nowadays, the classical green suitcase approach is *passé*. Bringing a suitcase full of cold-cash into the U.S. is not "cool" anymore. Modems, faxes and fast computers are the new style. In fact, according to the U.S. Treasury Department, about one trillion dollars are "turbo-washed" each and every year, worldwide. Roughly half of this amount is estimated to be drug money.

In the past, finding financial safe-havens was difficult for many would-be tax evaders. The Bible of fiscal loopholes, however, was published in 1988 by a Brazilian attorney and broker, Durval de Noronha Goyos Jr., the same attorney who, according to his peers, helped P.C. Farias to stash his millions overseas.[See Chapter 12.]

The book, entitled *Paraisos Fiscais, Planejamento Tributário Internacional (Tax Safe-Havens, International Tax Planning)*, lists more than 55 tax "safe-havens" and details the inner workings of tax and partnership dealings in the Dutch Antilles, England, Gibraltar, Isle of Man, Cayman Islands, Virgin Islands, Panama, Uruguay, Hong Kong and Luxembourg, among others.

Brazilians tend to favor those havens which fall under the British Common Law system. The concept of "Trust," previously restricted solely to Britons, is now used to protect the patrimony of whoever requests it. Each country tends to emphasize certain types of transactions over others. Individual transactions are favorable in Andorra, Ireland and Monaco. There, they benefit from low tax rates and secrecy laws. Partnerships and business firms, however, thrive better in Panama, Virgin Islands, Cayman Islands and Uruguay.

A specific case reveals the intricacy of capital flight. In 1989, one of the Medellin Cartel's biggest operations in the U.S. was dismantled. Through a sophisticated scheme, the Cartel laundered drug profits through jewelry outlets located in Los Angeles, Houston and New York. The "source" money was smuggled into the U.S. or transferred there through foreign banks operating under tight secrecy laws. Fake gold bars were dispatched to cover up the laundering operation, and "profits" from the "sale" of "jewelry" were deposited at banks in New York, later wired to Panamanian banks and from there into Swiss bank accounts. Subsequently, the money returned to Cartel sources in Colombia through that country's banking system, where part of it was reinvested in the drug business. The rest was used for the purchase of properties in the United States.

4

Forced Labor Revisited

Maryknoll NewsNotes

A November 1993 Americas Watch report, *Forced Labor in Brazil Revisited*, offers firsthand evidence that confirms the findings of earlier reports: in the inaccessible forests of the central and western states of Brazil, large landowners use forced labor to cut and burn enormous tracts of land for the purpose of turning the forest into cattle pasture. In addition to the abuse of laborers in the Amazon, the report also describes forced labor and conditions that approximate forced labor in other agricultural and industrial endeavors throughout Brazil.

Although Americas Watch has issued two other reports on forced labor in Brazil (February 1991 and May 1992), this is the first time that the human rights organization was able to document directly this most serious form of human rights abuse. On an investigative mission to Brazil in June and July 1993, a researcher entered two large estates near Alta Floresta, Mato Grosso. At the *Fazenda Pantera*, workers were recruited from Cuiaba with false promises of well-paying jobs clearing the forest and were told that they would not be charged for transportation, food or lodging. When the 70 men arrived at the *Fazenda Pantera* they found that they had been charged on credit for food, tools and materials for shelter (shacks made of plastic sheeting with no sanitary facilities).

The men at *Fazenda Pantera* worked from sun-up to sun-down six days a week. After being charged for food and tools, they would have earned less than $70 each for four month's work. In reality, none of the workers expected to earn anything. Several of the workers who attempted to escape from the *fazenda* were chased down, beaten, returned to the work site and threatened with death.

At another site, the *Fazenda WS*, 40 workers were recruited from the towns of Pontes and Lacerda in Rondonia to clear the forest. They were submitted to conditions similar to those at *Fazenda Pantera*. One work crew, who had spent three months clearing the forest, were told that after paying for food and tools, they had earned no money. The workers were supervised by armed overseers and could not leave the *fazenda* until they had finished their jobs and were allowed to leave.

The report indicates that the use of forced labor in non-Amazon settings appears to be on the rise and describes as an example conditions approximating forced labor at a sugar cane distillery in Ibaiti, Parana. In that case, workers were lured some 1,400 km (870 miles) from their homes by false promises of high wages, and were then left to work under miserable conditions for paltry wages. Although the workers were not physically impeded from leaving, a combination of fear and severe economic limitations made returning to their homes a virtual impossibility.

The 1992 report of the Pastoral Land Commission (CPT) notes a significant increase in the number of cases and persons exposed to nontraditional forced labor in recent years. Of 18 cases of forced labor, involving 16,442 workers, only four cases (128 workers) involved deforestation. The vast majority of laborers subjected to forced labor conditions were engaged in the following less traditional activities: sugar cane cutting (3,893 laborers); carbon production (8,800 laborers); coffee picking (60 laborers); lumber clearing and related activities (450 laborers); forcible eviction of land occupiers (60 laborers); other agricultural labor (3,051 laborers). In 1991 the CPT reported a total of eight cases involving 4,883 laborers in traditional and nontraditional forced labor situations.

In virtually all these cases certain common elements prevail: poor laborers are brought to estates or other work sites under deceptive circumstances; they are held against their will through acts and threats of violence; they are compelled to live and work in deplorable conditions; and, although the use of forced labor is contrary to Brazilian and international law, the perpetrators act with impunity. Despite the prevalence of this abuse, there has not been a single conviction of labor recruiters, gunmen or landowners for involvement in forced labor. Violators have gone free even on the rare occasions when the police have raided the offending *fazendas* to free workers held there at gunpoint.

Despite national and international condemnation, neither the federal nor the state governments in Brazil have designed a coordinated, effective program to eradicate forced labor. In some cases police authorities have been directly implicated in forced labor.

Americas Watch makes several recommendations for the eradication of forced labor in Brazil: enhanced funding for the federal police with money dedicated specifically to the suppression of forced labor; seizure of lands on which forced labor is practiced even without proof that the owner of the land was aware of the practice; diligent investigation of claims of forced labor by local authorities; and immediate reporting of all serious labor abuses to federal authorities.

[Editors' note: The full report referred to in this summary contains detailed suggestions for reforming the Brazilian goverment's policies on forced labor. To order copies of the full report, contact Human Rights Watch/Americas, 485 Fifth Avenue, New York, NY 10017-6104, tel. (212) 972-8400.]

5

Brazil's Labor Movement

Stanley A. Gacek

I n the late 1970s, Brazilian workers captured the world's attention by mobilizing massive strikes in the automobile industry of the greater São Paulo area. Defying the compulsory arbitration of the labor courts, they decided to directly confront the transnational auto companies and negotiated impressive wage gains. These labor militants also mobilized the celebrated *comissões de fábrica*, or factory commissions, which served as new vehicles for the negotiation of agreements and the resolution of individual disputes.

This *novo sindicalismo*, or new unionism, not only challenged the state-corporatist system of labor relations but threatened the entire military regime. Over the last fifteen years, it has made for three very noteworthy developments: 1) the creation of Latin America's largest and most dynamic trade union central, the CUT (*Central Única dos Trabalhadores*—Single Central of Workers); 2) the founding of a left-labor party known as the *Partido dos Trabalhadores* or Workers Party (PT), which has made extraordinary political and electoral advances on behalf of the Brazilian working class; and 3) the emergence of a radically democratic and politicized mass movement which is anti-corporatist and aspires to a contractual model of labor relations consisting of freedom of association, free collective bargaining, and a genuine right to strike.[1]

In order to understand the contemporary Brazilian labor situation, it is necessary to briefly revisit the history of Brazilian labor. During the Old Republic (1889-1930), Brazil was a predominantly rural society dominated politically by the local landowners, known as the *coroneis*. With the increased urbanization and industrializa-

tion of the early twentieth century, the old rural system of domination began to break apart. Urban labor organization burgeoned in
the large metropolitan centers and industrial employers brutally
crushed recognition strikes with local police. Nevertheless, a trade
union movement managed to solidify by the 1920s. Much of the
early organization was dominated by anarchists and Communists
who advocated the mobilization of work stoppages as a way of
organizing a general strike of the entire Brazilian working class.[2]

Thoroughly incapable of assimilating the forces of urbanization and modernization, the Old Republic collapsed alongside the
global economy in 1929. President Getúlio Vargas and his lieuten-
ants definitively overthrew the old regime in their "Revolution of
1930." As the new chief executive and de facto dictator of the Brazilian republic, Vargas created much of Brazil's modern corporatist state. During the *Estado Novo* (New State) period of 1937-45,
he outlawed the remnants of the old radical labor movement, building a new order based on the following corporatist principles: 1)
exclusive monopoly representation (only one trade union could
legally represent all of the workers of a professional category for a
given geographical area) and 2) the avoidance and suppression of
class conflict. This corporatist model of labor relations was officially enacted into law when Vargas promulgated the *Consolidação
das Leis Trabalhistas* (CLT), or Consolidation of Labor Laws,
Brazil's labor code for the past fifty years. Although the CLT has
provided legitimate status and material support to trade unions, it
also has subjected them to exceedingly rigid controls. It determines
the working conditions for most employment classifications, de-
fines the nature of collective bargaining and dispute settlements,
and establishes the norms for the creation and behavior of all labor
organizations.

Brazil's Labor Laws

The CLT empowered the Labor Ministry to define worker organization on the basis of "professional category" (i.e., metalworkers, bankworkers, commercial workers). The Ministry also had the

exclusive authority to determine whether a labor association would be recognized as a legal trade union.

The law also states that only one union is entitled to represent all of the workers of a professional category in a geographical area.[3] For example, all of the metalworkers of the city of São Paulo are represented by a single union. This Brazilian doctrine of single and exclusive union representation, which also applies to the federations and confederations, is generally referred to as *unicidade*.

Most of the trade union functions are carried on at the union level. In addition to distributing the legally mandated social welfare benefits,[4] these local unions conduct most of the collective bargaining with the corresponding employer unions.

The federation is the second rung in the official trade union ladder. The federation represents no less than five *sindicatos* of the same professional category or a related category, and generally has a state-wide jurisdiction. The law also authorizes the Labor Ministry to grant a federation the right to interstate or national representation.

The law requires the federation to "coordinate the interests" and join unions of its jurisdiction.[5] In practice, the federations selectively provide financial assistance to the unions of their territorial base. With the exception of certain professional categories, such as metalworkers, agricultural laborers and bankworkers, the federations have rarely assumed an active role in the mobilization of collective worker action, such as salary campaigns and strikes.

The confederations occupy the top level of the legally recognized union hierarchy. The CLT says that at least three federations of similar or related professional categories are necessary to form such an organization, which enjoys a national jurisdiction. Other than stating that confederations shall maintain their headquarters in Brasília, the CLT is practically silent about the functions of these national entities. From 1955 to 1964, confederations actively lobbied the national government for more largesse to the union movement. But with rare exceptions, the official confederations have seldom mobilized or collectively bargained for their membership on a national basis.

The law grants the official trade union structure the power to represent all workers of a given classification for a given area, even if those workers have not opted to join the union or pay a voluntary dues contribution. This entire structure is financed by a compulsory dues payment exacted from all workers, and euphemistically termed the "union contribution." The system requires an employer to check off the equivalent of one day's pay in March of every year for all employees under the CLT's jurisdiction. The Labor Ministry is ultimately responsible for the collection of this sum, and guarantees that the proceeds of the trade union tax are distributed on the following basis: sixty percent to the union, fifteen percent to the corresponding state federation; five percent to the corresponding national confederation; and the remaining twenty percent to the Labor Ministry.

Sources of Labor Militancy

Despite the persistence of a highly rigid corporatist system for over fifty years, contemporary Brazilian labor history has been punctuated by remarkable periods of intense radicalism and militancy. During the so-called "populist" period of the late fifties and early sixties, Brazilian labor militants managed to persuade the government to implement labor friendly policies and legislation. Under the progressive presidential administration of João Goulart (1961-1964), the Brazilian state actually relaxed the repressive mechanisms of the corporatist order, such as prohibition of strike activity. Labor leaders from the official corporatist structure were actively invited into the government's projects for agrarian reform and its formulation of economic policy.

Labor militants of the populist period took ample advantage of the more relaxed atmosphere by staging frequent strikes for both economic and political purposes. Yet none of this activity ever represented a serious threat to the corporatist system. The economic strikes leveled against employers were designed to secure the best tactical position in the state-directed arbitration process and to pressure a pro-labor government for more concessions in general. New class-wide organizations of the period, such as the *Movimento de Unificação dos Trabalhadores* (Workers Unification Movement), advocated more trade union sovereignty, including assemblies free of governmental supervision and the elimination of total state control over union funds. Even so, the movement still accepted the basic structure of trade unions and the existence of the union tax that kept organized labor dependent on the state.

The new unionism the late 1970s represented a fundamental departure from the corporatist status quo. The striking autoworkers of the greater São Paulo area categorically rejected the existing *de jure* order as a means of satisfying their economic demands. In 1978, the São Bernardo Metalworkers Union deliberately challenged the official labor court process, mounting a quick but overwhelming strike which produced a direct agreement with the auto companies.

The labor militancy of the populist period did not mean rejecting labor court intervention. One could argue that such a posture only made sense given the pro-labor orientation of the Goulart government. However, such an argument does not depreciate the political importance of the strikes of the late 1970s. The new unionists have not advocated a new and progressive labor court system with pro-labor judges. They have created experiments which shun anything even remotely suggesting an "enlightened" corporatism. Rather, the factory commissions exemplify the ultimate in labor voluntarism. They signify an independent worker initiative to settle economic grievances and bargain collectively, without any state intervention. The CUT's current project to establish independent collective contracts is an effort to sidestep the government.

The new unionists have also exploited the fully financed and all-inclusive corporatist structure. CUT militants spend a tremendous amount of time and effort on winning union elections. They also call for the destruction of the old system by advocating trade union pluralism and the elimination of the trade union tax.

The new unionism (1978 to the present) has been associated with the *autênticos*, a generation of younger and more authentic trade union leaders. The term was first used for those unionists who, in the 1978 congress of the *Confederacão Nacional dos Trabalhadores Industriais* (CNTI—National Confederation of Industrial Workers), actively opposed the conservative, pro-corporatist leadership of the confederation, accusing it of being "bureaucratic" and *"pelego"* (collaborationist). The authentic opposition was composed of union leaders who had no partisan links at the time, such as Luiz Inácio Lula da Silva of the São Bernardo Metalworkers Union and militants with ties to the PCB (the Brazilian Communist Party).

The new, authentic opposition founded the *Coordenação Nacional da Classe Trabalhadora*, (CONCLAT) in 1981, in an effort to build a new militant labor central which would join all Brazilian workers, regardless of professional category and geographical jurisdiction. The attempt foundered in 1983 due to a rift between the two groups. The new unionists, many of whom had become the founders of the Workers Party (PT), demanded a radical break with the corporatist order. The PCB-aligned faction, advocating an ideology known as "union unity" did not contemplate a thorough and complete rupture with corporatism. In fact, many who espoused unity believed that some of the state paternalism had done much to advance the entire Brazilian working class.

The new unionists founded the CUT in August of 1983 and the unity faction created the CGT (*Confederacão Geral dos Trabalhadores*—General Confederation of Workers) in March of 1986. The CGT advocated a more 'moderate' and 'pragmatic' view regarding the break with the corporatist order—which appealed to more conservative union leaders—and has become increasingly marginalized over the years. As of June 1992, the CUT reported 1,837 affiliated unions, representing a total of 17,739,000 workers. As of mid-1993, it was estimated that the CGT had about 600 affiliated unions, representing no more than three million workers. The only other significant Brazilian labor central is the *Força Sindical* (FS—Union Power), founded in March of 1991 by those unionists loyal to Luiz Antônio de Medeiros, former president of the São Paulo Metalworkers Union. As of early 1993, the FS had some 400 affiliated unions, representing 2.5 million members. Like the early CGT, the FS is seen to represent a more pragmatic "unionism of results."

Of all the centrals, the CUT unmistakably represents the greatest challenge to the corporatist regime. It has created a *de facto* pluralism by forming parallel state federations and national confederations (i.e., bankworkers and metalworkers) which enjoy more voluntary affiliations from the rank-and-file than do the official corporatist structures. CUT-affiliated unions have also challenged dependency on the state by remitting their sixty percent share of the union contribution back to the workers, financing themselves by means of a voluntary dues structure. And the CUT's proposal for an independent collective agreement would thoroughly preclude the compulsory interest arbitration process.

The CUT has unquestionably become the predominant labor central in Brazil. The CGT has suffered a precipitous decline in membership, and fails to offer any new or dynamic alternatives for Brazilian labor. Although the *Força Sindical* has demonstrated some impressive growth over the last few years, it is inextricably tied to the personality of Medeiros, whose future in politics and the labor movement has been threatened by a thoroughly misdirected and failed personal campaign for governor of São Paulo state.

We can expect the CUT to further actualize its anti-corporatist philosophy in the years to come. And if the *de jure* corporatist order is not officially changed through legislative reform, it will continue to suffer a legitimacy crisis given the *de facto* reality surrounding it. Alternative trade union structures, illegal strikes, and employers who prefer direct bargaining to governmental intervention, are all elements which will further erode the corporatist system.

Although Lula and the Workers Party failed to win the presidential elections of October 1994, the PT will effectively transmit the CUT's pro-labor and anti-corporatist ideology in the political arena. (There is no official institutional link between the two organizations but the CUT is organically linked with the Workers Party because the majority of the CUT's members are PT-affiliated.) Since the PT increased its representation in the Federal Chamber of Deputies from 37 to 49 seats and from one to five in the Senate, the CUT's agenda for labor law reform will be forcefully articulated in the 1995 session of the Brazilian Congress. And although President Fernando Henrique Cardoso successfully ran on a strongly neoliberal and pro-privatization platform, he will face effective and stalwart opposition from the PT should he seriously attempt to implement his campaign rhetoric.

Footnotes

1. For a full exposition of corporatism versus contractualism, see Tamara Lothian, "The Political Consequences of Labor Law Regimes: The Contractualist and Corporatist Models Compared," *Cardozo Law Review* 1001 (1986). Also see Stanley A. Gacek, "Revisiting the Corporatist and Contractualist Models of Labor Law Regimes: A Review of the Brazilian and American Systems," *Cardozo Law Review* (August, 1994).
2. Kenneth Paul Erickson, *The Brazilian Corporative State and Working-Class Politics* (University of California Press, Berkeley, 1977), 14.
3 A Brazilian *municipio* is described as being "roughly comparable to a U.S. county or township." Erickson, 30.
4. CLT Article 592 requires that *sindicatos* provide legal, medical, dental, pharmaceutical, maternity, education and day-care assistance, as well as libraries, recreation centers, and sports activities.
5. CLT, Article 534.

6

Labor's Development Critique:
An Interview with Durval Carvalho and Miguel Rossetto

Multinational Monitor

Durval Carvalho is the secretary for political action of *Central Unica dos Trabalhadores* (CUT), Brazil's national labor center. This secretariat works on issues of economic integration, labor law legislation, technological modernization, industrial policies, state-owned companies and working women. The secretariat also addresses issues of workers in the informal economy.

Miguel Rossetto, an officer in the local petrochemical trade union in Rio Grande in southern Brazil, was elected to the CUT national executive board in 1991. Rossetto is the head of the political coordination group on the integration of Mercosur, a planned common market for the Southern Cone of South America.

Multinational Monitor: **What impact does the restructuring of the Brazilian economy have on the population?**

Miguel Rossetto: Brazil has the ninth largest economy in the world. Our Gross Domestic Product in 1992 was over U.S.$414 billion. We have an industrial base that is relatively well-developed in many sectors. The agricultural sector is very strong in terms of diversified exports.

From 1991 to 1992, we had a 20 percent reduction in the workforce. We are estimating that we will have fewer industrial workers in 1993 than we had in 1980. And while the economy is now growing a little, industry is continuing to reduce the workforce.

In Brazil, there is great debate over the policies that were developed by the Collor administration to stabilize the economy. It is important to remember that inflation in Brazil reaches rates of around 27 to 30 percent a month. The administration of President Itamar Franco proposed reducing the fiscal deficit. The 1993 budget allotted 65 percent of federal funds to the payment of domestic and external debt services. Only six percent of the 1993 federal budget was allotted to social resources. So it is within this overall picture, with this terrible squeeze on wages, that the government maintains a recessive economic policy. It is opening the Brazilian market, opening up trade through agreements like Mercosur and continuing the push for privatization.

MM: **How has the political crisis affected the economic situation and the movement for labor rights and reform in Brazil?**

Durval Carvalho: The 1989 presidential elections were the first in 30 years. The military dictatorship had eliminated the people's right to vote for president.

The inauguration of president Collor in November 1990 brought in an administration that was totally committed to neoliberal, free market and privatization policies. We were confronted with inflation, the limited purchasing power of wages, and at the same time, a policy that eliminates any kind of economic or social role for the Brazilian state. Privatization of state-owned companies was undertaken indiscriminately, while basic social needs, like education, health care, housing and sanitation, were abandoned by the government.

The administration of Fernando Collor de Mello was extremely corrupt. To our surprise, the Brazilian media played an important role in exposing its corruption. This made it possible to create a massive people's movement, involving various sectors of Brazilian society, demanding that the president be impeached. We even managed to rejuvenate the student movement, which had played a very important role in fighting the dictatorship in the 1960s but had subsequently lost its political power and collapsed. With the movement that we created, we were able to pressure the president to resign. We interrupted the onslaught of the neoliberal agenda a little bit. And at the same time, the labor movement and grassroots movements managed to recover some energy for new battles.

I think that the political environment in Brazil today is going to heat up, because the Brazilian elite has become much more skillful at maneuvering and manipulating. Yet the *de facto* impeachment of the president as a result of people's pressure came as a surprise to the elites. It went beyond their control. Our success in that campaign opens new possibilities for getting back to the center of political activity in Brazil and offering an alternative.

In preparing for the 1994 presidential elections, the labor movement debated how to orient our political strategy so we could assume a more powerful and aggressive position in Brazilian politics. We need to offer a profound criticism of the social downgrading and deterioration of life in Brazil, while presenting an alternative political model in which the working class can build alliances with all those that are excluded in Brazilian society. And in Brazil, when we talk about excluded populations, we are talking about masses, about the majority of the people.

MM: **What social and economic conditions are you facing in your attempt to create a new national political agenda?**

DC: We are facing a severe economic crisis in Brazil. A combination of two phenomena is having profoundly negative impacts on Brazilian workers. From 1990 onwards, the Collor government steered the economy into a deep recession, causing an immense blow to the purchasing power of the working class. Companies are also going through a process of structural adjustment involving vast restructuring of production methods and managerial techniques, which is greatly undermining the role of human labor in the work process. So unemployment in Brazil today is structural in nature: we have unemployment due to the recent recession, but we also have unemployment resulting from the restructuring of the companies. Even if we get out of the recession, we will not have the same number of jobs as we did in the past.

Social indicators in Brazil today are frightening. Official data from the government statistical boards show that more than 60 million people in Brazil live at the poverty level. These people therefore do not have access to basic rights: education, housing, health care or jobs. And 32 million of these 60 million people are actually living beneath the poverty line.

There is a housing deficit in Brazil today of approximately 14 million houses. This creates a very serious social problem. Thousands and thousands of people in large and medium-size cities are squatters, occupying abandoned land or houses. The squatters make up a very important new grassroots movement in Brazil.

We have 62 million people in the age bracket of the economically active population. Of these 62 million, 48 percent work in the informal job market and are non-documented workers. And 60 percent of workers in the formal sector earn the minimum wage of about $120 a month.

We also have a serious problem with tax evasion: companies simply do not pay their taxes. This is the economic and social picture of Brazil today.

MR: A perfect example of the results of the free market model is cholera. Endemic diseases that had been vanquished return due to the worsening of social and health conditions. There is no soil treatment. Running water is not treated.

Despite the tremendous struggle we now face in Brazil, we are enthusiastic, because we think the political climate will encourage national debate on domestic and international economic policies.

7

New Directions for the Union Struggle:
An Interview with Altemir Antonio Tortelli

Paulino Montejo
(translated by Michael Pearlman)

O*Grito da Terra Brasil* (The Cry of Brazil's Land) is a movement created by diverse peasant organizations to pres-sure the Brazilian authorities by demanding agrarian reform and new agricultural policies. The movement marks a new milestone in the trajectory of the rural union movement in Brazil. The following interview was originally distributed by ALAI (*Agencia Latinoamericana de Informacion*) and features the ideas of Altemir Antonio Tortelli, vice-president of Latin America's largest and most dynamic trade union center, the CUT (Central Única dos Trabalhadores—Single Central of Workers), and Secretary-General of the National Department of Rural Workers of the CUT.

ALAI: **The Fifth Congress of the CUT took place in the last half of May 1994. What changes have taken place in the CUT because of this congress?**

Tortelli: First, let's recall how the Fourth Congress ended; with problems of unity, with much confrontation, two slates disputing each other, representing two positions that led to a confrontation that caused much wear and tear for the CUT.

After the Fourth Congress, we had to develop a process that would seek to minimally assure the governability of the CUT and establish a strategic plan with medium-term goals. But we had plenty of difficulty making the CUT function as a whole: problems in relations between some comrades have made it difficult to lead workers' actions in the last three years. The CUT still has internal challenges to overcome. We still have problems with united interventions, despite the fact that our responsibilities are now much greater.

But this didn't stop the growth of the CUT, which is now present in all the states of the country, in the different regions, and has maintained its principles in defense of combative unionism, of struggle, of profound transformation, of the project of a socialist society. It was also a significant actor in the process of impeaching the Collor government, as well as in the dismantling of the corruption schemes in the National Congress, against the failed revision of the constitution and in various actions against the economic plan of the current government. And we could have done more. Despite the fact that we're becoming more and more unified, we need to really consolidate the matter of our branches—rural, banking and metalworking—to have much stronger, united actions to strengthen the horizontal structure.

The Fifth Congress was an important step: despite all the differences, we succeeded in constructing a united program, debating the divergent questions and presenting a united slate.

Comparing the Fourth Congress with the Fifth, we left with a favorable balance-sheet on unity, a greater political balance and a favorable perspective. After ten years of existence, the CUT can't stop rethinking its role in the construction of a popular democratic project.

ALAI: **How does the CUT analyze the situation of the workers under the present regime [late 1994, President Itamar Franco], which has just launched a new economic plan criticized as an electoral maneuver on behalf of the government-backed candidate Fernando Henrique Cardoso?**

Tortelli: The neoliberal project is being introduced in an accelerated manner. We are suffering the consequences: unemployment, recession, wage cuts, lack of an agrarian policy, lack of an agrarian reform. The Itamar Franco government represents continuity with the Collor de Mello government.

The CUT is committed to explain to society, to the workers, what's behind this plan. We have no doubts; it has electoral objectives, but more important than that are the wage cuts that weigh on the workers. The plan might even lower inflation, but will be deficient because it doesn't consider agrarian reform, income distribution, job conditions, and investment in production, health and education.

ALAI: **How does the treatment of the rural question stand in the CUT? Does your election as vice president and your remaining in charge of training in the Rural Workers Department mean substantial changes?**

Tortelli: The problems are still great for the CUT to assimilate and take up rural questions. For example, the question of unionized small farmers; there's not an understanding of the importance of this sector among the whole of the CUT, unlike what's already been achieved in regard to wage workers. But things are being considered little by little. In the most recent period of mobilizations, we saw that CUT supporters have been treating the rural question with more care, and that the CUT is incorporating the capacity of struggle that this sector is displaying.

The unity of city and countryside is growing. In many states, a better understanding can be seen among the urban sectors, an assimilation of the importance of support to rural struggles, and the rural struggles are being incorporated in the plans and proposals of the CUT. We hope this perspective will be accelerated over the next three years.

ALAI: **What is the predominant vision today in the CUT in regard to the construction of unionism in the countryside? How do you personally see this question?**

Tortelli: It's certainly clear to me that we need to construct a different union project for the countryside, which will not be the project of CONTAG (the National Confederation of Agricultural Workers). Beginning with the CONTAG and the CUT's National Department of Rural Workers, we can build another project, a new CUT model for the countryside. This is the position of the CUT: to implant a new CUT structure for the countryside which is neither the Department nor the CONTAG, but a new structure that must come from the workplaces, that counts on concrete experiences, starting with the local unions, which must be more important than they are today, and vertical structures that really represent the workers. I think that CONTAG can join in to build this larger project.

ALAI: **Is *O Grito da Terra Brasil* an expression of this new reading of reality?**

Tortelli: I think that it's a question of an accumulation of maturity on the part of different organizations in the countryside that are seeking unity. *O Grito da Terra Brasil* shows that there's an accumulation of experiences and that we're building a new union model. Likewise, it reinforces the existing understanding in the CUT that the current model at the base, with a president and a municipal union, with a large structure, isn't really able to respond to mass actions, to permanent struggles and attacks, to the need for concrete victories by the workers. It continues the logic of "representing" the workers, leaving mass action in second place, prioritizing negotiations.

O Grito da Terra Brasil succeeded in associating negotiations with more prolonged mass actions to increase the strength of its pressure and win concrete things.

The political will demonstrated by the organizations in favor of unity is going to increasingly bring us to build much bigger mass actions and to be in the position to dispute for the leadership of agricultural policies and public policies in the countryside, so that they are really to the benefit of those who produce and create wealth and food for the country.

ALAI: **How does the CUT analyze the situation and perspectives of the current moment in Brazilian politics?**

Tortelli: We see that the Brazilian people are tired, tired of being tricked, of believing in miracles, of hearing promises that aren't fulfilled—tired of politicians.

The impeachment of Collor de Mello, the failure of the intended constitutional revisions, which revealed the incapacity of the right to articulate its own projects, the dismantling of the corruption schemes in Congress, are examples that it's possible to undertake changes, that the people still believe in the possibility of transforming the country.

8

Brazilian Guns Flood the Market

Rodney Mello

t was the March 1994 assassination of Mexico's presidential candidate Luis Donaldo Colosio that brought to light how powerful Brazil has become as a producer of guns. The weapon used by the alleged assassin Mario Aburto Martinez was a .38 Taurus manufactured in Porto Alegre, Brazil. The revolver started its trail in 1977 in a San Francisco gun shop when it was bought by a reluctant security executive who was against arming his company guards.

Forjas Taurus S.A. is not a late-comer to the gun market. The factory was founded in 1937 by a German immigrant to Brazil. Its big push, however, started in 1977 when Carlos Alberto Murgel and Luis Fernando Estima, two executives who were already working at Taurus, bought the interest of the American group Bunger Punta which had been controlling the company since the early 1970s. That's when the massive investment in the firm, which would amount to $30 million, started. More than 40 percent of the equipment was modernized and new technologies were introduced to eliminate waste and increase productivity.

Murgel and Estima started by buying Ifestel, a tool factory (Taurus has 15 percent of the Brazilian tool market), followed in 1980 by the acquisition of the Brazilian subsidiary of Italian giant Beretta. The Taurus International Manufacturing Inc. was created three years later with headquarters in Miami. It was supposed to be the beachhead of the company in the U.S., serving as the intermediary between the Brazilian factory and the American consumer. Since then, however, the American branch has grown into the third largest weapons factory in the United States.

Taurus is the third biggest manufacturer of handguns and pistols in the world. About 60 percent of the $85 million made by the firm in 1993 came from the United States. After all, 26 percent of all handguns being sold in the U.S. have the Taurus imprint. Americans annually buy about 150,000 of these handguns. And why the popularity? First, the price. The Taurus is cheaper than its legendary competitor, the Smith & Wesson. Besides, the company gives a lifetime guarantee to its products. Among the American clients are many police who have a love affair with the 357 Magnum, a weapon of great power and precision that can cost from $260 to $390. Another best-seller is the more expensive PT 101, whose price can go as high as $600.

Until 1990, exports accounted for 50 percent of Taurus's business. Today, this has increased to 74 percent, while the company exports to 78 countries. Without that, most of its 2,200 employees would be out of a job, since according to Taurus vice-president Estima, "the recession has paralyzed the Brazilian market and our sales in Brazil were cut in half in the last two years." While in normal times the American market is 10 times bigger for Taurus, in 1994 this disparity increased to 20 times.

Taurus president Murgel doesn't like to boast about his company's success, especially now, after all the macabre publicity that the firm has been receiving. "Guns are not the problem," he repeated to more than one reporter calling from all over the world after the Mexican national tragedy. "We cannot choose who buys our product," he declared to the weekly magazine *Isto E*. "This is a task that belongs to the authorities of each country." As part of its public relations, Taurus refuses to export arms to areas in conflict like Bosnia and promotes safe shooting classes in Brazil.

9

Hunger and Democracy Don't Mix:
An Interview with Herbert "Betinho" de Souza

Michael Shellenberger

B etinho is a co-founder of IBASE, the Brazilian Institute of Socio-Economic Affairs, one of the top 'think-tanks' in Brazil. Betinho, a hemophiliac, contracted the HIV-virus and is now suffering severely with AIDS. A long-time social critic, Betinho launched a national Anti-Hunger Campaign in 1993 to publicize the plight of Brazil's 32 million hungry citizens. In 1994, Betinho and IBASE started a jobs campaign to expose the structural causes of unemployment. He gave us this interview in his office at IBASE in September 1994.

"Nothing falls from the sky"

The roots of the Anti-Hunger Campaign can be found in Brazil itself, a country with a long history of hunger and misery. Nothing falls from the sky. In the 1940s, Josué de Castro wrote a famous book called *The Geography of Hunger* that raised the issue in a serious way. Later, Dom Helder Câmara launched a campaign called "Year 2000 Without Hunger" that mobilized a large movement here and internationally.

Meanwhile, hunger and misery grew, and 20 percent of the population fell into utter indigence. Today, 32 million people are hungry and in a state of total poverty.

What is the result of so much suffering? Increasing daily violence, calls for the death penalty, kidnappings, narco-trafficking, street-children and murder. The Anti-Hunger Campaign says look: democracy and hunger cannot co-exist.

"The dream has taken material form"

Eliminating hunger is not a utopian dream. Thousands of anti-hunger committees were formed and thousands of gestures of solidarity continue to be practiced. Today we have an immense movement, one without hierarchies, bureaucracies or corruption. There's no time for corruption. Whatever is collected is given away.

Raising people's consciousness is fundamental. Much more important than bringing bread, beans and rice to the people we must bring a new idea, a way of thinking that can change society. But we must remember what Einstein said: It's much harder to change an idea than to change an atom.

"Jobs aren't distributed in kilograms"

When we started the second phase of the Anti-Hunger Campaign, the Jobs Campaign, I was very concerned that we would only be complaining without providing the Campaign committees with the conditions to provide jobs. Providing food wasn't like that—it could be measured and distributed in kilograms. We always joke, "Jobs aren't distributed in kilograms."

What's surprising is that many of the committees discovered ways to generate work. One committee collected money from their community and transformed it into 150 minimum-wage jobs. They then employed 150 people to build a school, clean up the plaza and sweep the streets. Another community founded a bread-making center, providing both work and food. Another started a sandal factory.

Alongside the concrete work of creating jobs, we are pressuring the government for long-term changes. Today, public opinion is convinced that generating work is top priority. Before, there was a lot of talk about growth and development, but not about creating jobs. Of course, there are thousands of things to be changed. There are gigantic steps we still must take but history is now beginning to move in the other direction.

"The neoliberal economic model is old, worn-out and defeated"

In Brazil today you have a certain schizophrenia between social and economic policy. Our social policy tries to minimize suffering through band-aid solutions; our economic policy produces misery and rationalizes the organization of social apartheid with totally unsustainable arguments.

Why is this? Because our elites are the worst. Our people, our workers, our artists and our intellectuals are fantastic. Geniuses. But our elites are very stupid, very cynical and very cold.

Neoliberalism is an affirmation of the interests of the elites who refuse to show their true face. Neoliberals say they are defending the market because they don't have the courage to show their true identity. The neoliberal economic model is old, worn-out and defeated. Unfortunately, it is still the dominant way of thinking among our idiot elites here in the Third World.

I ask, why don't the neoliberals just say outright, "We are the oligopolies. Leave it to us to make production decisions and determine prices"? That would be more honest. Instead they say: "There aren't any oligopolies, there aren't any monopolies. All that exists is the market. Leave everything to the market and all our problems will be solved." Look, leaving everything to the market is exactly what got us into this mess.

A day will arrive when these ideas are shot down and the neoliberals will be judged by history as complicit. I've been struggling against neoliberalism for years and will only stop when it has been buried in a cemetery far away without any possibility of being resurrected.

"When the neoliberals talk of the market, we talk of citizenship"

An ethic that doesn't condemn hunger and poverty doesn't have the slightest value for society. It's fundamental that society rethink its tolerance, complicity and co-existence with hunger and misery. We must declare war on poverty.

When neoliberals say that poverty and misery are inevitable

consequences of human society we say no, it doesn't have to be that way. Whoever thinks that poverty and misery are irresolvable problems should get out of the way. We affirm that people, not economic models, make history, and that every economic model has an author and represents certain interests.

Let me give you an example. Here in Brazil there's a region in the state of Minas Gerais called Paracatu' that has the largest plantation of beans in Latin America. About 100 feet away is a *favela* where people are dying of hunger. The farm's grain silo is guarded like a bunker. We're the third largest exporter of food in the world; no Brazilian should go hungry.

"Our movement is moved by outrage, not by sadness"

Let's reread the Human Rights charter of the United Nations— not the charter of the IMF or the World Bank, but the United Nations. What does it say?

All people have the right to eat. Children have the right to play and be happy, not to be thrown out into the streets or underneath bridges. Everyone has the right to work at a decent wage. Everyone has the right to education and health care. Everyone has the right to honest information free from manipulation by powerful interests.

We must fulfill the UN mandate, and we must do it in a way that respects the environment, the seas, the rivers, the air and future generations.

No longer will I accept any argument for the perpetuation of hunger. I won't accept any economic policy or theory that tries to justify, rationalize, or make us accept hunger and misery as a natural, human fact. I reject as perverse, this kind of cynical thinking. Hunger, and the kind of thinking that perpetuates its existence, must be eradicated.

"We must democratize the state"

Our government is very curious. A supposedly public entity, the state has been appropriated by private interests. Though business elites constantly talk of the market, they live at the doors of the government, asking for all the guarantees, protection, financing and favors the state can provide. This is true principally when businessmen need government contracts or need laws that facilitate their business. So what you have is a business class dependent on the public sector, with an anti-public sector discourse.

The modern state must represent public, not private, interests. In this sense the government has a decisive role to play. The massive struggle against hunger must have the power of the state to achieve structural changes. We need an agrarian reform that would orient production toward attending to the needs of society. We need an industrial policy to create new jobs and to resolve the contradictions created by new technologies. We need basic education and health care that guarantee these elementary rights. Economic activity must be public activity.

State industries are responsible for an incredibly large part of the GDP. The President can say, "I don't like the current head of Petrobras. He's out." He sits down, writes it out, and the head of one of Brazil's largest industries is fired. This is absurd. When Collor was president, Petrobras had five Executive Directors in one year. Of course you later had everyone calling for the privatization of Petrobras because it was being destroyed from the inside.

Currently, the President nominates all the heads of state-owned industries. Whatever and however he wants it, the president hires and fires the CEO. The President is the largest businessman in the world. We don't have state industries. We have presidential industries.

An alternative is to democratize these industries. Make them public and democratize them. The response, I always insist, must be horizontal, from the bottom up.

"The Cold War is over, but the social war is still there"

We have disarmed nuclear bombs, but we haven't disarmed the social bomb. And it's not just here in Brazil: there are about 20-30 million hungry people in the U.S., according to Hunger '94, and millions of hungry people in Europe. At the international level we must say enough!

Either this is a planet for all of its inhabitants to live, eat and have their rights respected, or let's admit outright that the earth is divided between the haves and the have-nots—then we'll see if war breaks out. If there's a war how will it be? An affluent white minority will be up against a mass of very poor and hungry people. Will the affluent minority live in bunkers? Will they migrate to the moon?

"We must call on all peoples to get aware and take action"

If we do this we'll change our public policies, our governments and eventually, we will do away with hunger and misery. This should be a fundamental part of every government program.

No longer can I say, "Hey, I'm a sociologist, a political scientist, none of this has to do with me," or, "Hey, I'm a middle-class citizen, I pay my taxes—damn the rest."

Throughout the campaign, people would ask me, "What can I do?" Look, I'm not going to tell you what you should do. You are a citizen, you are capable of deciding on your own. Invent something! Use your ability and intelligence to do something! Don't ask to be excused from your responsibility.

10

The 1994 Brazilian Elections and US-Brazil Relations

Ken Silverstein

American dominance of Latin America is long-standing. Yet the neoliberal revolution of recent years has brought about a deepening of U.S. political and economic influence in the region. Only Brazil, due to its size and aspirations, has been somewhat reluctant to enter more firmly into the U.S. orbit. With the October 1994 election of Fernando Henrique Cardoso as president, however, Brazil will almost certainly abandon much of its moderately independent stance.

Across Latin America, neoliberal governments have eagerly embraced the U.S. agenda for the region.

• Under Carlos Salinas Gortari, Mexico entered into the North American Free Trade Agreement (NAFTA) and has sold off hundreds of state-run firms. The country's economy is now so linked to the U.S. that American companies, in the words of Brazilian analyst Rene Dreifuss, can "plan with Mexico as part of the overall productive chain."

• Argentina has followed a similar economic path, lowering trade barriers and courting foreign investors. President Carlos Menem's foreign policy has been so subservient to Washington that political scientist Andre Fontana complained, "He not only does what they (the U.S.) ask and what they demand, but he goes beyond that and adds what he supposes they want."

• Chile, long cited by the IMF and World Bank as a "model" for the region, is actively lobbying to be the next country to enter into a free trade agreement with the United States.

Like the other countries of the region, Brazil has moved closer to Washington, especially after neoliberal Fernando Collor de Mello was elected in 1989 (championed by the U.S. press as a crusading reformer, Collor was impeached in 1992 for gross corruption). Soon after taking office, Collor ended an "undeclared moratorium" on Brazil's $100 billion-plus foreign debt, which had been implemented by his predecessor, José Sarney, and quickly moved to improve relations with creditor banks and multilateral lenders. In April of 1994, that process was finalized when Brazil signed an agreement with private lenders rescheduling $49 billion in debt.

Collor also pushed ahead with privatizations, despite broad public opposition, and agreed to phase out the so-called "market reserve" policy, which was designed in the 1970s by the then-military government to protect the domestic computer industry from foreign competition.

Even so, Brazil remained far more aloof from the U.S. than any country in Latin America other than Cuba. The reason is not hard to see: with nearly half of South America's population and economic output, Brazil sees itself as the natural leader of the region, and the only Latin country which can hope to challenge the U.S. (that view is held not just by the left but by nationalistic conservatives as well).

"Brazil is an undeniable pole of economic and political attraction," retired diplomat Luiz Souto Maior wrote in a 1992 article in the Rio daily *Jornal do Brasil*. *"*An increase of U.S. strength in the area will tend to dilute our regional influence." Former President Sarney has spoken more directly to the issue, saying that negotiating with the U.S. was difficult because if Brazil made all the concessions that American governments have demanded, it would "have to give up being a great presence in the world of the future."

From the U.S. point of view, greater economic integration with Latin America is extremely attractive. The market system, at the national and international level, favors the strongest. With an economy that is far more efficient, less dependent on trade barriers and five times larger than all of Latin America combined, the U.S. is sure to reap the lion's share of the benefits resulting from the neoliberal "free market" reforms. In the last few years, Latin America has emerged as the fastest growing market for American exports. Furthermore, as Dreifuss points out, Latin America is, for the U.S., the only area of expansion that remains open without the questioning of external forces.

For Brazil, a hemisphere-wide free-trade pact as envisioned by Bill Clinton and George Bush, is far more problematic. João Paulo dos Reis Velloso, a former planning minister under the dictatorship, has said that increased free trade in the region could give the U.S. a captive market for its manufactured goods and turn Latin nations into a "backyard" for dumping obsolete American products. In regard to Washington's call for free trade, says Reis Velloso, "There's a need to see that the U.S. is defending its own interest and not necessarily ours."

Brazilians are, of course, aware that "free trade" is not necessarily a two-way street. While Latin nations have been slashing tariffs and trade barriers, the U.S. continues to protect and subsidize non-competitive sectors of its economy. Huge agricultural subsidies, for example, have helped American companies to undersell Latin producers, especially in the area of grains and foodstuffs.

Brazil, with the region's most solid industrial base—which means it is most likely to come into conflict with U.S. companies—has frequently been the target of unilateral American trade sanctions. Elevated tariffs against goods such as paper and appliances cost Brazilian manufacturers hundreds of millions of dollars. Glass, ceramics and orange juice have also faced stiff barriers in the U.S. market.

José Marcio Camargo, an economist who has advised the Workers Party, says Latin American governments long overprotected their internal markets and that some sectors can be liberalized with positive results. But he believes that it makes no sense to reduce trade barriers across the board, as most Latin governments have been doing in response to U.S. demands. "We need selective protection with a coherent industrial policy—companies need to know which sectors will be favored, where the government plans to invest, etc.—*not* no protection and no industrial policy."

Another potential conflict is in the crucial area of technology. According to Dreifuss, the restructuring of world production resulting from fantastic leaps forward in technology—"the transformation of multinational corporations into gray matter firms and the transformation of the North into a scientific-industrial park"— has led to a greater need to control "know-how." For Brazil, which is trying to move into sensitive areas such as computers, satellites, biotechnology and optics, developing an independent technological base is of vital importance.

Such a step has not been viewed with great enthusiasm by U.S. governments. For years, the U.S. justified this stance on the grounds that Brazil had sold weapons to countries such as Iran and Iraq. Of course, so did the United States and many of its key allies.

David Fleischer, a political scientist at the University of Brasília, says that only full acceptance of U.S. dominance in the region— and abandoning intentions of developing an independent high technology sector—will allow Brazil access to the resources it has been denied. "The bottom line," he says, "is who is going to control decisions on local industrial development, Brazilian companies or multinationals? Will it be autonomous [development] or dependent?"

The "market reserve" for the computer industry, which was ended in the early 1990s after years of U.S. pressure, is especially revealing in regard to the conflict over technology. While the market reserve resulted in Brazilians paying higher prices for less sophisticated equipment, it also allowed the country to develop a $7 billion local industry, the sixth largest computer market in the world. The number of domestic companies in the sector shot up from 9 to 350 in just a decade.

Even the left, which traditionally backed the market reserve, recognized that the policy as originally devised had bogged down by the late 1980s. But such critics favored reforming the policy— for example, by requiring companies to invest 5 percent of their gross sales revenues into research and development—not scrapping it entirely, as has now been done.

The market reserve's success is seen when comparing Brazil's computer industry—employing an estimated 50,000 people—with those of countries such as Argentina and Chile which have no formal policy in this area. Those nations have a combined annual market of less than half a billion dollars and together employ fewer than 10,000 people.

As Fleischer points out, Brazil, more than any other Latin country, has witnessed important growth in the use of computer products. He says, "In Chile, you can buy anything you want but there is no development of an autonomous R&D sector ... Chilean manufacturers that want to computerize an assembly line can't get the technology from a local firm so it has to be imported. That's fine if you play by the American rules but if not, you may have problems."

Foreign policy has also produced conflict between the U.S. and Brazil. Unlike some key Third World countries allied with the United States, such as Indonesia, Brazil has not blindly followed the U.S. lead in its relations with other nations. Even during the 1964 to 1985 military dictatorship the government maintained independence in some important areas, most notably in establishing friendly ties to leftist regimes in the former Portuguese colonies of Angola and Mozambique. Collor was on warm terms with Fidel Castro and Brazilian companies have negotiated important commercial deals with Cuba.

At the global level, Brazilian governments frequently have used international forums to demand a more equitable distribution of world resources between North and South (even while vigorously working to prevent a fairer distribution of resources nationally). "Brazil is far too poor and unjust a nation to be a major player on the world stage," Mexico's Jorge Castaneda wrote in a 1990 article. "But it has become a sufficiently democratic country, and its economy is strong and large enough for it to play an important role in the post-Cold War state of U.S.-Latin American relations."

Given Brazil's size and strength, it is unlikely that Cardoso will be as assiduous as Menem of Argentina in seeking to oblige the United States. However, Brazil's new president, who boasts of his warm friendship with Vice President Al Gore, will almost certainly move to strengthen Brazil's links to the United States.

Look for Brazil to be far more accommodating in key areas such as the external debt, foreign policy, trade barriers and foreign investment. Cardoso is also likely to speed up the government's privatization program and make new concessions in the crucial area of "intellectual property rights," long a sore spot between the two countries.

The payoff from such a posture is uncertain. It *is* certain, though, that Brazil's efforts to establish a "great presence in the world of the future" will at least temporarily be put on hold.

11

Their Bright Shining Knight in Brazil

Ken Silverstein and Alexander Cockburn

The greatest game in the Americas in the fall of 1994 was the election of the president of Brazil. The stakes were vast. With roughly half the population and economic output of South America, Brazil is a pivotal force in the hemisphere. It also bulks mightily in the balance sheets of major North American banks, to which Brazil makes major interest payments on its $118 billion external debt.

To Washington the dangers of a swerve to the left by Brazil are always vivid. Back in the early Sixties, the menace of land reform prompted the Kennedy brothers to send Gen. Vernon Walters to Rio de Janeiro to confer with the Brazilian military about rectifying the situation. A coup soon followed.

The threat today is the socialist Workers Party and its leader and presidential candidate Luis Inácio Lula da Silva. During Lula's 1989 campaign against Fernando Collor de Mello a prominent corporate leader, Mario Amato, warned that "800,000 businessmen [would] leave the country" if the socialist were elected.

Since the October 1994 elections we have heard remarkable testimony about the efforts of international banks to stop the Lula threat and install as president a reliable major-domo for capital, Fernando Henrique Cardoso, a promoter of austerity, privatization, and the standard catechism of the neo-liberals.

The bankers' plotting began in April 1994. At that moment Lula was far ahead in the polls, in an economy spiraling into chaos as monthly inflation neared 50 percent. These are not conditions to which bankers normally adopt a forgiving posture. But fear of Lula was paramount.

Brazil's private creditors signed an agreement which rescheduled $49 billion worth of Brazilian debt. The IMF backed the deal by putting up $1.5 to $2 billion to buy zero coupon bonds issued under the agreement.

Simultaneously, Cardoso, then Brazil's finance minister, was preparing his anti-inflation package, the *Plano Real*. The timing was deftly handled. The debt rescheduling was announced just before Cardoso stepped down from the finance ministry to announce his presidential bid. Introduction of the *Plano Real* was delayed until July 1.

Why was the *Plano Real* not implemented when Cardoso was still finance minister? Answer: it would have fallen apart too soon. An official in the U.S. Federal Reserve system spoke to us off the record, with remarkable frankness: "The *Real* was carefully calculated to produce the maximum effect," the Fed man told us. "If it's such a great plan, why didn't they introduce it in January instead of waiting until mid-year? The answer is that it would have run out of steam by now and people would be looking for somebody's head to chop off." He predicted that the *Real* will restrain inflation until late year — after the fall elections — at which point the Brazilian economy will "deteriorate rapidly."

To underline the point, this official sent a recent story in *LDC Debt Report*, a newsletter for Third World investors, citing opinion of the *Real*: "Some [suspect] that the plan is a jerry-rigged quick fix meant to catapult its architect, Fernando Henrique Cardoso, into the presidency."

This official also remarked that the April bail-out, organized by the banks, "could easily be seen as outside interference in the presidential campaign." Behind the backstage maneuvering, the Fed official spots the hand of William Rhodes, a Citicorp vice chairman and the man charged with coordinating the negotiating posture of U.S. bankers in talks with Brazil and other Latin debtors —four of whose governments have acknowledged his power by bedizening him with resplendent decorations of state.

The Fed man, who tersely described Rhodes as the "Emperor of South America," pointed out that when the terms of the deal are fully implemented, Brazilian interest payments will bring Citicorp roughly $400 million per year.

Brazil's international creditors, the Fed official continued, have "broken kneecaps" to ensure that Brazilian state and private companies regain access to credit on European markets. Such loans shore up the debt accord—and, indirectly, the *Plano Real*—by allowing Brazil to raise foreign exchange useful in meeting the terms for rescheduling.

In the 1989 presidential campaign, Lula criss-crossed Brazil denouncing the extortions of the international banks that drain billions of dollars from the country's economy. The media titans of Brazil ran a ferocious campaign against him and the Workers Party. With an assisting chorus from the international press they offered the thief Collor as a shining knight who would solve Brazil's problems. Now Cardoso fills the same role.

Today, 50 percent of Brazil's wealth is held by the richest two percent of the population. Only in India are there such horrible chasms between rich and poor. Can any nation in the Third World escape the bankers' pincers? Although many Brazilians pinned their hopes on Lula, the Northern bankers have once again strained every sinew to help the local elite ensure that he never gets the chance.

James Carville Heads South

The high-stakes Brazilian election reached deep into Washington, and into the client portfolio of a man with a 24-hour White House pass and unlimited access to the president's ear: James Carville.

During the run-up to the October 1994 elections, the Brazilian press contained hints that a leading, unnamed, American political consultant was advising a top presidential candidate. Evidence gathered by the Washington newsletter *CounterPunch* points to the self-proclaimed "populist" Carville as the American counselling

Fernando Henrique Cardoso, the bankers' choice.

Carville, it appears, was hired in mid-1994. He did not list Cardoso, or any Brazilian client, on a financial disclosure statement filed in June. The filing came after Republicans complained that Carville and the three other close Clinton advisors who hold permanent White House passes—Mandy Grunwald, Stan Greenberg and Carville's partner, Paul Begala—should be required to reveal whom they work for while advising the president.

Carville is said to have several assistants on the ground in Brazil, whither he travelled at least three times prior to the October 1994 elections. His chaperon while there is Eduardo Jorge Caldas, one of Cardoso's top aides.

Carville's low profile on the Brazilian account is apparently in compliance with a demand of Cardoso's political group, the Brazilian Social Democratic Party (PSDB), which fears that disclosure of Carville's activities would provoke an uproar in Brazil. One informant told us that a wealthy businessman might be paying for the work, under the pretense that he was simply seeking an outside analysis of the Brazilian political climate. The businessman would receive the consultants' recommendations and pass their work on to the PSDB, thereby providing plausible deniability to all parties.

Several other D.C. firms, we have been told, worked with Carville on the Cardoso account. These include Grunwald, Eskew and Donilon—headed by Clinton's intimate, Mandy Grunwald— and the public relations firm of Chlopak, Leonard, Schecter and Associates.

The total fee being paid to the U.S. consultants is believed to be in the neighborhood of one million dollars. Big money, but not a burden to Cardoso's campaign, which was flush with deposits from businessmen terrified at the prospect of a Lula victory. Someone familiar with the negotiations between Carville and the PSDB said, "They [the party] have got more money than God."

Carville failed to return numerous phone calls requesting information about his work in Brazil. But a staff member at Chlopak, Leonard, Schecter & Associates confirmed that the firm was working for a Brazilian political group. Carville and "several other consultants," the staffer told us, were also involved in the effort. Robert Chlopak, the staffer said, was working on the account. Chlopak did not return phone calls.

Asked who was handling the firm's Brazilian account, an employee at Grunwald's office said that Kate McDonald was the relevant party. McDonald, too, did not return phone calls.

Back in June 1994, Carville and Clinton's three other outside advisors announced their decision to file disclosure statements. In a June 10 op-ed piece in *The Washington Post* the quartet presented themselves as idealistic crusaders unfairly attacked by the Republicans. "We have turned down offers from some of the largest corporations in the world," they wrote. "We have tried hard to meet the high ideals our president has set." In the case of Brazil, it seems they missed the scheduled appointment with these "high ideals," or couldn't find them.

12

Brazil's Controlled Purge: The Impeachment of President Collor

Theotonio dos Santos

The issue of corruption has captured the attention of citizens around the globe. In Italy and Brazil, the battle against this ancient scourge seems to have assumed a newly effective form. In Italy, many politicians and business leaders have seen their careers and reputations shattered. In Brazil, a president was impeached and faced criminal prosecution on corruption charges, and a warrant was issued to arrest his closest aide.

Nevertheless, the difference between the two cases is obvious. In Italy, the entire political and business oligarchy is in crisis. In Brazil, the oligarchy managed to fix the blame on two people: Fernando Collor de Mello, a small-time politician catapulted onto the national scene by the country's major economic powers, and the businessman Paulo Cesar Farias, the president's chief legal advisor and campaign treasurer. The oligarchy has emerged unscathed.

The congressional investigation into President Collor and P.C. Farias implicated some of Brazil's most important business people, but no formal charges have been laid against them. Although popular mobilization was a crucial factor in the president's impeachment, the fact that Collor went free makes a mockery of that display of public outrage. The only person behind bars is the U.S. mechanic William Black, who is serving a sentence in the United States for falsifying documents for Farias' Miami-based air leasing company.

Corruption is nothing new in Brazil or Latin America. In the 1950s, Carlos Lacerda led a broad morality campaign against President Getulio Vargas, who had been elected by a wide margin in 1950. Lacerda charged that the Vargas government was mired in a "sea of slime." The campaign culminated in calls to impeach the president. Backed by the U.S. government and U.S. business interests, as well as by a portion of the Brazilian armed forces, Lacerda was preparing a coup to overthrow Vargas. The plan was foiled, however, when Vargas suddenly committed suicide in August 1954. In the political testament he left behind, Vargas blamed international capital and its local representatives for his fall. The political upheaval sparked by Vargas' death and his final testament partially deflated Lacerda's morality campaign. It took on new life, however, in the figure of Janio Quadros.

Quadros was elected president in 1961 by pledging to bring morality to the government and struggle against the oligarchies, despite his extensive commitments to those very forces. When Quadros suddenly resigned after only seven months in office, Vice-President João Goulart—a political rival and heir to the Vargas legacy—assumed power. Goulart found himself the object of a vicious campaign accusing him of corruption and subversion. Under the anti-corruption banner, the military—with the support of Lacerda and the U.S. government—ousted Goulart in a 1964 coup, inaugurating a dictatorship that lasted 26 years.

Fernando Collor, the first directly elected president after the years of military rule, ran as an anti-corruption candidate. As governor of his home state of Alagoas, Collor fired highly paid government employees and promised a government of public morality. It was his well-publicized campaign against "maharajahs" in government that gave him the credentials to run for president. His enormously expensive, modern advertising campaign cast him as a superman: a lone hero in an American Western battling all sorts of corrupt individuals. His statement, "Anyone in my government who steals goes to jail," became famous.

It seems incredible that a partyless politician with no clear commitments to the oligarchy—except to some wealthy relatives and

TV Globo, the national television network—could become president of a country with 150 million inhabitants and about 90 million voters. Collor's election was a legacy of the dictatorship that had outlawed political parties, but it was also to some extent a repeat of the Janio Quadros episode.

Brazilians have not been able to create solid party structures, and are still seeking political leaders who can stand up to the powerful and the corrupt. Thus, they reason, the fewer ties to organized social forces a candidate has, the stronger he will be. Perhaps Collor's victory was the expression of the last flicker of hope in such a solution.

But who was Fernando Collor de Mello? A wealthy party-going womanizer, with a cultivated playboy image, he was a man who led a fast and easy life. Persistent rumors circulated—later confirmed by his younger brother Pedro—that during his youth in Brasília, he experimented with cocaine and LSD. The son of a senator of the old National Democratic Union—the party of Carlos Lacerda—Collor understood how powerful a vote-getter moralistic demagoguery could be. His uncle Lindolfo Collor was a cabinet minister in the first revolutionary Vargas government in 1930, but broke with Vargas two years later. Lindolfo then turned to Mussolini's fascism for ideological inspiration, which led him to the Brazilian fascist movement, known as integralism. Fernando also venerated Mussolini, and was reputed to be as hot-tempered and prone to violence as his father, who once killed a senator in the midst of a session of Congress.

None of this gave his campaign sponsors pause. At first, they appeared not to have thought his candidacy would go far, and aspired to negotiate a spot for him as vice-presidential candidate on the ticket of a more established political party. That political formula was actually suggested to Mario Covas, the Brazilian Party of Social Democracy (PSDB) presidential candidate. Covas ruled it out however, perhaps because he regarded Collor's support as weak: at that point he had only a five percent rating in the polls.

As Collor moved into first place in opinion surveys, he began to create his own power clique. In the second-round run-off, he faced Luis Inácio Lula da Silva, the labor leader and candidate for the leftist Workers Party (PT). Taking advantage of the panic among the business oligarchy at the prospect of a socialist president, Collor's campaign treasurer, P.C. Farias, acquired enormous contributions totaling $100 million, far exceeding what the campaign required. It is not unusual in Brazil for candidates to pocket such excesses themselves; what made this episode different was its scale. It later became known that Collor and P.C. Farias squandered $25 million of "campaign left-overs" on genuine maharajah-like spending sprees.

The newly elected Collor formed a cabinet composed of unknown personalities and some conservative politicians. The public was led to believe that he would be the country's savior. They even went along with the president's ill-fated attempt to curb inflation by freezing $115 billion of the $150 billion in the country's bank accounts on his first day of office. During the president's first two years in office, at least 13 different cases of alleged corruption arose, forcing Collor to remove many top officials. Then, he decided to form a new government made up of distinguished citizens and conservative politicians. The media claimed that with the bandits in the president's entourage out of the way, the new team would resolve everything. But inflation, after a period of decline, increased once again, and wages continued to lose purchasing power day by day.

Collor's presidency was a family affair, with political and family matters—ranging from the routine to the scandalous—thoroughly intertwined throughout all levels of government. On the routine side, his brother-in-law Marcos Coimbra was one of the mainstays of his administration, and his sister Ana Luiza de Mello was continually under fire for meddling in the government. Moving toward the scandalous, his wife Roseane has been accused of embezzling funds from the large state charity she oversaw. The Supreme Court launched an investigation into her activities. Even Collor's mother, Leda Collor de Mello, joined the fray. Moving things from the scandalous to the ridiculous, she pleaded in the press with her son not to risk his life by flying jets without a pilot's license and driving Ferraris at high speed. The country was under the aegis of the "Republic of Alagoas," to the disgust of many in the establishment. The oligarchy and the conservative middle classes were horrified at the monster they had created.

Finally the dam of impunity built by Collor over two years began to wash away under the pressure of those who found their interests harmed by his brutal assaults on both private and public assets. As is usual in these kinds of cases, attacks began from the side. Allegations of corruption dogged P.C. Farias and other low-level officials throughout the spring of 1992.

Then the bomb of domestic strife exploded. In an exclusive interview in the news weekly *Veja* in May, Fernando's brother Pedro accused the president of using P.C. Farias as a "front man" for illicit kickbacks and influence-peddling schemes that netted millions of dollars. These accusations resulted in an investigation by a 22-member congressional committee. It seems that Pedro was provoked when his control over the Collor de Mello family media empire in Alagoas was threatened by a rival media group headed by Farias. Fernando's attempts to seduce his brother's wife Teresa also aroused Pedro's wrath. Pedro began by attacking Farias, but gradually took aim at his brother, the president.

The public was hesitant at first to turn against their president. Polls in late June indicated 67 percent of Brazilians wanted Collor to remain in office. But new revelations began to tarnish the president himself. His brother went on the offensive, talking to every media outlet that asked. Pedro asserted that the president was the ring leader and P.C. Farias simply his henchman. Although Collor claimed that he had severed his ties with Farias in 1990, the Brazilian magazine *Isto E* reported that Collor's personal secretary routinely paid the family's household and personal expenses out of a checking account fed by Farias. Collor's unwillingness to take specific measures against P.C. Farias was a sign to many that he too was guilty.

The congressional inquiry became a Pandora's box, continually unearthing shocking new evidence. Congressmen scrutinized more than 30,000 checks drawn on accounts linked to Farias which revealed a host of fiscal subterfuges by Farias and financial links between Farias and Collor. Congressional testimony and these checks revealed that P.C. Farias had set up in each of the main state agencies a group of representatives who skimmed millions through fixed bidding practices on government contracts. In addition, it became known that Farias had extorted millions more from Brazil's main business people, both national and multinational, no doubt in exchange for his services within the presidential circle. A network of bank accounts registered under false names was also discovered.

The congressional investigation turned up countless examples of greed that had virtually no limits. It discovered that Collor and his cohorts had set up a *caixinhas*, a "kitty" in which to collect off-the-books funds. In small, closed meetings, they set the goal of collecting two billion dollars. According to gossip in Brasilia, they held a party one year later to celebrate their first billion. Evidence that emerged in June 1994 from investigations by police and Kroll Associates, the international accounting firm, suggested that in this way Farias amassed about $1.4 billion.

More serious yet were P.C. Farias' possible ties to drug traffickers. Farias did favors for politicians of all stripes with a fleet of planes that periodically flew out of the country on a route very close to that used for drug contraband. Pedro Collor said a Miami banker had told him that he had serious misgivings about the source of P.C. Farias's wealth. The banker speculated that such a large amount of cash could only come from drug trafficking. Suspicions were further increased when the Collors bought a $4 million apartment through the services of Guy de Longchamps, a man with ties to international drug trafficking. Subsequently, a figure linked to organized crime in Argentina gave a detailed interview to *Isto E* accusing P.C. Farias of being directly involved in drug trafficking. This avenue of inquiry was immediately suspended and forgotten.

P.C. Farias went on the offensive and threatened to bring a lot of people down with him if these charges were pursued. The president too began to fight back. He went on television several times to deny any wrongdoing, and to insist he was the victim of special interests trying to thwart his economic reforms. His words failed to convince the Brazilian public of his innocence. The leaders of three opposition parties that normally have little to do with one another—Lula (PT), Tasso Jeireissati (PSDB), and Orestes Quercia (PMDB) came together to call for the president's impeachment.

Struggling for his political life, Collor called on Brazilians to show their support by wearing green and yellow—the colors of the national flag—at a mass demonstration. Few heeded his call. Instead, thousands of Brazilians wearing mourning black marched through the streets. Pro-impeachment demonstrations involving hundreds of thousands of protesters were held in a number of cities, in an uncanny replay of the 1983 "Direct Elections Now" campaign. Many of the demonstrators were students, quickly dubbed "painted faces" for the colorful paint they applied to their faces. The television networks—earlier hesitant to impugn Collor—now zestfully covered the protests. The vast majority of Congress members and governors also cast their lot against the president.

Collor had by then lost the unconditional support of the Globo TV network which had brought him to power. The oligarchy, now aware of the enormity of the mistake it had made, was looking for an out. The only possible route was impeachment. But who was to succeed the president?

Members of the oligarchy were loath to see Collor's vice-president, Itamar Franco, come to power. Franco, a former PMDB senator from Minas Gerais state, lost his bid for the governorship of his home state in 1986. He was a consistent foe of the military dictatorship, while Collor had collaborated with it. He had also led a congressional committee investigating corruption in the Sarney government in the late 1980s. Collor selected Itamar as his running mate because he needed an honest, established politician from a populous state to round out his ticket. This partnership was awkward and full of political and personal frictions from the start. Itamar was renowned for taking nationalistic stands. He opposed Collor's neoliberal market reforms, including privatizing state industries. He had also opposed Collor's first economic plan in which private savings were frozen.

The armed forces, on the other hand, were inclined to support Franco as a suitable replacement. Collor had angered the military by destroying the National Information Service, closing nuclear research sites, signing the agreement committing Brazil to the nuclear non-proliferation treaty, and drastically reducing the military budget. The armed forces did not favor dismantling the state, and feared that the excessive opening of the national market to foreign competition might sink the nation's industry and advanced technological research apparatus.

Franco's support among the armed forces was perhaps the most decisive factor impeding efforts to depose the vice-president along with Collor. The loose-cannon governor of Bahia, Antonio Carlos Magalhaes, a right-wing populist and faithful servant of Globo TV, and Globo's president, Roberto Marinho, led a campaign to drop Itamar. At the opposite end of the political spectrum, the far-left flank of the PT called for general elections, inadvertently supporting the agenda of the oligarchy, which wanted to pass over Franco.

This maneuvering occurred as a pageant of civic spirit unfolded on the streets, broadcast nationwide on all the TV channels. Congress professed fidelity to the popular will and prepared to impeach the president. Collor played his last card by resigning before the Senate reached a verdict. But under popular pressure, the Senate decided to go ahead with the trial, convicting Collor by 76 to 3 on charges of official misconduct. By then, the Attorney General had brought criminal charges against Collor for "passive corruption" and "criminal association." The nation's elites were united in their abomination of the felon. By the date of the impeachment vote, Collor faced solid opposition from Congress, Brazil's major business groups, the major media, and 23 of 26 state governors.

Vice-President Itamar Franco was named acting president for the remaining two years of Collor's term. Policymakers were initially elated and triumphant. They gloated that they had dutifully obeyed the wishes of the citizenry. Seizing advantage of the positive image it had acquired because of the impeachment vote, Congress decided to move up the date of the plebiscite on Brazil's system of governance. Brazilians, however, thwarted their ambitions, voting overwhelmingly against weakening the presidency by changing to a parliamentary system.

The Brazilian elite grew unhappy with the Itamar Franco government, which was at odds with it over economic policy. That may be why the legal proceedings against ex-President Collor for criminal activity moved so slowly. It may also partly explain why P.C. Farias has been treated so gently, and has even managed to go into hiding and perhaps flee the country when he should be in jail.

Brazilians are still waiting for justice to be done. Calls for public morality did not prevent Paulo Maluf—a true symbol of the corruption of the dictatorship era—from winning the mayor's race in São Paulo in November 1992. Not even the revelations of corruption that surfaced during his mayoral campaign have harmed the presidential prospects of this authoritarian former governor of São Paulo and leader of the right-wing Democratic Social Party. Maluf's constituency is made up of the very same conservative sectors that tried to overthrow Vargas and that supported the overthrow of Goulart in the name of public morality. Maluf's past has been forgotten, and he is presented as an honest and moderate politician. At one point in 1994, he ran second behind Lula in polls asking people who they would prefer as their next president.

It would seem that more important issues are at stake. Yes, the truly corrupt must be punished. Corruption, however, is embedded in a much broader and more complex political process. Corruption is just one facet of the general control of the state by private interests. Ultimately, state subsidies to the private sector or oligarchical interests are more harmful than the irregular transfers and commissions, known as "corruption."

[Editors' note: On December 12, 1994 the Supreme Federal Court of Brazil cleared Fernando Collor of corruption charges, claiming that the prosecution had failed to prove its case against the former president. Brother Pedro died from brain cancer in December 1994. Mother Leda Collor unsuccessfully attempted suicide via an overdose of drugs and has remained hospitalized in a coma since September 1992.]

13

"Don't Kidnap Me, I'm a Professor"

Marshall Berman

In August 1993, I made a visit to Brazil. It was my second visit. The first was in August 1987, a few months after my book, *All That Is Solid Melts Into Air*, appeared in a Brazilian edition. To my amazement, the book hit the charts, and all sorts of Brazilians wanted to meet me. The United States Information Agency picked up the tab (it evaluated me as "a counter-cultural figure who is also a deeply patriotic American"). I gave dozens of speeches and interviews; got into a public argument about public space with Oscar Niemeyer, the architect of Brasília, a city with no public space (NIEMEYER CHAMA BERMAN DE IDIOTA, said a headline in *O Globo*); received many gifts, the most precious from an Umbanda priest, a statue of Zé Pelintre, the Afro-Brazilian Umbanda god of the city and of night in the city (he looks like Sporting Life in Porgy and Bess); and had the time of my life.

In the summer of 1993, I got to do *Flying Down to Rio, Part Two*, this time with my wife, Shellie Sclan. We went as guests of the PT, (*Partido dos Trabalhadores*, the Workers' Party) and of the city of Porto Alegre. Once more we were locked into a format that devoured every minute and gave us no time to relax or reflect. I had to tell big lies to free us from our handlers for a few hours alone. We didn't have enough time in Rio or São Paulo. When we finally got to go to the beach, up in Bahia, it rained. But we got to see so many vivid environments, and to meet so many smart, sweet people, and even though we saw things from a special perspective, we saw a lot.

In Porto Alegre, and in the South as a whole, people are largely blond (even the poorest, most ragged people), descended from German colonists who hacked family farms out of the jungle a century ago. Cities are relatively prosperous, with highly skilled populations (lots of scientists and engineers) plugged into world computer and biotech industries. City governments appear both adept and humane. They have spent money and energy trying to create jobs for the poorest people. Porto Alegre has a high-tech municipal enterprise for waste disposal, recycling and environmental cleanup; when the new system supplanted the old, biohazardous city dump, the men and women who had lived by scavenging in the dump were retrained, incorporated into the civil service, and given skills that will be increasingly marketable. The young mayor, Tarso Genro, and his commissioners, are rightly proud of their work. Porto Alegre reminded us of some progressive provincial cities in America—Minneapolis, for instance—that work wonderfully, but aren't so interesting. Kids who have grown up there are civically proud but spiritually bored; they dream of life in bigger, nastier, messier cities like Rio or São Paulo or Paris or New York.

In the North, in Bahia, which Southerners patronizingly call "Little Africa," many people are black, descendants of African slaves, but most look like what North Americans would call "Latino." (In the South, most people look like what North Americans would call "white.") In Salvador, Bahia's capital, we saw some of the sharpest polarities in Brazil: a lavish, glitzy tourist sector along the ocean, and an enormous network of shanty towns (the Brazilian word is *favelas*) just a little bit inland. *Favelas* exist everywhere in Brazil, but Porto Alegre's seem almost luxurious compared with Salvador's, where the shacks are folded into precarious gullies, subject to lethal mud slides every time it rains, where you can see the walls shake in the wind and smell the raw sewage that runs in the streets. In Salvador's *favelas,* the congestion is as intense as any place in New York; there's not an inch to spare. Half a mile away there are splendid postmodern skyscrapers that belong to national banks or to the Bahia state government, built on lavish suburban plazas that are empty of people and landscaped as if they had all the space in the world.

We saw immense, sublime modern ruins, abandoned factories near the waterfront that once kept the city's poor people at work; they reminded me of my old South Bronx. But there was another ruin of a kind that I haven't seen in the United States: abandoned schools and hospitals whose construction was stopped before they could open; broken promises of a welfare state that never worked.

What happened? The cost overruns, we heard, were grabbed by giant construction companies, some private, some public, all profoundly corrupt and untouchable. When we saw the vast, empty state government plaza, I asked why the local poor people didn't try to start a *favela* here. The answer was, because they'd be shot for treason. Nonchalant fatalism was the attitude that most marked people in the North.

Between North and South are Rio and São Paulo, two of the most fascinating cities in the world: Rio, where a spectacular mountain/ocean topography, with miles of gorgeous beach, frames an urbanism of colonial palaces, plazas and gardens, hundreds of beautiful vernacular Bauhaus and Art Deco apartment blocks, and a flashy, glamorous, vaguely sinister pedestrian street life; maybe the most alluring city in the world (perhaps tied with Venice), and one whose citizens often feel drunk and drugged on their allure. São Paulo is as different from Rio as Los Angeles is from New York; it contains few landmarks, it's impossible to navigate without a car, but it spreads forever and ever, and contains dozens of cities within it—Italian, Japanese, Korean, Arab, Jewish, industrial, intellectual—you drive past carburetor factories on the way to the art museum. São Paulo has a full-fledged industrial sector, and all the paraphernalia of industrialism that have virtually disappeared from the United States.

São Paulo is the birthplace of the PT and its greatest source of strength today. The party grows out of a militant labor movement, rooted in CIOesque industrial unionism, but also in white-collar unions. It represents itself as a fusion of the Metal Workers Union from the northern industrial suburbs and the Bank Workers Union downtown. The PT has a program and a world outlook surprisingly close to that of *Dissent* (Irving Howe would have enjoyed its critique of Latin American Leninism) and about 34 million voters. The PT has won more than 40 percent of the vote in national elections, and Lula, its charismatic leader, who began his career as a metalworker, could well be elected President some day. The PT program evokes European social democracy today: sophisticated about public health, worker safety, environmental destruction (plenty about the Amazon), racism, equality for women. It pointedly does not feature nationalization. When I remarked on this, I was told that a great deal of Brazil's economy is nationalized already—including some of its most rapacious corporations, especially in oil and iron extraction—and that it hasn't done the workers a bit of good.

One of the high points of the trip was an encounter with a group of PT shop stewards from the Metal Workers' Union, at union headquarters in São Bernardo, an industrial suburb just north of São Paulo. They seemed mostly in their upper twenties and thirties, about a third were women, couples held hands and smooched while I spoke, a couple of women nursed babies, older kids ran and jumped around at the other end of the cafeteria where we sat. My Brazilian translator and I spoke for about an hour and a half—too long, I feared—but the shop stewards kept our discussion going till maintenance people came to close the hall. They asked complex questions about multinational companies, computers and robotics, about the destruction of the environment, about modern art and anti-art, about the decline of the American labor movement, about the conflicts within American feminism, about the fall of the USSR. They were as thoughtful and lively a group as I've ever talked to, and I thought Brazil would be lucky—indeed, any country would be lucky—if people like them should come to power.

One of the things that holds Brazil's radically contrasting scenes together is a system of mass media with a nationwide reach. There are several daily national newspapers, a decent facsimile of the *Wall Street Journal*, a couple of news magazines in the *Time* class. But everybody's primal source is the *Globo* TV network, whose stylish graphics and sexy yet insipid programs are often seen by as much as 90 percent of the households in the country. Globo is the leading producer of *telenovelas*, Brazilian soap operas, which are broadcast in prime time, feature steamy sex scenes (alas, not in the three hours we saw), and draw a higher proportion of the total audience than anything Americans can imagine. The plots and characters of these programs are said to define the staples of Brazilian conversation; they provide a legitimate pretext for any two strangers to talk. In addition, they are dubbed into Spanish and sold to the entire Spanish-speaking world; Brazilians take pride in this as a symbol of their country's cultural strength.

Our driver in São Paulo, a student and participant in radical theatres, has no television set himself and can't stand these shows; but as "a cultural worker among the people," he can't afford to appear ignorant of their latest twists, and the morning papers publish summaries of the coming action every day. Brazil is full of clubs that watch these shows and vote approval or disapproval of their plots. Clubs' letters, some with thousands of signatures, often lead the network to annul marriages, drive companies out of business, afflict their characters with sudden death or miraculously bring them back to life.

Two years ago, President Fernando Collor de Mello was impeached by the nation's Congress. But on the day he was brought down, this tremendous event rated only a minor place on page one. Far more prominent, with bigger headlines, a more highly charged story in much greater detail, was the murder of a leading *telenovela* actress by the actor who played her lover on television.

Among the Brazilians we met, people close to the labor movement and the PT were the most optimistic about the future. People who worked for universities, or who worked in the health professions or social services, saw a prospect far more bleak. Three things made them depressed and anxious: Brazil's inflation, the chronic decline of its public services, and daily fear and anxiety about violence.

Brazil has one of the most dynamic economies in the world, with productivity and exports growing around 3 percent every year. But its productivity has been sapped by chronic inflation. For the past year, the inflation has been rising a little over 1 percent a day.

This means, for instance, that price tags in stores mean very little: every day a new master price list goes around; if the store you're in hasn't yet received (or figured out) its list, they will take the figure and the date on the tag, and jack the price up accordingly.

People who work for large corporations and organizations make direct-deposit deals with banks that give high interest rates (30 percent a month, say) indexed to the previous month's inflation. ("Indexed" is a life-and-death word in Brazil.) People do as much of their business as possible by check, even buying drinks in a bar. Cash machines are everywhere; people wait till the last possible moment before withdrawing cash from their high-interest accounts.

We couldn't find any clear consensus on why the inflation had gotten so bad, but everyone seemed to agree that parasitic state corporations (there are over seven hundred, many run by military officers) were a big factor in it, and no one had any confidence in the government's capacity either to clean them up or to sell them off. Meanwhile, people talked angrily about a "new class" that has gotten rich on currency speculation and sapped the national economy's productive power.

Luís Schwarz, my publisher, was selling more books than ever last year, and had three of the top ten national best-sellers, but almost went broke because several of the big banks, after taking huge losses in world money markets, withdrew their credit lines from small businesses. Luís has never loved capitalism, but he always thought that at least it had a coherent system of meanings: you make money if you sell a commodity that people want, you lose money if you don't. Now he sees it as pure theater of the absurd.

What upsets people most, though, is the violence. Shellie Sclan: "Everybody seems to live in a *favela* or behind a fence." All the Brazilians we met felt that in recent years the violence has gotten a lot worse. They fear turf wars and shoot-outs by well-armed drug gangs, but also random stick-ups by coked-up *pivetes*, twelve-year-old street kids with guns, and kidnappings by crooks who have run out of rich victims and democratized their business, working their way down into the lower middle class. Now they grab people who often have little or nothing to give, and sometimes this makes them mad and they kill. (A t-shirt on sale in Porto Alegre's public market said, *"Don't Kidnap Me, I'm A Professor"*—in other words, a person without capital, slim pickings.) They talk about the *arrastão*, a maneuver where pickup gangs of fifty or a hundred boys descend from the *favelas* and sweep the beach or the Avenida Atlantica, robbing and stabbing everyone in their path. (Last year the big drug dealers decided these kids were attracting too much attention and jeopardizing serious business, so they cut off some of their hands.) Everybody felt that the quality of Brazilian life, so informal and mellow not so long ago, has turned brutal and paranoid today. This was most striking in Rio, where several people talked about how they "grew up on the beach" but fear to go there now. Middle-class apartment houses in Rio and São Paulo have security systems far more ambitious and elaborate than their equivalents in New York or Chicago. Single-family houses have iron fences that in effect place the house in a cage; although, thanks to the grace and finesse of Brazilian design, it's easy for householders to forget the iron cages they live in.

At the end of July 1993, just before we arrived, the violence exploded. Rio's beautiful domed Baroque Catedral de Candelaria, in the old center of the city, is home to hundreds of *pivetes*, who sleep on its porches and benches. Now and then they engage in what North Americans might consider legitimate work, but mostly they live by begging, small-time drug dealing and theft. They are locked in unending struggles with the Military Police, who suspect them of everything (about half the time they are right), and who are said to shake them down. One night in July, a group of Military Policemen converged on the church and fired point-blank into the crowd, killing nine kids and wounding dozens more.

Why did they do it? Were they punishing the kids for failing to pay protection? Or did they come looking for somebody, but the search got out of hand? Or were they just having drunken fun? Or what? Nobody seems to know. A couple of the cops who were involved have been arrested (many others weren't), but nobody thinks they will do hard time. All the time we were in Brazil, people couldn't stop talking about the mass murder. But their talk went round and round in futility. Nobody thought the state had institutions with enough authority to get to the bottom of it and this juridical bankruptcy evoked their worst memories of military dictatorship, which after all wasn't so long ago. (Brazilians consider 1981 the watershed year in the life of their still fragile democracy.) Did "the public" hate those kids so much that it would tolerate mass murder and throw away the rule of law that it had fought so hard to secure? Our friends were afraid of the answer.

In Brazil during the summer of 1993, there was much talk about the violence of underclass boys: violence done by them, violence done to them. After a while, I came to feel that there was something weird about this talk. It had a pathos and an emotional intensity that seemed to take on a life of its own. Brazilians ordinarily love conversation, but once a Brazilian started talking in this vein, there wasn't anything I could say, except "Gee, that's terrible." For instance, I couldn't say the United States also has very high levels of violence, and I couldn't say that discourse about violence has all sorts of symbolic weight in American political culture. (I did say it, but even the best listeners wouldn't hear.) But after awhile, I began to see what Brazilian discourse of violence is really all about. One story told to us several times was that the World Bank had delivered a message to Brazil, saying the country had one-third too many people. We felt this had an apocryphal ring, but we could see the point: there is a solid, thriving industrial economy here, but many millions of Brazilians who are totally outside it, and who have no imaginable way in.

The educational system does nothing to help them. Brazilian children are tracked far more rigidly than Americans. One thing that everyone we met insisted on is that it is impossible to get into college without going to private school. But private schools in Brazil offer no scholarships. And there is no system of community colleges, and nothing like the high school equivalence exam, and no way to move into higher education if you're late getting out of the gate, and no cultural pressure to get poor kids into and through college, and no institutions for workers' education (though the PT seems to be trying to create some). So a crucial feature of adolescence in Brazil is a very personal encounter with class barriers that are peremptory and absolute. And most kids who go through this encounter, as all kids must, are doomed to end up as permanent losers. When Brazilians talk about their dead-end kids, they tell themselves something like this: "Of course they'll do anything, because there isn't anything out there for them." Because they see no signs of anything turning up for these kids, they judge them beyond help or hope, and they see their number as bound to grow and grow.

This drama is a story we should know all too well. Yet American culture has more second acts, more entrance and exit lanes, more holes to fall into, but also more holes to crawl out of. Our poor people haven't quite reached the tragic pass of poor people in Brazil, a country that feels inexorably split between the *favelas* and the fences.

14

Beware the Tanks

Carlos Ravelo

T he revelation came as a surprise during a January 1994 interview with Manchete TV network. "I want to say something extremely serious," said Justice Minister Maurício Correa, matter-of-factly. "Not long ago, some people called on President Itamar Franco with the mission of convincing him to endorse a coup." The people to whom Correa referred were never identified. The president himself downplayed the matter and the military reaffirmed their disposition to uphold the constitution. Questions still linger. How serious was the idea of a Fujimorization of the Brazilian system? Like Peru's Fujimori, Franco has a short fuse when criticized by the press and although the country has no guerrillas, Brazil's problems with corruption sometimes seem to need a little extra help from somebody strong, preferably wearing khaki. The military wouldn't dare any coup, say some political observers. Can they be that sure?

Less than a decade after they abandoned control of Brazil's destiny by leaving it in the hands of civilian politicians, one of the Western Hemisphere's largest military establishment has again let its heavy *sotaque* (accent) be heard ... this time loud and clear!

After pronouncements made earlier by then-Finance Minister, Fernando Henrique Cardoso, that the military's 21 billion *cruzeiros* budget was to be cut by at least 40 percent, the Armed Forces' top brass took a bold step forward—apparently with the implicit support of President Itamar Franco—and "de facto" placed Cardoso's austerity plans into a rapid about-face.

Roman Cure

"If we should have to leave our white-washed bones upon the sands of the deserts, so be it—but be ye aware of the choler of the Legions!" These words of warning are attributed to Marcus Flavinius, a Centurion in the Imperial Roman Army, who rose to the forefront of the Roman power structure. Now those same words are being repeated by Brazil's Army Chief-of-Staff, General Benedito Onofre Bezerra Leonel. The coincidence is ominous.

President Itamar Franco's support against any cutbacks in the Armed Forces budget was, by default, a hard blow to Finance Minister Cardoso's ego and political credibility. At a moment when the rest of the government is reeling from a budgetary slash to the tune of $82 million, which also affects the average person on the street, the sacred military cow seems to be untouchable. Three of its offspring are just as sacred: a nuclear submarine, Brazil's space program, and an interceptor plane project—the AMX—currently being researched jointly with the Italian government.

Navy Minister Ivan Serpa flexed his muscles quickly too. After being informed of the proposed cuts, he emphatically stated: "No, I don't agree. How would you like to have your salary cut in half?" A close friend of President Franco, Serpa spearheaded a veiled threat of mass resignations among top military officers. Further compounding the problem, complaints and concerns were conveyed by all military branches, at each and every level of the chain-of-command. General Gilberto Serra, spokesperson for the Army, indicated that "the cutbacks will (effectively) shut down the Army." Brigadier Cherubin Rosa, Jr. of the Air Force stated: "The Brazilian Air Force has reached an operational rock-bottom; only emergency-type operations are feasible, but none of a military nature."

Low Profile Defense

As far as military expenses *per capita* are concerned, Brazil occupies the 73rd spot out of 140 countries worldwide. Brazil pays an average of $7 per citizen per year to maintain a functional military structure. That compares to an average per capita expense of

$10 in Mexico, $35 in Argentina, $55 in Chile, $395 in England and more than $1,000 in the United States.

Salaries of rank-and-file are also perilously low in Brazil. A Staff Sergeant in the Army earns a mere $300 per month; a simple private only makes $30. But in spite of the heated debate on this issue, so far there has been no mention of a coup a la 1964. "The military does not have any power-taking plan like they had prior to 1964," says military analyst Roberto Lopes, "although Brazilian society does not yet know what they want from their Armed Forces."

One exception, however, is Reserve Colonel Pedro Schirmer. From Rio de Janeiro, he publishes *Ombro a Ombro* (Shoulder to Shoulder), a radical magazine in which he actively supports and promotes "Hard and drastic measures against misguided democratic policies." Schirmer has been in contact with other radical South American *golpistas* such as rebel officers Mohamed Ali Seineldín— currently serving a life sentence in Argentina—and General Francisco E. Visconti, of the Venezuelan Air Force, currently ex- iled in Peru after his failed coup attempt. Both are collaborating with Schirmer by writing articles for his journal.

Old Boys Network

The apparent mutual attraction between Itamar Franco and the military is nothing new. During his tenure as Mayor of Juiz de Fora, in the state of Minas Gerais, during the 1960s and 1970s Franco was on excellent terms with the military commanders of the 4th Army Division and the 4th Military Regional Headquar- ters, both stationed there.

In fact, President Franco often left his offices in the Palácio do Planalto solely to appear at certain military ceremonies. Under coun- seling from his closest advisors, however, Franco refuses to en- gage in any controversy involving military versus civilian issues.

Almost 30 years after the 1964 coup, some of the military seem to long for their past role in Brazilian society. During the 20 years of military dictatorship their role was simple and forceful: to fight the "red menace," keep law and order and, if at all possible, promote progress. To this day, however, they still believe that they are the "safekeepers of institutionality," whatever that might mean. If Brazil's unending crisis were to place institutional stability at a risk, then they would presumably intervene.

And it is precisely the fear—and the dishonor—of having their budgets cut even further, that has prompted the top brass to voice their demands. Warns Deputy (Congressman) Jose Genoíno, "Any displeased and mistreated military structure will end up creating political problems." Considering Brazil's past experience with the military and their longing for the past, he may be right.

Messianic Mission Impossible

Nineteen sixty-four is seen by many as a turning point in Brazil's political history. This was the year of the military coup. Nevertheless, Brazil's experience with a case of "the reds"—as far as the military is concerned—dates back to 1935 when *Gaúcho* general Getulio Vargas came to power. The reform forces that subsequently propelled and empowered President João Goulart in the 1960s, further exacerbated internal divisions within the armed forces.

Slowly, a messianic vision crept into the minds of the top brass; the theory was that the military had to "clean up the house." Hardliners then took control, after Marshall Castelo Branco's tenure. It was General da Costa e Silva who in reality took control and exercised power in a heavy-handed and politically uncompromising manner.

The 1960s were also a time of global social turmoil; guerrilla movements were widespread on a worldwide scale. One group which the military mistakenly identified as the ideological wing for the leftist movements was the Catholic church due to its support for agrarian reform movements.

As early as 1961, after President Janio Quadros resigned, and after then Vice-President João Goulart's visit to Chairman Mao's China, suspicions by the military were suddenly aroused, almost resulting in a military coup. Several high-ranking generals even intended to halt Goulart at his presidential inauguration. Payback time arrived three years later, carried out by the same group that was unable to topple Goulart in 1961.

By the late 1960s, many within the rank-and-file began to quietly voice their dissatisfaction with the negative turn of events. The Armed Forces began to feel resentment against those few who were tarnishing their image in Brazil and abroad. The messianic-militaristic viewpoint was slowly changing into a corporative outlook, a more businesslike approach to the military's social role.

The current approach and outlook of the military can be measured by the attitude and words of one of its most outspoken representatives, Federal Deputy Jair Bolsonaro. He also happens to be a captain in the reserve, and was elected mostly through the support and votes of military men and their relatives. "They've desisted from trying to save the nation," he states, "and are just trying to save themselves." His words have the ring of undeniable truth. In any case, Brazil's military and its political role continue to be a magician's hat and Pandora's box, rolled into one.

15

The Black Hole

Rodney Mello

Where is the money of one of the richest economies in the world? In the deep pockets of those with many crooked, imaginative techniques and no sense of citizenship and solidarity. Brazil has been losing tens of billions of dollars to these thieves.

With a foreign debt of more than $110 billion, Brazil is the champion of the Third World Big Debtors Club. This amount, accumulated during decades of impulse borrowing and free-spending-cum-money-disappearing acts, pales, however, in comparison to what corruption and embezzlement cost the country every year. According to estimates of the government itself, the country loses $80 billion a year due to the fraud of those who don't pay their federal taxes. When you add losses due to waste and negligence over the past few years, the bill rises to an estimated $140 billion.

This explains why most of the people get poorer by the minute while a very small number gets richer with the public's money. And the bill would be even bigger if we added all the money the country loses through smuggling, all the resources wasted on the local and state levels, and all the dollars sent overseas through illegal channels. The $60 billion figure for waste and negligence is a conservative number, since it is based on only 22 cases of corruption and waste uncovered since the beginning of the Collor years, which started in 1990. Ex-president Fernando Collor himself was impeached and exposed as the leader of a gang.

The government chest was raided and depleted from all sides. Social Security, unemployment benefits, programs to assist children and fight hunger, resources destined for schools, funds to combat the drought in the Northeast and to build roads—nothing escaped the greedy hands of an unscrupulous minority.

Some Exemplary Cases

The Budget Mafia: Representatives involved in this scandal, in which politicians had their hands greased by big contractors in exchange for "little changes" in the budget, received more than $100 million. This is only the money that could be traced through bank accounts. João Alves, a representative from Bahia, had moved more than $50 million through his 13 banking accounts since 1989, the year he started manipulating amendments to the budget.

Public charity: There are suspicions that one third of the $152 million distributed through *Ministério da Ação Social* (Social Action Ministry) to philanthropic organizations between 1989 and 1992 ended up with crooks such as congressional representative Fábio Raunheitti from Rio.

PC: PC Farias, the ex-treasurer of president Collor's campaign, hasn't paid more than $100 million in taxes he owes through his companies. In only two years during the Collor administration, he increased his wealth by $1 billion. PC has become a symbol of decadence and the patron saint of all corrupt politicians.

Health: The acquisition in May 1991 of 2.6 million syringes by the Health Ministry without bidding resulted in a loss of $42 million. Yearly, $1.5 billion are lost in this sector.

Children: In 1991, Maria de Fátima de Omena, the ex-president of the *Fundação Centro Brasileiro para Infancia e Adolescencia* (an organization to assist children), along with her husband, Francisco das Chagas Porcino, was accused of pocketing more than $1 billion.

Food: A 1992 CPI (Parliamentary Inquiry Committee) revealed that only $3 of every $10 destined by the federal government to fight hunger ever reached the people for whom the money was intended. FAE (Foundation to Assist the Student) bought $128 million in overpriced food the same day minister Carlos Chiarelli left the Education Ministry in 1991. In 1990 the LBA (Brazilian

Legion of Assistance) bought almost 200,000 *cestas básicas* (basic food baskets for the poor) at a 20 percent inflated price. There were more than $6 billion in losses due to the diversion or waste of grain, according to a study in January 1993.

Social Security: A gang of swindlers in Rio caused losses of $550 million to the INSS (National Institute of Social Security). Another $5 billion was lost through work overcharged to the FGTS, an unemployment benefits agency.

Contractors: It is unusual for contractors to overcharge up to 100 percent. In 1990 the government spent $24.8 billion in public works. Pharaonic works are common. The Xingó Hydroelectric Dam was over budget due to overcharges, costing $1.5 billion, and *Ferrovia do Aço* (Steel Railroad) wasted at least $200 million. There was also an overcharge of $302 million in the construction of new dams in the Northeast.

Taxes: The IRS estimates that only half of the money due to the agency is ever collected. This means an annual loss of $80 billion.

16

Jungle of Myths

New Internationalist

How much do you know about the Amazon rainforest? And how much of it is true? With many false beliefs flying around, it can be a difficult task to differentiate the facts about the Brazilian rainforest from the fiction.

"The Amazon rainforest is the lungs of the world," is one of the most common misrepresentations. In fact, the Amazon uses as much oxygen as it produces. Otherwise, it would be getting bigger all the time. The rainforest is, however, critical to the climate of the region. Its destruction would bring dramatic and unpredictable changes.

"Deforestation of the Amazon by burning is a principal cause of global warming," is another favorite misconception. If the entire Amazon rainforest were burned over the next 20 years, it would each year contribute about 20 percent of the carbon reaching the atmosphere to produce the "greenhouse effect." This would still be less than half the amount produced by the burning of fossil fuels (oil and coal) in the industrial world alone.

It is easy to imagine that logging is the biggest cause of deforestation. It is true that logging—particularly of hardwoods like mahogany—often plays a part in starting the clearing process. But clearance for cattle ranching is by far the biggest cause of deforestation.

Many people assume that this cattle ranching produces beef "used to make hamburgers in the US." In reality, the Amazon is a net importer of beef. Exporting meat is difficult because foot-and-mouth disease is endemic in the area. The main use of cattle ranching in the Amazon is as a device for claiming land and for speculation rather than the production of beef.

"If the forest were cleared the land could feed the hungry," is still heard these days. But this fails to take into account the fact that the soils of the rainforest are thin and poor. They degrade and erode quickly after clearing. Only a carefully planned mixture of agriculture and forestry could sustain a large population.

The claim that "there are too many people in the Amazon today," is countered by the fact that there are probably no more people living in the forest today than there were at the time of the European invasion in the 16th century.

"Landless colonists are to blame for torching the Amazon," may seem plausible to many but it is untrue. The culprits are overwhelmingly large-scale landowners. Settlers clear smaller areas and cultivate them more intensively.

Finally, there is the commonly held belief that "at this rate the Amazon rainforest will disappear by the year 2010." This is unlikely. The Brazilian government claims that only five per cent of the forest has been cleared. Some studies suggest a figure of 20 percent, but between ten and 15 percent is more probable. Clearing and burning reached a peak in 1987 when there was an exceptionally dry burning season, and landowners, fearing agrarian reform, wanted to secure their claim to the land. The pace has slowed down since then but it does not mean that people have stopped suffering.

17

What Future for Amazônia?

Ignacy Sachs

M any people in the industrialized countries would like Amazônia to be preserved exactly as it is, and transform it into a vast nature reserve. Some of these advocates of the non-development of Amazônia attach the highest priority to safeguarding planet Earth and at the same time regard human beings as parasites. Others point out that the Amazônia forest plays a major role in counteracting the greenhouse effect, and wish to see it act as a gigantic filter so that 500 million cars can continue to consume fossil fuels.

The Current Context

The non-development of Amazônia is totally unacceptable both to the people who live in the region and to Brazilians in general. The gratuitous advice handed out to the people on the spot may well be seen as a kind of ecological colonialism as long as the industrialized countries of the North refuse to change their ways of life and patterns of consumption.

Let these countries prove their sincerity by proposing to the United Nations a specific program for the reduction of energy consumption in industrial societies.

Let them also provide the countries of the South with access to the scientific and technical knowledge that is needed to develop the immense biological heritage of the Amazônian forest within a framework of sound ecological principles. For this long-term task, Brazil and the other countries of Amazônia need the capacity to carry out their own *in situ* research.

For tropical countries, biotechnology opens up considerable possibilities based on progress in the production of biomass and the
range of products that can be derived from it. Eventually we may
see the emergence of a new "plant-based industrial civilization," a
particularly interesting prospect for tropical countries. Mr.
Monkombu S. Swaminathan, a former President of the International
Union for Conservation of Nature and Natural Resources, believes
that a new form of civilization based on the sustainable use of renewable resources is not only possible but essential. The vision of
this Indian scientist coincides with the intuitions of the Brazilian
sociologist Gilberto Freyre, who in the 1960s founded a seminar
on tropicology at Recife.

At present, however, biotechnology seems to be so effectively
shielded by a wall of patents that people in developing countries
are wondering whether it will become an instrument for the North
to recolonize the South. The industrialized countries could relax
their position on patents and intellectual property rights, and establish more open forms of access to science and technology.

In 1989, Mr. Rajiv Gandhi, then Prime Minister of India, suggested that a 0.1 percent tax be levied on world revenue and its
yield of $18 billion be used to establish a world fund to finance
research into environment-friendly technologies and their free distribution to all interested countries. Nothing came of this proposal
but it relaunched the debate on the financing of environmental protection and development.

Another possible course of action would be to create a network
linking Asian and African researchers to Brazilians and other Latin
Americans who are seeking to harness the renewable resources of
humid tropical ecosystems, a process that should harmonize three
objectives of what is known as ecodevelopment:

• the promotion of greater social justice in the name of the ethical principle of synchronic solidarity, with development being regarded as a step toward a civilization based on the equitable sharing of possessions;

• self-development in harmony with nature rather than through
domination of nature, in the name of the ethical principle of

diachronic solidarity with future generations;

• the pursuit of these two goals through a search for a kind of economic efficiency that is not restricted to a concept of business profitability which often takes no account of ecological and social costs.

In addition to such measures, however, international cooperation must primarily be directed at improving the general economic environment of Latin American countries. In other words, solutions must be found to the problems of debt, terms of trade, and protectionist barriers in the industrialized countries.

The internal challenges posed by the development of Brazilian Amazônia are as vast as the size of this immense area which has captured the imagination of so many and inspired so many exaggerations.

Dreams and Realities

There is a golden legend which portrays Amazônia as a region of fabulous wealth, a mirage which has lured generations of adventurers. A variant of this legend, inspired by the philosophy of the Enlightenment and some of our ethnologists, paints a picture of noble savages living happily in perfect harmony with nature.

There is also a legend which describes Amazônia as a green, impenetrable hell, protected by tropical diseases which afflict all intruders.

These contradictory pictures are reflected in opposing conceptions of the region's future. Some see Amazônia as the world's last great economic frontier, a place of incalculable mineral, hydraulic and plant wealth. Others believe that the abundance of its vegetation is an illusion and that its soils are poor and subject to erosion as soon as the forest is felled. Haphazard exploitation of Amazônia's mineral wealth and the growing number of big dams, combined with chaotic colonization leading to massive deforestation, will rapidly turn Amazônia into a desert.

What are the facts?

A precondition for successful development is the abandonment of the dominant model of predatory exploitation of the region's natural resources, a model which takes no account of social and environmental costs. The random pursuit of growth is just as unacceptable as nondevelopment.

For twenty years or more, several factors combined to accelerate deforestation. These factors were:

• geopolitical imperatives leading to the settling of Amazônia along purpose-built roads;

• the idea that Amazônia could absorb refugees displaced by the industrialization of agriculture in southern Brazil and by the persistence of unequal land-ownership structures in the northeast;

• the decision to favor large-scale animal husbandry, which is quite unsuited to the natural conditions of Amazônia and leads to speculation in land;

• hopes that the region's mineral wealth could be used to alleviate the burden of foreign debt;

• the establishment of a great industrial center in the duty-free zone at Manaus.

As a result of these policies, now revised, Amazônia has lost between 300,000 and 400,000 square kilometers of forest.

There has also been rapid urbanization. Ten million of Amazônia's 17 million people today live in cities (Manaus and Belém each have over 1 million inhabitants). There are many shantytowns which are so exposed to the risk of epidemics that the living conditions of the people who live in them and in the cities undoubtedly constitute Amazônia's most acute environmental problem today.

Outside the urban centers, the population lives in widely scattered settlements along the banks of streams and rivers and practices a subsistence and gathering economy. The creation of "extractive reserves" has brought a measure of relief to the *caboclos* and *seringueiros* (peasant farmers who tap rubber) whose existence is threatened by land speculators. These people live in extremely precarious conditions which could be improved by more rational exploitation of the forest's natural products, but this can only be envisaged as part of a long-term solution for the whole region. The *seringueiros* want their share of economic, social and cultural progress, which implies a dynamic vision of the transformation of the extractive reserves into poles of ecodevelopment.

The indigenous populations, long the victims of adventurers and colonists, enjoy considerable rights under the Brazilian Constitution, and the Government has promised to earmark 198 million acres of land for 250,000 indigenous people throughout Brazil.

A New Strategy

The aim of Brazil's current environmental policy is to promote a strategy of ecodevelopment rather than a strategy of development at all costs. This is a laudable goal, but it will not be easy to achieve, either in Brazil or in the other Amazônian countries.

It must be accepted that ecodevelopment in Amazônia depends on policy changes outside the region. Land reform and reform in agricultural policy must be carried out in the rest of Brazil in order to reduce the flow of migrants to Amazônia. Likewise, forest resources must be protected by an ambitious reforestation program elsewhere than Amazônia. The FLORAM Plan prepared by the Institute of Advanced Studies of the University of São Paulo proposes that 49 million acres of forest be planted outside Amazônia in thirty years, at a cost of $20 billion.

Within Amazônia, the first step is to divide this heterogeneous region into some twenty sub-regions, each with its own strategy. The global problems of Amazônia call for solutions adapted to local ecological and cultural conditions. Social diversity is a counterpart to biological diversity.

The main thrust of these efforts must be directed toward the rehabilitation of already deforested land and, as far as possible, to increasing the density of the population in these areas, so as to halt the advancing frontier of colonization and prevent further deforestation. Efforts must be made to create an archipelago of connected "development reserves" so as to guarantee the protection of virgin forest and the habitat of the indigenous population. Such an approach presents many difficulties, but it still seems more realistic than creating a proliferation of natural reserves.

Agroforestry which makes judicious use of local plant species (especially the enormous potential of fruit trees), aquaculture, high-yield agriculture and horticulture in the *varzeas* (highly fertile floodland) and small-scale animal husbandry are promising techniques. Knowledge of the environment acquired in the course of the centuries by local populations may provide a useful starting point, hence the importance of ethno-ecological studies.

Technical skills based on the know-how of local populations and inputs from modern science can meet the needs of small modern family farms. The use of local energy sources exploited on a limited scale would also make possible the gradual development of small packaging and transformation industries.

An efficient network of production and marketing cooperatives would provide an institutional framework for these ecodevelopment strategies. In the medium term, such cooperatives would make it possible to provide decent living conditions for a much larger population, while respecting the vulnerable ecosystems of Amazônia. They would also slow down the exodus to the shanty-towns and the proliferation of uncontrolled gold mining.

The objective must be to make Amazônia habitable by abandoning the colonial vision of an area producing resources which are drained away to the outside world. There remain the far more difficult problems of reducing the social and ecological costs of mining and hydropower, improving the living conditions of the urban masses, and controlling tropical diseases, especially malaria.

Contrary to a widespread prejudice, enough is known about Amazônia for us to advance along the road of ecodevelopment, without neglecting research. Successful projects and promising local initiatives can be found in the interstices of the predatory development model. These solutions may be seen as the precursors of a new paradigm of development.

18

The Rubber Tappers Under Fire Again

Linda Perney

n April 1992, two officials of Brazil's National Council of Rubber Tappers (CNS) spent a week in New York City. They came as part of a delegation of the Alliance of the Peoples of the Forest, an umbrella organization that represents a coalition of grassroots movements in Brazil. Together with leaders of several groups of indigenous peoples, Pedro Ramos and Antonio Macedo were guests of honor at Amazon Week II, held at New York University. They participated in panel discussions. They gave press conferences. They met with schoolchildren. They were honored at a reception at the United Nations. They had the best seats in the house at the Ritz, where Milton Nascimento sang for their cause. Then Ramos and Macedo went home to Brazil, where somebody tried to kill them.

At issue was land conflict in Amazônia. It is the same dispute that killed union leader and environmentalist Chico Mendes in December 1988. Mendes, one of CNS's founders, was a defender of extractive reserves, an alternative proposal for agrarian reform.

In a country where 44 percent of the arable land is owned by one percent of the population, the path toward agrarian reform has been strewn with bodies. The Pastoral Land Commission, an organization that is run by the Catholic Church and organizes against violence in Brazil's rural areas, estimates that 1,658 members of movements related to land disputes were murdered between 1964 and 1991. Only 12 of the alleged killers have ever gone to trial; five of them have gone to prison. Darly Alves, the man who ordered the murder of Chico Mendes, is in jail largely because of the international uproar over the CNS leader's death—or so claim spokespeople for several human-rights groups.

Ramos and Macedo are heirs to Mendes's vision and struggles. Both are hardworking grassroots organizers. Both have a deep connection to the land and its peoples. Both have Mendes's gifts of oratory and leadership, but neither has received the international attention that protected Mendes for a long time.

In Amazônia, land reform has meant creating extractive reserves, which the CNS managed to introduce into Brazil by almost superhuman efforts. Under the extractive-reserve system, rubber tappers and other indigenous peoples are granted concessions for use of the land they have traditionally occupied. The land, however, remains the property of the nation as a whole.

As they stand now, the reserves are administered by extractive peoples' co-operatives, or unions. In the state of Acre about 3.75 million acres have been designated extractive reserves; additional reserves in the states of Rondonia, Amazonas, and Amapa cover about the same area.

Two years ago the reserves were established by a presidential decree that named IBAMA—Brazil's environmental protection agency—as the agency responsible for demarcating the reserves and giving the forest peoples the structural conditions to operate them.

But there has been ongoing conflict over how the reserves will be demarcated. Reform advocates have been targeted for attack by large landowners. The attacks on Ramos, Macedo, and a third colleague, Gomercindo Rodrigues, are symptomatic of the attacks on the movement as a whole.

Antonio Luis Batista de Macedo is a strongly built man with curly, undisciplined hair and flimsy wire-rimmed glasses. He lives in Cruzeiro do Sul, the second-largest town in Acre. His friends say he is more of a poet at heart than a union organizer, and he seems most comfortable singing romantic ballads, accompanying himself on the guitar. Still, he is one of the most influential leaders in the CNS.

Macedo grew up among the Kaxinawá Indians, and he speaks a

number of Indian languages. One of his childhood friends is the Indian leader Sia Kaxinawá; this and similar friendships have been instrumental in forging new alliances between indigenous groups and the *seringueiros*. Macedo says it was these friendships that almost got him killed.

In early August, Moises and Francisco Pianko, two Kampa brothers—members of an indigenous nation that Macedo has helped defend in conflicts with Brazilian government agencies—traveled to Brasilia to lobby for official demarcation and appropriation of the nation's reservation. At the same time, they denounced people they called invaders, who, they said, were using the reserve as a base for cocaine trafficking.

A month later Macedo led a group of census takers into the Upper Jurua Extractive Reserve. They stopped at Vila Taumaturgo de Azevedo, some 125 miles upstream from Cruzeiro do Sul. Macedo says that as he stepped out of a store, he was set upon by a man who knocked him to the ground, put a revolver to his head, and pulled the trigger three times. The gun misfired. Macedo then heard his attacker say it didn't matter, because he really wanted to get the two Kampas. Macedo says there were witnesses to the attack but they did nothing. He later identified his assailant as a member of a family accused of drug dealing.

On September 24, according to Macedo, some of his neighbors saw a car drive past his house twice. One of them recognized the driver as the man who had earlier attacked him. That night Macedo was awakened by the sound of someone trying to break into his house. He dashed to the front door, and his shouts brought neighbors running, in time to see two men drive off on motorcycles.

Physically, Pedro Ramos de Souza is almost the direct opposite of Macedo. When he gets up to speak in public, he seems almost frail. He is slight and nervous, a chain-smoker who chews on the insides of his cheeks when he is not dragging on a cigarette.

Ramos thinks and speaks in paragraphs, not disjointed phrases. His arguments have the precision, imagery, and seamless closing of a Bach fugue. While much of the CNS leadership, including its president, Julio Barbosa, lives in Acre, vice-president Pedro Ramos leads the budding extractivist movement in eastern Amazônia, which is based several thousand miles away in Macapá, the capital of Amapá.

On July 20, the night before a public debate on the environmental impact of a highway that will cut through the Rio Cajari Extractive Reserve, Ramos was severely beaten in the doorway of his house. The next morning neighbors found him lying unconscious in the street. He later told friends that if his dog hadn't gone after the attackers he would be dead.

But the most controversial of the recent attacks on CNS leaders took place in the Acre state capital on September 17. As he walked toward the offices of the Acre State Environmental Institute (IMAC), CNS adviser Gomercindo Rodrigues was accosted by two armed men; when he tried to flee, he was shot in the throat and abdomen. Doctors in Rio Branco were unable to remove the bullet from his throat, so he was transferred to São Paulo.

Rodrigues identified his assailants by pointing at photographs. Two men were arrested.

CNS members claim that the attack was prompted by Rodrigues' work. He has been instrumental in organizing many of the successful *empates* (standoffs) against local people who have tried to survey or cut tracts of extractive reserves. Moreover, Rodrigues received telephone threats while in the hospital after the attack. He would never get out alive, said the callers.

Their opponents have attempted to spread scandalous rumors about Ramos and Macedo. It has been suggested by some that Ramos was engaged in an adulterous affair. Macedo has been accused of raping Indian girls. Brazilian tradition has not been broken: No one has been tried in either of the two attacks.

Meanwhile, the cycle of violence continues. Because of their activism, the rubber tappers remain the most visible target. The rubber tappers say they are tired of attending masses for their murdered colleagues. They want to put a stop to attacks on the forest peoples.

19

Prostitution Comes to the Indigenous Amazon

Gilberto Dimenstein

The Yanomami, intrigued by his green eyes, watched him. They were afraid, thinking that he was an apparition. After all, they had never seen a man with green eyes. With time, they grew accustomed to Dr. Marcos Pellegrini who, in 1986, was the first white man to come in contact with a tribe of Yanomami Indians from the Moxafe region in Roraima. To get there, Marcos undertook a week-long journey, three days of which were on foot in the heart of the jungle.

For a number of months, Marcos lived with this tribe, learning its customs which had not yet been tainted by "civilization." It was a harmonious society, without epidemics or hunger. Hunting, fishing and agricultural production provided enough for all.

But after Marcos, thousands of men arrived with their dredges, revolvers and mercury. It was the invasion of the *garimpeiros* in search of gold.

In 1991, Marcos, now a doctor at the National Health Foundation and the Indigenista Missionary Council (CIMI), returned to visit this tribe. Green eyes and blonde hair no longer impressed the Yanomami. A number of them had other interests: women offered themselves to him in exchange for gifts. The health of the tribe had deteriorated. Marcos noted the appearance of various illnesses, among them gonorrhea. An old woman asked him a question which seemed strange at first: "Aren't there any white women?"

Afterwards, he understood. These people had met only men— soldiers and *garimpeiros*—who represented invasion and illness. They were not accompanied by their wives, and took advantage of the indigenous women. Sex, so natural in the bosom of the community, had become a product with an exchange value. In this way, prostitution made its appearance in the tribe: sex was paid for with rum, medicine, clothes and food. The tribe had even stopped growing crops and were in need of food.

Marcos is currently working with the tribes of the upper Purus region in Acre. There, he has also noted the sexual abuse of indigenous women and children — especially by the *marreteiros*, hawkers who travel by boat selling their wares. They carry rum with them to pay the women.

I had the opportunity to interview the former *cacique* Raiaou, who lives in the indigenous reserve of São Lourenço, in the municipality of Assis Brazil. Raiaou, who spoke in the Jaminauá language which a local guide translated for me, admitted to having been the victim of this rum introduced by the *marreteiros*. One day, one of the men asked to sleep with his daughter in exchange for 12 bottles. The deal was struck. The old *cacique* had no complaint until the men asked for his wife.

"Then, I said: 'Respect me, you son of a bitch,'" Raiaou recounted, repeating the gesture he had made with his arm. He said the phrase "son of a bitch" not in Jaminauá, but in Portuguese.

During my stay in Rio Branco, I discovered various Jaminauá families wandering around the city. A team of television reporters approached a family to ask for an interview. The reporters were caught off guard when the girls insistently offered their bodies in exchange for a little food or money.

Not only the *marreteiros*, but also the soldiers scattered among the different garrisons of the Amazon are responsible for the attacks against women and children. The doctor and anthropologist Antonio Maria de Souza, a researcher at the Emílio-Goeldi museum in Belém, has gathered dozens of testimonies of the "general"—a sort of gang rape of indigenous girls that the soldiers engage in.

"It was common practice until very recently for a group of men—generally off-duty recruits—to catch an Indian, often a young one," Antonio says. "They would take her to a deserted place and force her to do 'the general.' In other words, they would gang-rape her. These rapes occurred innumerable times despite the punishment of some aggressors. In the city, you hear people say that the Indian girls like it."

The commander of the Fifth Special Borders Battalion of the Army of São Gabriel da Cachoeira, Colonel Francisco Abrao, does not appreciate the accusations against his soldiers. "It is the Indian women who try to rape my soldiers when they are in heat," he says. "I must protect my soldiers because they cannot respond to all these longings."

20

Popular Struggle and the Preservation of the Amazon

Pastoral Land Commission

The Brazilian Amazon, since the decade of the sixties during the military dictatorship, has gone through an accelerated process of human occupation. This occupation for colonization projects was accomplished by the dislocation of huge groups of people from the Northeast—who were beaten down by the drought in the 1970s—and by owners of small holdings and landless people from the South of the country. The objective was to diminish the social conflicts and, alleging motives for national security, to promote the occupation of the Amazon Territory. Many groups of rural workers were settled in the region, principally along the Transamazon Highway.

The majority of these projects, however, did not guarantee the conditions necessary for a dignified standard of living for the settlers and were implanted at very high ecological costs. Most of the financial incentives designed to promote the colonization of the Amazon were actually swallowed up by large agro-industrial enterprises, many of them connected to multinational corporations. The dislocation of huge migrant groups served to open up and prepare the region for the implementation of these big projects. Huge areas of forest were, and continue to be, cleared and converted into pasture. This policy was protected by the law, as deforestation was considered profitable. Cattle ranchers received the greatest economic incentives under the plan. Clearly, the government, the multinationals and the national companies are responsible for the accelerated destruction of the tropical rainforest.

On the other hand, for many years the Amazon had been inhabited by riverside dwellers, rubber-tappers, Indians, rural workers and small farmers, who in their interaction with nature never caused the devastation that is seen today. These less well-off social groups were capable of formulating alternatives to satisfy their needs and contribute to their development, with compatible social programs in their midst. Their participation is indispensable in the elaboration of projects relating to production and the preservation of the environment. They can offer their knowledge from working the land as well as their commitment to preserving the environment. Their perspective is pivotal for development projects seeking to utilize adequate social technologies which preserve the environment and are economically viable.

In addition to well-known problems such as deforestation, burning land to raise cattle, and the exploitation of wood for export, there is another destructive practice: predatory fishing conducted by big fishing ships with ice containers. This is causing scarcity and even the extinction of various species of fish in the rivers of the Amazon, bringing hunger to the river dwelling population.

Confronted with these environmentally destructive practices, government agencies, the European Community, the World Bank, and many others have proposed alternatives for sustainable development in the region. These initiatives have provoked more problems than solutions, both for the preservation of the environment and for the local population.

The "Echea Project," which advocates the production of fish in aquatic cages, exemplifies the contradictory nature of some proposals. According to studies by the University of Manaus, this project may be deleterious both in social and ecological terms. The "Echea Project" could interfere with the local production of 5 billion roe (fish eggs).

Secondly, the proposal plans to incorporate local fishers as the main labor force. This would transform their community into a fishing factory, thus marginalizing their traditional activities and their peaceful interaction with the environment. Thirdly, this project is opposed by the communities of the region because its objective is the development of fishing for export without concern for the local population.

Confronted by this challenge, some riverside communities have developed their own projects for the preservation of lakes and rivers seeking to guarantee the livelihood of their communities and to preserve the environment. Their policy consists of choosing lakes for their fishing needs, using only safe methods and instruments, and using lakes for breeding (sanctuary lakes) where fishing is prohibited. The communities have formed fishing committees, or "committees for the protection of fish," whose task is to organize the protection of lakes and rivers. These committees also have the goal of sensitizing small farmers not to destroy the banks of the lakes and rivers.

The committees also mobilize community members to expel the big fishing ships that invade the lakes and conduct predatory fishing. These committees often face hostility. Armed confrontations have occurred in Tefe, Parintins and Itacoatiara.

The struggle of the indigenous people for the demarcation of their lands and for the preservation of their reserves is also among the popular initiatives for the preservation of the ecosystem, and the preservation of the livelihood and culture of the Amazonian population. In spite of resistance from the highest ranking members of the Brazilian Army, in 1991 a legislative proposal ordering the creation of the Yanomami reserve was approved. The struggle of indigenous people for autonomy is certainly the most explicit example of the necessity to plan for the preservation of the Amazon ecosystem. This preservation can be accomplished by taking into serious consideration the local population, its living conditions, its struggle for survival and its legal rights.

Preservation is especially relevant to the case of the Brazilian Indians because of the abuse experienced due to poor health care and the invasion of their lands. We need to continue to be attentive because there are many pressures from the military and economic groups that the demarcation of the reserve be reconsidered.

Another example of grassroots struggle for the preservation of the Amazon is the movement of the rubber-tappers for the demarcation of extractive reserves. In spite of the financial difficulties created by the drop in the price of rubber in the international markets, these reserves are a means to preserve the environment and guarantee the preservation of the culture and way of life of the rubber-tappers.

The peasants of Acre, through the creation of a cooperative of ongoing cultivation of trees in Nova California, are developing cultivation adapted to the Amazon region, for example Brazil-nut, *Cupuaçu* and *Pupunha*. The objective is to produce high quality food while guaranteeing greater economic gains and the preservation of the environment.

The grassroots initiatives searching for truly sustainable forms of survival do not restrict themselves to the Amazon region. The state of Espirito Santo, which is the site of deforestation of large areas for extensive cattle ranches, has also seen rural conflicts.

Aracruz Celulose, the world's largest producer of celulose (Prince Philip of England is one of its stockholders) has begun the cultivation of huge plantations of eucalyptus which deplete the soil. The government department for the "Protection of Nature" promoted this project, while agreeing with the policy of Aracruz and spreading terror among small farmers. Under the cover of false ecology, these departments, with the support of Forest Rangers, are not allowing the small farmers to use a rotation system to cultivate their land.

The small farmers have known for a long time how to live in the Atlantic Forest. In order to face this new situation and to overcome the terror spread by the police, the farmers have organized a farmers association for mutual support. They have established an agreement committed to preserving the native forest, to reforesting devastated areas and to enforcing the replanting of burned areas with native seedlings.

Ecology and Agro-Chemicals

"I went to spray insecticide on the tobacco plantation. I was wearing only shorts and a t-shirt. The next day I got a headache. I took some aspirin and went to bed. It was worse and I went to the hospital at Massaranduba. I remained there like that but it got worse and worse, I had pain in my arms and chest. A doctor from Curitiba sent me for intoxication exams and said that I would have problems in my arms. There have been 8 years of treatment for nothing. I feel pain and tiredness in my arms and chest. I cannot work because I am very weak." The testimony of Vilmar Becone, a 32 year-old farmer from Santa Catarina state and a victim of agrochemical poisoning, is illustrative of the human and ecological consequences of today's model of agricultural development.

One result of the so-called "green revolution," implemented by North American companies during the 1960s, was the heavy use of agro-chemicals. With the excuse of increasing productivity, this technique benefits industries related to agriculture, in this case, machine and agro-chemical industries. This has led to the abuse of agro-chemical products, including chemicals already forbidden in first world countries, so the industries can profit with no concern for human and ecological damage. Tens of thousands of farmworkers have been poisoned. Thousands have been killed.

Reacting against this predatory system, small farmers all over the country have carried out experiments with new agro-technologies which do not damage the environment. These initiatives, which try to eliminate agro-chemicals to produce higher quality food without damaging the population's health, have low costs and guarantee the small farmers' survival. To carry out these projects, small farmers are creating associations of ecological agriculture.

Land Reform: A Necessary Condition for Democracy

President Collor was relatively successful in running the country through a political marketing strategy. From August 1990, with the propagandistic announcement of the Federal Government's "Rules of Economic Policy Towards Agriculture," until the more recent version, the so-called "Land Program," nothing concrete happened.

The Collor government showed no political will to implement

Land Reform, but concealed these true intentions. This attitude was made clear by the positions of the Agricultural Land Reform Cabinet. It made at least five different announcements that the government would begin a land reform program in Brazil, and nothing beyond propaganda has happened.

However, the Federal Government's own numbers on land concentration and social problems in Brazil speak for themselves and demonstrate the urgent need for land reform.

Data from the 1985 rural census conducted by the Brazilian Institute of Geography and Statistics show that approximately one percent of rural landowners control almost 45 percent of the total agricultural land. This ranks Brazil among countries with the highest levels of land concentration in the world.

Brazilian agriculture has had serious environmental and social consequences. The burden of implementation of today's agrarian and agricultural policies, which exclude the majority, has fallen upon millions of peasants and rural workers. The policies ignore social and environmental damage because they are based on the intense exploitation of natural resources and labor.

Agriculture in Brazil mines the land. It removes the richness of the soil with no concern for conserving natural resources or for minimizing environmental damage. It consumes natural resources as if they were inexhaustible.

The plan to modernize Brazilian agriculture came from a monolithic perspective with only one main objective: to increase productivity without considering social and environmental questions. This view is related to policies set by the IMF and First World countries who believe that they have the right to dictate the priorities and, in the international division of labor, to assign tasks to the Third World countries according to their First World needs. For Brazil, the priority is to produce profits on the international market in order to pay interest on the foreign debt and to produce cheap raw materials. The Brazilian people have learned through their own pain that development does not depend on the improvement of macro-economic growth rates, but must mean a better quality of life for the population reflected in dignity, jobs and food. The reactionary modernization of agriculture has strengthened the hand of monoculture and large landowners which form the basis of Brazilian agriculture. The system of large farms has been the main cause of rural violence, human suffering and environmental degradation.

Dependence upon cattle ranching destroys nature in the Amazon and kills the possibility of self-determination for indigenous populations, peasants, rubber tappers and fishers.

In recent decades, the growth of land concentration, financially supported by the Brazilian state, has generated the expulsion of rural populations to the large cities. The intense rural exodus has made the large cities almost non-viable: slums, criminality and lack of basic services like housing, health care and education. New generations have no future in the country. The slavery of young girls and the killing of street children are indicators of this reality.

Faced with a dim future, we again propose Land Reform. It is not a limited struggle of peasants and rural workers. It is the basis of a profound social reform with benefits to the whole society. It is the cornerstone of any alternative development with redistribution of wealth, based on socially adapted technologies which do not destroy the environment. It is committed to the possibility of self-determination and production of food for the population.

A successful land reform program is necessary in order to allow millions of politically excluded people to exercise their citizenship. To think about democracy also means to think about the redistribution of power, which today is concentrated in the hands of a few. Land reform is a *sine qua non* for the achievement of real democracy.

21

Extractive Reserves: Economic and Social Alternatives for the Tropical Rainforest

Marcus La Tour

> "Behind every ecological problem there is a social problem and behind every social problem there is an economic problem."
>
> Paulo Roberto Silva

I n 1985 the Brazilian National Council of Rubber Tappers proposed "extractive reserves" as an alternative to the ecologically destructive practices of cattle ranching and slash and burn agriculture overtaking the Amazon. It wasn't until 1988 that the dream of thousands of rubber tappers and environmentalists became a reality. In what was considered an unlikely move at the time, President José Sarney signed an official decree establishing extractive reserves in the Brazilian states of Acre, Amapa and Rondonia.[1]

Extractive reserves are legally protected tracts of rainforest from which sustainably harvestable non-timber forest products, such as latex rubber, Brazil nuts, resins and fruits are collected and marketed regionally and internationally. While the land is owned by the Brazilian government, the products of extraction are managed by, and benefit, local communities. Whereas slash and burn agriculture, cattle ranching and logging all entail clearing massive areas of forest, extractive reserves produce economic gain without cutting or burning trees.

Because forest dwellers derive income from the land, while doing relatively little damage to the forest system, extractive reserves have been advanced as a melding of what is often seen as two distinct issues, but which are in fact two sides of the same coin: forest conservation and economic development.

Seringueiros—the Rubber Tappers

Rubber tappers *(seringueiros)* have lived and worked in the Amazon rainforests for over 100 years. These people, whose lifestyle is well adapted to the rainforest, practice a variety of sustainable economic activities. While "tapping" rubber from wild rubber trees is their main pursuit, they also collect Brazil nuts and other non-wood products for commercial sale and their own consumption.

Rubber tappers, until very recently, have been subject to an exploitative system of debt peonage called *aviamento*. Under *aviamento*, rubber tappers are required to sell all their products to, and buy all their provisions from, a powerful rubber baron or *seringalista*. Rubber tappers, as a result of these terms of trade, end up "held captive" by ever increasing debts to the *seringalista*. Unfortunately, many tappers in the more remote parts of the Amazon still work this way.

In the 1960s, as domestic subsidies for rubber production lapsed and Malaysian rubber flooded the Brazilian market, many of the traditional rubber barons withdrew from the land, seeking more lucrative business. Most rubber tappers, however, stayed; fishing, hunting, and selling rubber and other forest goods to traveling merchants. About the time many rubber tappers gained their independence from the rubber barons a new threat loomed. The Brazilian government, in an effort to modernize the Amazon, began to sponsor development schemes such as road building, cattle ranching and colonization projects. Government tax incentives encouraged cattle ranchers to burn forest and establish pasture. As more and more forest went up in flames, ranchers came into conflict with rubber tappers and Indians over the issue of land ownership.

Many tappers organized to protect their homelands. Often, whole communities of unarmed men, women and children traveled to where the trees were being felled to plead with the cattle ranchers' workers. This form of protest, called an *empate*, proved successful on many occasions as endangered areas of forest were saved from destruction. Cattle ranchers, for their part, reacted savagely to these demonstrations, ordering assassinations of rubber tapper leaders. Thousands of rubber tappers were coerced off the land and into the cities. Over 40,000 rubber tappers fled to Bolivia.[2]

But tappers, empowered by their organizing success, joined forces with other forest peoples and resisted. In 1985, rubber tappers and forest gatherers with a shared history of economic exploitation and forced eviction created the National Council of Rubber Tappers. It was during one of these early meetings that Chico Mendes, a major figure in the tapper movement, suggested extractive reserves as a grassroots alternative for land reform for the Amazon. The idea is simple: allow forest peoples to live on the land and communally manage the forest resources they know best. Rubber tappers took their case to the Brazilian Government, international lending institutions and the international environmental community. After considerable lobbying, extractive reserves were granted.

While over 75 million acres of Amazonian rainforest are now "officially" protected in extractive reserves, there is no enforced protection and no government subsidies. Much of this land is still under constant threat of invasion by cattle ranchers and displaced settlers from other regions of Brazil.

Violence and Conflict Over Land in the Amazon

The establishment of Brazilian extractive reserves has been a point of conflict and even violence between rubber tappers and wealthy cattle ranchers who prefer to see the forest converted to pasture. While rubber tappers have used nonviolent tactics to attain their goals, politically powerful cattle ranchers organized the Ruralist Democratic Union, or UDR, which resorts to intimidation, torture and even murder to achieve its ends. International attention focused on the plight of the tappers movement when Chico Mendes was killed by the son of a cattle rancher on December 22, 1988. UDR has hired gunmen to kill local tapper and union leaders such as Wilson Pinheiro, Ivair Higino and many others.

Incomplete Accounting

While barren, infertile, weed-ridden cattle pasture represents short sighted "quick cash" profit, standing rainforest represents a resource base capable of helping people into perpetuity.

In fact, environmental economists estimate that over a period of 50 years, the gathering and marketing of non-timber forest products can generate over twice as much income as either cattle pasture or timber plantation.[3]

Recent economic analysis of land use in Amazônia reveals a tragic irony. While some believe that "development" activities such as cattle ranching advance Brazil's economic progress, the reverse is true. National accounting schemes that encourage cattle ranching and logging activities have failed to consider the role of extractable non-wood forest products. Forest foods and medicines collected and sold by rural peasants in small markets, while often not calculated in the national accounting scheme, are a significant source of sustenance and commerce for the local populace.

A 1988 study by researchers Robert Mendelsohn, of the School of Forestry at Yale, Charles Peters of the Institute of Economic Botany, and Alwyn Gentry of the Missouri Botanical Garden indicates that standing rainforest is worth more from an economic standpoint than converted to any other use. The researchers calculated the market value of the non-wood renewable resources on a one hectare (2.47 acres) plot of rainforest close to the city of Iquitos, Peru. They then computed this value as an annuity over 50 years, less harvesting and transportation costs. The Net Present Value (NPV) of the forest was calculated at $6,820 per hectare. In comparison, the NPV of a timber plantation was estimated at $3,184, and a "good" Amazonian cattle pasture at only $2,960. It is important to note that the last two figures are based on the unproven and dubious assumption that plantation forestry and grazing lands can be sustainable land-use practices in the tropics.

The Problem with Rubber

Production of rubber in the Amazon is hampered by South American leaf blight, a destructive fungus which increases costs and lowers productivity of Brazilian rubber production. Southeast Asian rubber plantations, unaffected by this fungus, are able to produce rubber more cheaply than rubber tappers in the Amazon. The Brazilian government, eager for self-sufficiency, has long subsidized domestic rubber by setting price controls that encourage national production. When these subsidies falter, as they have in the past and threaten to in the future, rubber tapping becomes a marginal economic activity.

But rubber is by no means the only Brazilian extractive product of economic significance. There is a growing market for rainforest products. While Brazil earned only $6 million from extractable products in 1975, non-timber forest product exports were $58 million in 1985. While not all of these products came from the forests, Brazil nuts and palm hearts from the Amazon accounted for 60 percent of this value.[4]

For extractive reserves to be more productive, products other than rubber need to be identified, researched and marketed. The potential for identifying and extracting new commercially valuable fruits, spices, sweeteners, pigments, oils, fragrances and perhaps most importantly, medicines from tropical forests is enormous.

The Future

Extractive reserves are a wise investment in the future. Like any long-term investment, they require support, money and patience. As stewards of the forest, rubbertappers need our assistance.

If Brazilian reserves can prove that a standing forest is worth more than a burned or logged one, other rainforest countries could implement similar strategies. Peasant communities in the Peruvian Amazon have set up lake and forest reserves provide fish, rubber, fruits and other products on a sustainable basis.[5] Villagers along the Tahuayo River in Peru are working to get government approval for an 800,000 acre extractive reserve. In Guatemala, half of the Maya Biosphere Reserve (3.7 million acres) is designated as extractive reserve. A group of Harvard Business School students have released a promising report on the potential for marketing non-timber products from Borneo called "Project Borneo."

The widescale "marketing" of the rainforest could, however, be a problematic issue. What effect will the increasing extraction of industrial quantities of nuts, fruits, plants or other forest products have on local ecology? How can the extraction and marketing of new products genuinely help local forest peoples? Rubber tapper leaders are quick to point out that extractive reserves should not be seen as a final answer to the problem of deforestation in Amazônia, but as part of a plan of reform which addresses the vast social and economic inequalities of modern Brazil. Programs to redistribute farmland, reform farming practices and halt population growth are essential.

Rainforests are worth far more than any current "market value." As tropical ecologist Philip Fearnside noted: "The question of whether Brazil should allow its Amazonian forest to be destroyed is not related to direct economic costs and benefits. If financial benefit is insufficient, one should not cut down the forest but rather alter the economic equation until conservation becomes profitable." (Fearnside, 1989)

How You Can Help

• Reduce your consumption; buy sustainable, organic products that do not contribute to rainforest destruction.

• Rubber tappers need financial, material and technical support. Contact the Amazônia Campaign at RAN for specifics.

• Join the Rainforest Action Network to keep yourself up to date on current actions, boycotts and letter writing campaigns:

• 450 Sansome St., Suite 700 San Francisco, CA 94111, Tel. (415) 398-4404 Fax (415) 398-2732

• Rua Alexandre Farhat, 206 Bairro José Augusto - C.P.: 424 Rio Branco, AC - Cep: 69900, Brazil   Tel.(0115568) 229-9645 or 224-9063 Fax (0115568) 224-3622.

Footnotes

1. Fearnside, P.M. "Extractive Reserves in Brazilian Amazônia; An Opportunity To Maintain Tropical Rainforest Under Sustainable Use" *Bioscience,* Vol. 39, No.6, June, 1989. Also see Fearnside, P.M. "A Prescription For Slowing Deforestation in Amazônia" *Environment,* Vol. 31, No. 4.

2. Allegretti M. and Schwartzman, Stephen. "Extractive Reserves: A Sustainable Development Alternative for Amazônia. Report to World Wildlife Fund" (US Project- 478), 1987.

3. Peters, Gentry and Mendelsohn, "Valuation of an Amazonian Rainforest" *Nature,* Vol. 339, June 29,1989.

4. Ryan, J. "Goods From the Woods" *World Watch,* Vol. 4, no. 4, July/August, 1991.

5. Schwartzman, Stephen. "Marketing of Extractive Products in the Brazilian Amazon," Environmental Defense Fund, October 29,1990.

22

Clowns Up the River: The Amazon's Health and Happiness Project

Charles L. Johnson

C*harles Johnson turned up this bit of positive news from the Amazon. He describes a kind of appropriate rural assistance that is too small and sensible for the World Bank, too remote from Brazil's political and economic turmoil perhaps even to survive, but too good a model to lose.*

When most folks think about poverty in the Third World, the prevalent image is one of urban crowding in *favelas* or *colonias*. These are words for the shantytowns that "symbolize what is wrong" with the countries where they exist.

Outside of its major cities, the Brazilian Amazon is not known for *favelas*, although the poverty is nonetheless real. Isolated communities appear as islands of misery in the midst of splendor. These are places that suffer from a lack of resources, detached from the amenities that "civilized people" enjoy.

Water, Water, Everywhere. . .

But not a drop that is potable without treatment. Though many species of Amazon wildlife depend on the flood cycle for their survival, it can be hazardous to humans. Rainy-season flooding means less land for farming, fewer pastures for livestock, more difficulty in catching fish and pollution from human waste that mixes with the drinking water. The result is disease caused by poor sanitation and undernutrition.

This describes the situation faced by Dr. Eugenio Scannavino when he arrived in Santarem, a city in the heart of the Amazon, near where the Tapajos and Arapiuns Rivers meet the Amazon River. It was early in the 1980s, and Dr. Eugenio had just finished a stint in the *favelas* of São Paulo. He could see that there was little medical care outside of Santarem, and an even shorter supply of technological skills for utilizing the area's available resources. It wasn't long before he developed a plan to deal with these problems—the Health and Happiness Project (*Projeto Saude e Alegria*).

Founded in 1984, the project soon came to a halt due to a lack of funds. It got off the ground again in 1988, and since then has become a popular and effective means of improving the quality of life of people living in virtual isolation; there are no roads connecting the 19 communities and 94 settlements which the project covers, other than the rivers. It reaches more than 20,000 people.

The 32-member staff is divided into seven sections: Health, Education, Art, Communication, Rural Production Development, the Information and Research Center, and Administration.

If any undertaking is to be successful, it first has to get the attention of its target, which is every member of the community. What better way than to stage a show, an idea that led to the creation of the Great Mocorongo Health and Happiness Circus. (*Mocorongo* is the local name for people living in this area.)

Send in the Clowns

The Circus is a lot more than a bunch of clowns and jugglers and tightrope walkers. Behind the masks and greasepaint hide doctors, nutritionists, veterinarians, agronomists, educators, and other community-development experts.

When the circus rolls into town—make that "sails into town"— it is first of all a call to work. The Health and Happiness team uses the spectacle as a means of generating excitement in order to promote its three main community-oriented objectives: health, rural development, and maintaining the local culture. The show is a drawing attraction that helps teach people about health care, how to boost production, and how to improve other activities such as gardening, small-animal raising, handicrafts, rubber tapping, teacher training and tree raising. The key is environmental education.

The H&H staff quickly focused on two emergency needs: health care (there were few medicines, almost no clinics, and a slew of misconceptions about good health practices) and improving the output and variety of foods available (especially during the flood season, when fish become scarce and most people subsist on a mixture of manioc flour and water known as *chibá*).

The first programs to be carried out reflect these priorities: "Contamination and Illness Cycles," "Life and Environment Cycles," "Community Health" and "Human Ecology."

Is Health What You Haven't Got?

As the project was getting underway, community members were asked about their conception of health. They tended to define it as "getting sick and then getting well." Since there were essentially no clinics or medical personnel, prevention was mostly an unknown process. A clinic, for most people, was a place where you went only when you were severely sick or hurt. The low economic level precluded any sort of investment in this area. And when one lacks the means and the know-how to stay healthy, the result is, not surprisingly, a fatalistic attitude toward death and illness, poignantly reflected in the high infant mortality rate.

Once the emergency situation was under control, the time came to go beyond merely treating injuries and illness and providing medicines. The next phase involved training what are called "health monitors" in each community. These people learn medical skills at a paramedic level: first aid, giving vaccinations and performing emergency tooth extractions. Equally important, they teach community members the fundamentals of good health, stressing preventive measures. As far removed as these communities are from medical facilities, fast action is often required to combat chronic problems. Diarrhea is one example. Among North Americans, the word has a somewhat humorous connotation—the "trots" and so forth. But among these riverbank people, it is a matter of deadly seriousness, especially in the case of infants. Sudden dehydration through diarrhea in young children is a common killer. It can be treated with a homemade oral rehydration solution of sugar and salt in water. Other simple yet lifesaving methods include adding a chlorine solution to polluted water to make it safe to drink.

Monitors are the educational link in making their fellow community members aware of the effective home remedies at hand. The name "monitor" is significant since these workers are also taught how to keep records to track the status of public health in the community, as well as to detect and advise health authorities of impending problems, such as threatening outbreaks of disease. This is truly a "bootstrap" program, in that trained monitors fan out into surrounding areas to pass on their skills to others. H&H estimates that these monitors are now able to handle upwards of 70 percent of health problems, evidence of their crucial role within the project.

It is common for children to be left in charge of their younger siblings when mom and pop are out farming, hunting and the like. Consequently, H&H has created a Kiddy Monitor program, whereby children between the ages of six and fourteen are taught basic skills that they apply to caring for their brothers and sisters.

These programs indicate a core concept of H&H: To endeavor to involve 100 percent of the people in the decisions that will lead to improving their quality of life.

Realizing the need to break away from the fish-and-*chibá* cycle, the project has put teeth into its nutrition program. It has a team of agronomists that work with farmers to show how the quality and yield of local plants can be improved, with a number of experimental farms now in progress. A veterinarian provides small animal raisers with support, knowing that increased production means a diminished need to deplete wildlife in the surrounding forest.

In the belief that knowledge of the environment enhances respect for it, the H&H approach strives to make community members aware of the resources available in the surrounding forest— food, curatives, housing and potential income—while emphasizing the need to properly use and preserve these resources.

Education forms part of an ambitious H&H project intended to revamp teaching methodology along two lines. First, the overriding philosophy is that teaching should be tailored to local realities, drawn from the geography, climate and culture of each community. This concept stems from the fact that in Brazil, education curricula are based on a national "standard" that reflects little of the country's vast cultural spectrum. Secondly, learning should be based on game-playing; things that are fun sink in deeper. With their obvious reflection of the good feelings produced by the circus, games are an important educational tool that can be applied to virtually every activity. After all, it's much more exciting to learn about bees if, for example, for a brief while you can actually be a bee.

A Day in the Life

As the H&H boat chugs in, it is greeted by the community amid much hullabaloo. Since many of the staff show up in clown garb, the walk into town often becomes a mini-parade, jugglers juggling and musicians playing.

But hold everything. Business before pleasure. During the day, activities are mainly divided between checking and doing. In conjunction with health monitors, children are examined and weighed (especially the newborn), expectant mothers are given checkups in the presence of midwives, community health status records are updated, and immediate medical problems are treated. Each community has a Mothers Club, one of whose duties is to work with nutritionists to learn how the family diet can be improved. This may include pointing out the medicinal herbs that are found nearby, plus tips such as using ground eggshell as a handy source of calcium, or sticking a rusty nail in an orange to furnish iron to combat anemic deficiencies. Another program that ties in with the Mothers Clubs is called "Women: Body and Soul." It deals with a wide range of subjects, such as mother-child relations, body awareness, cottage-industry production and handicrafts.

Experts in the Rural Production section work with community members in many agricultural areas. Included are chicken and pig raisers, rubber tappers and farmers who are being taught to develop new and more nutritious species of plants, particularly the ubiquitous manioc. Another good tip is the use of the termites that abound in the region as a source of protein for feeding chickens.

In communities with a school H&Hers meet with children and teachers to check on programs such as proper tooth-brushing techniques or the tree nursery, a popular activity among children. Part of the Fruition project, the latter is an attempt to preserve and upgrade local varieties of trees, as well as to introduce useful species that are not found in the region, such as certain citrus fruits.

As the day wears on, preparations begin for the evening performance of the circus. Once again, the goal is educational entertainment. No way is it merely a show for the people, it is a show with the people. The local pavilion is made ready, costumes are prepared, and skits are rehearsed. H&H acrobats set up their gear—they, too, often pass on their skills, training aspiring tightrope walkers, jugglers and other performers.

Not long after night falls, the curtain rises. The circus is open to everyone; it is a showcase for local talent such as musicians, storytellers, hams and anyone else who might have something to contribute. Those with well-hidden abilities can slap on a little greasepaint and clown around. This is no spectator-in-the-bleachers event but most definitely a hands-on production reminiscent of street theater. At each performance, the community joins with the H&Hers to put on skits with a message: the benefits of forming co-ops; how contagious diseases are spread; the causes and prevention of undernutrition; the dangers of drinking untreated water. These "household hints" are intended to save lives, rather than make your shirts a whiter white or remove that nasty stain from your carpet.

Some places have formed what's known as a Headcold Choir, which sings about respiratory problems that can result from neglecting a simple cold or from the overuse of medicines.

By the time the evening's festivities have ended both H&H staff and community members have had quite a workout. And this is a project that works. Its ingenious blend of learning and having a good time leaves people feeling good in body and spirit.

Visits normally last three to four days. H&H staff members may also come to call under specific circumstances—the agronomy section, or the medical team in case of a disease outbreak, and so on. A recent event of great significance has been the cholera epidemic in Latin America. It is to the credit of the Health and Happiness Project that cholera has thus far been kept away from the areas where the project operates. This is most likely due to three factors: the effectiveness of the health-monitor program, the three years that the project's Hygiene, Rural Sanitation and Diarrhea Prevention Program has been implemented, and the widespread use of chlorine solution to create potable water.

The *Caboclos*—Preserving a Culture

The current world focus on the Amazon has almost exclusively dealt with the Indians. Very little has been said about the ethnic group that makes up the great bulk of the Amazon population—the *caboclos* (Brazilian for mixed Indian and white: the majority of the population in the area covered by the H&H Project). The *caboclo* culture is perhaps less flamboyant than that of the Indians. There are no tribes of *caboclos*, no ritual dances, no tribal gods (or Hollywood movies). However, translating the somewhat high-falutin Portuguese word *acervo*, these people are the "storehouse" of folklore in this part of the Amazon, a valuable body of knowledge.

Herein lies another goal of the project: to keep alive a culture threatened by two problems confronting most developing areas, rural flight and the encroachment of the outside world. Here's where the Communications Sector steps in. Besides documenting activities, great efforts are dedicated to recording the *caboclo* culture. As always, the key is to get people involved, as evidenced by the program's name, "Grassroots Communications."

Teenagers and youth—being the most likely candidates to skip town and head for the big city—are encouraged to become what the project calls Local Correspondents. They are given the task of documenting the local life, which may range from interviews (oral history) to acting as recording secretaries for meetings of community groups. There is also Live Radio, with recorded material first "aired" to the community itself in a simulated broadcast (at a circus performance, for example) and with some material taken to Santarem for actual broadcasting as part of a Rural AM program. Toward this end, Grassroots Communications provides training in the methods of broadcasting. There are also community and intercommunity newspapers that offer prospective journalists a chance to work in this medium, as well as serving as a tool for the exchange of ideas.

Other popular media forms are educational photo-comics with plots developed by community members and then shot by the H&H crew, and a News Wall, a large bulletin board where community news, photos, and other items are posted. The outcome is two-pronged: media skills are taught, while the people gain increased awareness of their culture and how they can improve it.

The Information and Resource Center puts out the word about the project, along with serving as a center for research on present and future activities. It works with virtually all media—still photography, video, and audiotape recordings—to compile data on community life and lore. The archives of the IRC are available to anyone who would like further information on the project.

The Future of the Project

Project scheduling is naturally keyed toward expansion, aimed at reaching more and more of the isolated communities in the mid-Amazon. The ultimate goal is for these communities, through their health monitors, teachers, mothers clubs and other involved groups, in tandem with general awareness campaigns, to be self-sufficient to the greatest possible degree. It's good to know that your problems are being solved, but even more satisfying is the sense of pride in realizing that you have taken an active part in the process.

The demand cannot be underestimated. As neighboring communities learn about the project there is an increasing number of requests for information, assistance and training. The Health and Happiness Project is a nongovernmental organization administered by the Center for Advanced Studies in Social Care. Its main headquarters are in Rio de Janeiro, and there is a regional office in

Santarem.

In mid-1991, government funding for the H&H Project was put on hold for ten months. The circus came to a halt. This was not the first time a shutdown had occurred. The subsequent release of governmental funds in no way implies that the flow will be constant. For this reason, the project is attempting to assemble backers to ensure that at least current work will not be halted. Any type of support is useful, including donations of money or equipment.

Additional information on this project may be obtained from the following addresses.

Projeto Saude e Alegria (CEAPS)
Rua Paulo Barreto, 23 Botafogo
CEP 22.280-010
Rio de Janeiro, BRAZIL
tel (55) (21) 266-7896
FAX: 266-7897
Email (AlterNex): Ax!ceapsrio

Projeto Saude e Alegria
Av. Borges Leal, 2284
Cx Postal 243 CEP 68.040-080
Santarem—Para, BRAZIL
tel. (55) (91) 523-1083
FAX: 523-1083

23

Kids Out of Place

Nancy Scheper-Hughes and Daniel Hoffman

I n Brazil, a poor, ragged kid running along an unpaved road in a *favela* or playing in a field of sugar cane is just a kid. That same child, transposed to the main streets and plazas of town, is a threat, a potentially dangerous "street kid."

On July 23, 1993 eight young "street children" (*meninos de rua)* were gunned down as they slept near the Candelaria Church in downtown Rio de Janeiro. The Candelaria massacre brought renewed attention to the plight of street children, their "elimination" at the hand of death squads, and the wrenching poverty that characterizes life for vast numbers of urban residents in Brazil.

The pattern of violence reflected in the Candelaria killings, though remarkable in its degree, is in no way new. In 1981 Hector Babenco's film *Pixote* stunned audiences with its brutal portrayal of the institutional and street life of marginalized children in Brazil. Filmed during the final years of a waning military dictatorship, *Pixote* focused on the generation forgotten by the Brazilian "economic miracle" of the 1970s.

In the ensuing decade the situation of marginalized children seems to have gotten worse.

Underlying the current formulation of the street children's crisis is a deep preoccupation with the future of Brazil, and with the increase in public violence that seems to have accompanied the economic crisis and transition to democracy. With the demise of the former police state, the structures that had kept the social classes safely apart and the "hordes" of disenfranchised, hungry and "dangerous" *favela* (shantytown) children at bay also disintegrated. Suddenly, street children seemed to be everywhere.

Urban violence itself may not have actually increased with democratization. What has changed significantly is both the official discourse and the popular representations of marginalized children in Brazil over the past three decades. In the 1960s in the Northeast of Brazil, street urchins were a fairly familiar feature of urban life. They were commonly referred to with a blend of annoyance and affection as *"moleques"* (ragamuffins or rascals). *Moleques* were "street-wise" kids who were cute and cunning, sometimes sexually precocious and invariably economically enterprising. They tried to make themselves useful in a myriad of ways, some of these bordering on the criminal and deviant. Many *moleques* survived by "adopting" an affluent or middle-class household for whom they did odd jobs in exchange for the right to sleep in a courtyard or patio.

Despite new legislation asserting the rights of children, street children in Brazil are viewed as a public scandal and a nuisance. They are now referred to either as "abandoned" children or, alternatively, as "marginals." The first denotes pity for the child (and blame for the neglectful parents), while the second denotes fear. Both labels justify radical intervention and the forced removal of these "pests" from the urban landscape.

What is rarely articulated but nonetheless quite clear is that street kids are poor children in the wrong place. A street child is, like our definition of dirt, soil that is out of place. Soil in the ground is clean, a potential garden; soil under the fingernails is filth. Likewise, a poor, ragged kid running along an unpaved road in a *favela* or playing in a field of sugar cane is just a kid. That same child, transposed to the main streets and plazas of town, is a threat, a potentially dangerous "street kid."

The very notion of a "street child" reflects the preoccupation of one class or segment of society with the "proper place" of another.[1] The term is a manifestation, albeit a semiconscious one, of a kind of symbolic or psychological apartheid Safely confined to the *favela*, the poor child or adolescent is invisible to the better-off city dwellers, and therefore of little interest or concern. Only when the child steps outside of his or her area is that child perceived as a problem about which "something must be done."

From the point of view of the *favela*, however, there is nothing inherently problematic about a child, especially a male child, flowing over into the main streets of the town. The street—especially the city center—is, after all, the primary site of employment and economic survival. As long as he or she doesn't get in trouble with the law in the process of surviving, the child who can negotiate the realm of the street is seen as resourceful and self-reliant.

In the context of his own environment, the street child is nothing more than a "kid." The very term "street child" has no meaning in the shantytown. Indeed, it is almost never used as a term of reference or identification, although *favela* mothers will sometimes lament having permanently "lost" one or more boys "to the streets."[2] Here, the term "lost" and "street" are used to describe a poor child's declaration of independence from his home and his parents. But under ordinary conditions, to be a *favela* boy is to spend the better part of the day—and often the night as well—"*na rua*," in the street. Homes are overcrowded and mother's "*amigo*" or current boyfriend may make demands for privacy that preclude older kids sleeping at home. "Home" for many male *favela* kids is not so much a place to eat and sleep as an emotional space—the place where one comes from and where one returns, periodically.

For *favela* girls, the alternation between home and street is more problematic. The same home conditions that propel their brothers into the street affect them as well, but a *favela* girl must always declare a fixed assignment and a fixed destination in the street. Surveillance of the immediate whereabouts of daughters is a perennial preoccupation of *favela* women who themselves must often be out working for long periods of the day. From the age of seven or eight, *favela* girls are assigned child-tending and other domestic tasks that keep them close to home. But girls who are quick and savvy are often very useful to their mothers in dealings with the "somebodies" of the street, including shopkeepers, coffin makers, clinic doctors, patrons, political leaders and clergy.

Most "street children" are today, as they were in the 1960s, "supernumerary" or "excess" kids, the children of impoverished and often single or abandoned women. While they may be quite economically independent, street kids remain deeply emotionally dependent and attached to the idea of "family." When nine-year-old "Chico" was asked if his mother loved him, he looked back incredulously. "She's my mother; she has to love me," Chico said, although both Chico and the questioner knew that his mother had tried to give him away several times to distant relatives.

Street kids in Bom Jesus da Mata—most of them boys—tended to be sentimental on the topic of mothers, their own in particular. When asked why they beg or steal, or why they live in the streets, poor children often replied that they were doing it to help their mother. Most share a percentage of their earnings with their mothers whom they visit each evening. "Fifty-fifty," said Giomar proudly with his raspy, boy-man voice. "Oh, *che*!" his nine-year-old friend Aldimar corrected him. "Since when did you ever give your mother more than a third!"

A band of street children, who had attached themselves to Nancy Scheper-Hughes' household in the 1980s, liked nothing better than to be invited inside to use her flush toilet, to wash with soap and hot water, and, afterwards, to flop on the cool floor and draw with magic-marker pens. Their sketches were curious. Most drew self-portraits or conventional intact nuclear family scenes even when there was no "papa" living in the house or when the child had long since left home for the streets. These homeless children also favored religious themes—the crucifixion in particular—colored in with lots of bright red wounds. Cemeteries and violent death were also a frequent theme. Yet their self-portraits were often surprisingly smiling and upbeat.

The street offers both opportunity and danger. There are many ways to be a child of the streets. Most work selling candy or popsicles, guarding cars, carrying groceries and other parcels, or shining shoes. While most street kids return home at night to sleep, some alternate nights of sleeping outdoors with sleeping at home. A very small number of children actually live full-time in the streets, rarely if ever going home to visit.[3] This minority is, however, very visible, greatly feared, and they fuel the stereotype of the "dangerous" and "uncontrollable" *menino de rua*.

These street children do not so much run away or choose the streets as they are thrown out of homes where hunger, abuse, poverty and neglect make life under bridges and in bus station restrooms seem more peaceful than life at home. Such children of the street are predictably more associated with gangs and drugs, and are the most common target of adult exploitation, violence and death squads.

While most of those who actually live in the street are boys, young girls may also enter the anonymous space of the street, often escaping abusive homes or exploitative work as junior domestic servants. The vehicle of their "escape" is generally prostitution.[4] Domestic work in the context of semi-feudal Northeast Brazil is not infrequently described by favela girls and older women as "slavery," so that a flight to the streets and even to prostitution can be seen as acts of self-liberation. "The first time I sold my body was the first time I felt that it belonged to me." said one young "runaway" from the rural Northeast who chose the streets of São Paulo and prostitution over domestic servitude in Pernambuco.[5] Because these girls frequently live in brothels, prostitution may remove them somewhat from the dangers of life on the street. Yet they suffer increased risks of HIV infection, pregnancy and sexual abuse.

Indeed, food and affection exchanged for sex is common among Brazilian street kids, the majority of whom are initiated into sex by nine or ten years of age in the big cities. Both street girls and street boys are often used for passive anal intercourse. Street girls in Recife are frequently raped by men, including policemen. Younger street boys as well as street girls are vulnerable to rape by older street boys.[6]

Street children—typically barefoot, shirtless and seemingly untied to a home or a family—are separated from all the laws and roles that confer propriety, rights and citizenship. In family-driven Brazil, the street child is barely a person, and is vulnerable to the

worst forms of exploitation, abuse and manipulation. This is revealed in the proliferation of derogatory names for poor street children: *pivete* (thief), *trombadinha* (pick pocket), *maloquiero* (street
delinquent), *menor* (juvenile delinquent) and *marginal* (criminal).[7]
Each term denies the validity and personhood of the child or adolescent and transforms him or her into a dangerous and disgusting
object, one to be removed with violence and impunity.

Bolstering and justifying the open warfare on street kids in Brazil
are rumors, radio reports and sensationalized news stories about
crimes committed by street adolescents. The popular news weekly
Veja reported that in the central plaza of São Paulo street children
commit over 32,000 thefts and robberies a year, each child allegedly committing an average of three thefts a day.[8]

Further fueling the panic among middle- and upper-class people
were news reports of the *arrastão*—or sweep—in which large rov-
ing gangs of poor adolescents allegedly streamed across the elite
southern beaches of Rio de Janeiro robbing anyone within reach.

Many street children *do* survive by committing petty crime.
Almost all of the street children we interviewed in 1992 at a shelter in Bom Jesus volunteered that they stole things, or that they
used to before they mended their ways. Stealing, they said, was
"*um jeito*"—a way of getting by—an unfortunate means of survival, not something they were proud of. There is a natural evolution from begging to stealing as begging becomes both humiliat-
ing and more difficult for the older child. When street children
begin to show signs of physical maturity, they are chased away
from public spaces and rarely evoke compassion or a handout from
people on the street. Stealing is the next phase in the life cycle of a
street child. When a younger child was continually pushed away
from us at the street shelter in Bom Jesus by older kids who denied
that the child had ever really been a street kid, the little one vehemently protested, "*Eu pedia, eu pedia!*" ("but I begged, I begged!").

Brazilian street children live in daily fear of the police, state
children's asylums, anonymous kidnappers, death squads, and
(more fantastically) imagined child-and-organ stealers.[9] Their lives
are characterized by a profound sense of insecurity. The seemingly

far-fetched rumors of street kids kidnapped for overseas adoption or mutilated for their organs coexist with an active roundup of street urchins, thousands of whom disappear each year into state-run reform facilities that are viewed with suspicion and horror by shantytown residents. "You won't ever turn me in to FEBEM (the misnamed state institution for the well-being of minors), will you, Nancy?" Scheper-Hughes was made to answer many times over. "They kill children there," little Luiz insisted. The more she denied that this could be so, the more the children ticked off the names of friends who had been "roughed up" or hurt at one of the reform schools. "Why do you think that they built the FEBEM school so close to the cemetery of Bom Jesus?" asked Jose Roberto, age 12, with fear in his voice.

Until the enactment of the new Child and Adolescent Statute (1990) which recognized the legal rights of minors incarcerated without due process, almost 700,000 Brazilian children and adolescents were locked up in FEBEM or related reform schools.[10] The film *Pixote* recreated the life of children in a FEBEM facility, portraying conditions of everyday violence and vulnerability where criminalization, rather than reform or education, was the only possible outcome. In spite of the new legislation, the disturbing conditions dramatized in *Pixote* have not changed. On October 22, 1992, in a FEBEM facility in São Paulo, a 24-hour rebellion resulted in one death, 40 wounded, and over 500 escapees (350 of whom were recaptured). The daily *Folha de São Paulo* reported that those adolescents returned to the 1,200-inmate facility were beaten severely by state functionaries. In a subsequent investigation a state legislator claimed that the youths were "caged up like animals." "Not even in maximum security are prisoners treated this way," a prosecutor said, commenting on 100 youths who were kept locked up 24 hours a day in cells without ventilation or bathrooms. A director of FEBEM confirmed that the adolescents were being kept naked in the buildings "for reasons of security."[11]

Reform of the FEBEM system—a central demand of child advocates and an implicit provision of the 1990 Child and Adolescent Statute—remains elusive. The primary function of these "correctional" institutes continues to be the removal of unwanted children from the public sphere.

In addition to the thousands of children who fill Brazil's special reform schools, significant numbers of children are illegally detained in prisons alongside adult offenders. This appears particularly true of smaller municipalities that lack specially designated facilities for minors. The practice is in flagrant disregard of the new Brazilian Constitution with its bill of rights for the child. The newly appointed Children's Judge of Bom Jesus allowed us to visit a few dozen minors being held without bail in the local prison. The children were incarcerated, the judge explained, for their own safety. Outside they were already "marked for extermination" by local hit squads, he said, and they had been rejected by family members as well as feared and hated by the local population for whom their deaths would be counted as a relief.

In one cell of the local jail we found "Caju" and "Junior," 15- and 16-year-olds whom Scheper-Hughes remembered as cute street urchins attached to her household in 1987. "Caju" was elected to represent the street children of Bom Jesus at the first national convention of street children held in Brasilia in 1986, when street children from all over Brazil converged on the capital to voice their grievances and demand their human rights. Now, five years later, both boys were accused of assault, and Junior, of the rape of another street child. Thus were they transformed into precocious "little men" jailed and held accountable for their chaotic street behavior.

As a guard at the jail in Bom Jesus reflected: "the life of a young marginal here is short ... It's like this: for a *menino de rua* to reach 30 years of age, it's a miracle." The Federal Police reported that close to 5,000 children were murdered in Brazil between 1988 and 1990.[12] Few of these deaths were considered worthy of investigation, which is hardly surprising given that police officers are themselves perpetrators of many of these crimes.[13] Most of the victims are adolescent males between the ages of 15 and 19, a dangerous time, especially for the children of black *favela* dwellers.

The specter of violent and sudden death looms close for poor adolescents and for street children especially. This is no less true for the children of a relatively small municipality such as Bom Jesus (population 50,000) than for those of major cities. Street kids of Bom Jesus had no difficulty identifying the names of murdered friends and companions.

A few of these adolescents lost their lives in acts of random violence after having fled to Recife, the regional capital. Some were murdered when caught in the act of petty theft, or were the victims of vigilante "street justice." Still others died at the hands of death squads, their murders unresolved.

In 1991 *Veja* reported that the public morgue in Recife received approximately 15 bodies of dead children and adolescents a month. Black and brown (mixed race) bodies outnumbered white bodies 12 to 1, and boys outnumbered girls by a ratio of 7 to 1. In 80 percent of the cases, the bodies had been damaged or mutilated.[14] The local human rights organization GAJOP characterizes the routine assassinations of poor adolescents as an unofficial death penalty which is carried out "with chilling cruelty and without any chance of defense whatsoever."[15]

Brazilian journalist Gilberto Dimenstein, in his forceful denunciation of violence against children, *Brazil: War on Children*, emphasized the complicity of off-duty policemen, hired killers, and store owners in the death squads.[16] Typically, it is store owners who pay to have "undesirable" adolescents and children eliminated. A similar conclusion was reached in a report by the São Paulo chapter of the Brazilian Bar Association, which indicated that "the military police and death squads paid by shantytown shopkeepers killed most of the nearly 1,000 street children slain here in 1990."[17]

Dimenstein writes that support of human rights for children in Brazil is confined to a relatively small minority, and that to make a case for the rights of children is perceived by many as "an attack on decent people's rights to walk down the street in safety."[18] Underlying this sentiment is a perception that street adolescents are dangerous criminals with little chance of reform. Discourses regarding human rights, including rights for children, easily come into conflict with popular concerns for public safety, leading some to claim that human rights are the "privileges of bandits."[19]

Support for death squads, "private justice," lynchings and lethal tactics by the police are related to widespread perceptions that
the justice system does not work, and that police are inefficient,
corrupt, and frequently themselves involved in crime.[20] Residents
of poor neighborhoods are often the strongest supporters of violent, extrajudicial solutions to local crime, a phenomenon that has
been, in part, attributed to the lack of security in these communities. As one observer writes, "people are usually asking the police,
whom they fear and accuse of being violent, to be violent 'against
the side that deserves it'."[21] The poor, it appears, feel every bit as
besieged by crime, if not more so, as the rich and middle class do.
They tend to accept extreme forms of private justice, even though
they are likely to become the targets of its abuses.

Thus, each time a troublesome young street child was swept up
in a police raid or was physically attacked or "disappeared" in Bom
Jesus, people said nothing. Some residents were even sympathetic
to these violent attacks on other people's "bad children," and would
occasionally murmur under their breath, "Good job, nice work!"

The tolerance for violence is also a legacy of the dictatorship.
Throughout Brazilian military rule (1964-1985), the civil and military police were heavily implicated in the disappearances, tortures
and deaths of suspected "subversives." Although the process of
democratization has been fairly rapid since 1982, it has yet to check
the extraordinary power of the civil and military police over the
poorer populations. The police are called upon to enforce, often
violently, the apartheid-like codes that keep the poor and the black
"in their proper place." Indeed, race and race hatred have emerged
as popular discourses that justify violent and illegal police actions
in shantytown communities. Death-squad persecution is directed
at a specific class and color of shantytown resident. Consequently,
young black males are increasingly a threatened population.

The problem of "street children" is emblematic of a larger di-
lemma in Brazil: a failed economic model that has relegated a vast
proportion of the population to misery. Out of this arises the specter of the homeless and abandoned street child, perceived by the
more affluent classes as a blemish on the urban landscape and a

reminder that all is not well in the country. Unwanted and considered human waste, these tattered, mainly black children and adolescents evoke strong and contradictory emotions of fear, aversion, pity and anger in those who view their own streets and squares as "private places" under siege. But unlike other forms of debris, street kids refuse to stay in the dump (the *favelas*). Instead, they often stake out public and elegant spaces of the city to live, love and work, thus betraying the illusion of Brazilian "modernity."

By invading the city centers, frequenting the public parks and upper-class beaches of Rio de Janeiro and Recife, and engaging in petty crimes against the middle class, street children defy the segregated order of the modern city. Street children are poor kids in revolt, violating social space, disrespecting property, publicly intoxicating themselves, and otherwise refusing to conform or to disappear. The risks and hazards of this inchoate domestic rebellion are great: illiteracy, toxicity from inhalant drugs such as glue, chronic hunger and under-nutrition, sexual exploitation and AIDS. It is this overall configuration of risks that leads child advocates in Brazil to defend the right of the child to be in the street, while recognizing that a life of the streets can only be self-destructive in the long term.

The new Brazilian Constitution and the subsequent Child and Adolescent Statute recognize the rights of children and the obligation of the state, civil society and parents to protect these rights and to provide for the needs of children as individuals in a special condition of dependency. The National Movement of Street Children (MNMMR), an organization of street educators and children's advocates, is at the forefront of legislative reform and the movement to engage and empower street children in their own environment: in the parks and plazas of the city. The MNMMR helps street children to form their own organizations, to develop their own leadership, and to articulate their own demands, so that individual acts of survival can be translated into collective acts of political resistance. The Street Children's Movement activists recognize the anger and indignation of street adolescents as appropriate to their marginalized and precarious existence.

The outcome of the struggle for childhood in Brazil will weigh heavily on the success of activists in the MNMMR and other organizations that share its vision of a new society in which all children are valued. For all its power, however, the Brazilian street children's movement has been unable to strike at the source of the problem. Until Brazilians reverse the chaotic economic and social conditions that cause desperately poor parents to "lose" their children to the streets, childhood for the vast majority in Brazil will be a period of adversity to be survived and gotten over as quickly as possible, rather than a time of nurturance to be extended and savored.

Footnotes

1. This and related themes are elaborated in D. Hoffman, "Street Children and the Geography of Exclusion in Brazil," in Nancy Scheper-Hughes and Carolyn Sargent, eds., *Child Survival*, 2nd Edition (Berkeley: University of California, forthcoming).
2. See Nancy Scheper-Hughes, *Death Without Weeping* (Berkeley: University of California Press, 1992) p. 469.
3. For a useful discussion of street children and family life, see *Childhood and Urban Poverty in Brazil: Street and Working Children and Their Families*, Innocenti Occasional Papers, The Urban Child Series, UNICEF, 1992.
4. See Gilberto Dimenstein's *Meninas da Noite* (São Paulo: Editora Atica 1992) concerning prostitution rings and the near-enslavement of adolescent girls in the North of Brazil, and his chapter in this book.
5. The young woman gave this testimony at a consciousness-raising meeting for young (mostly migrant) sex workers in São Paulo organized by a grassroots AIDS awareness group.
6. The rape of street girls by policemen has been reported by Ana Vasconcelos, founder of the Casa de Passagem, a support and shelter project for street girls in the northeast city of Recife.
7. *"Menor"* literally means "minor" in Portuguese. In the context of Brazil, it is stigmatizing, and specifically applied to poor adolescents who are assumed to be criminally inclined.
8. Maria Simas Filho, Eliane Azevedo and Lula Costa Pinto, "Infancia de raiva, dor de sangue," *Veja*, May 29, 1991, pp. 34-35
9. See Nancy Scheper-Hughes, "Theft of Life," *Society* 27(6), Sept.-Oct. 1990, pp. 58-63.
10. See Anthony Swift, *Brazil: the Fight for Childhood in the City* (Florence: UNICEF International Child Development Center, 1991).
11. Agencia Ecumenica de Noticias (AGEN), through the computer network Peacenet, November 19, 1992.
12. *Journal de Comércio*, June 19,1991. See Ben Penglase, *Final Justice: Police and Death Squad Homicides of Adolescents in Brazil* (New York: Human Rights Watch/Americas, 1994) for an excellent analysis of extrajudicial violence and murder against poor adolescents, including street children, in Brazil. Available

from Human Rights Watch, 485 Fifth Avenue, NY, NY 10017-6104.

13. Penglase's *Final Justice* describes the many obstacles to achieving convictions in death-squad killings, particularly when cases involve the military police and the military justice system. See also Gilberto Dimenstein, *Brazil: War on Children* (London: Latin America Bureau/Monthly Review Press, 1991); and MNMMR et al., *Vidas em Risco: Assassinatos de Crianças e Adolescentes no Brasil*, Rio de Janeiro, 1991.

14. Maria Simas Filho, Eliane Azevedo, and Lula Costa Pinto, "Infancia de raiva, dor de sangue," *Veja*, May 29, 1991, pp. 34-45.

15. Gabinete de Assessoria Juridica as Organizaçoes Populares/Centro Luiz Freire (GAJOP), *Grupos de Exterminio: A Banalização da Vida e da Morte em Pernambuco* (Olinda: GAJOP, 1991)

16. Dimenstein, *Brazil: War on Children.*

17. Quoted in "Brazil's Police Enforce Popular Punishment: Death," *New York Times*, November 4, 1992.

18. Dimenstein, *War on Children*, pp. 63-67

19. Teresa Caldeira describes these transformations in public life in contemporary São Paulo in her dissertation *City of Walls: Crime, Segregation, and Citizenship in São Paulo* (University of California at Berkeley, 1992).

20. Caldeira, *City of Walls*, p. 179.

21. Caldeira, *City of Walls*, p. 187.

24

Toil for Tots

Carlos Ravelo

Although the Brazilian Constitution forbids work before the age of 14, about two million children between the ages of 10 and 13 are working in Brazil. In some states, 36 percent of the children in that age group are at work. And surprisingly enough, the violations are not just among poor families.

A recent investigation by the Brazilian Institute for Geography and Statistics (IBGE) has destroyed certain prevailing myths relating to Brazil's labor market. For example, it was always thought that most working children were located either in large cities or in the northeast. It has been determined that the vast number are children who live in rural areas and work with their parents mostly in the southern part of the country.

Most children in the southern states of Paraná, Santa Catarina and Rio Grande do Sul between ages 10 and 13, and living in the rural areas, work. And, although most of these children work an average of about ten hours per week, they are not the hunger-driven, uneducated street children or shantytown dwellers prevalent in the larger cities. Most go to school, have decent meals and are well clothed and taken care of by their parents. The research was initiated under the auspices and recommendations of world renowned sociologist Herbert (Betinho) de Souza who has guided the "campaign against hunger" in Brazil.

Working children between the ages of 10 and 13 make up fifteen percent of all working children and roughly three percent of the country's total work force of 66 million. In the larger urban centers like São Paulo, minors make up an insubstantial number of the total work force: in São Paulo's case, roughly 47,000 children are working out of a population of about 1.5 million children. That is about three percent of children working, as compared to 36 percent in the South, 29 percent in the Northeast and 21 percent in the Southeast.

As presented by *Veja*, a Brazilian weekly magazine, the Derlam family, in a rural town outside of Porto Alegre in the state of Rio Grande do Sul, is a prime example. The father, Geraldo and the mother, Cloreci, both worked as children. Today, their daughters Joseane (12) and Fabiane (14) help the parents collect and load dozens of boxes of oranges harvested by them at their farm. The daughters gather more than half the harvest. The work ethic is passed from one generation to the next, regardless of what Brazil's federal constitution has to say about the matter.

The financial crisis that has shaken Brazil since the late 1980s has turned this practice into a matter of survival. But another important finding is that a substantial proportion of these children work without being paid. The states of Paraná, Santa Catarina and Rio Grande do Sul in the South and Piauí in the Northeast head the list of states with the highest percentage of unpaid child labor.

25

Targeted for Death: Brazil's Street Children

Paul Jeffrey

B atman looked down on the children sleeping in a huddled mass under the movie theater marquee. *Batman O Retorno* had come to northeast Brazil, but the movie's hero could do nothing for the poor waifs seeking only a moment of peace in which to dream of a different world.

The streets of Recife and other Brazilian cities are more dangerous these days than Gotham City. And the children themselves are fighting back, supported by an increasing number of churchpeople.

Homeless children languish in other South American countries as well. According to UNICEF, 100 million children live on the streets of the world's cities, an inordinate half of them in Latin America and the Caribbean. Throughout this region, 78 million children live in what the United Nations considers "extreme poverty." Half the region's children are poor, and a majority of the region's poor are children.

In addition to facing hunger and want, poor children contend with increasing violence from those who make them scapegoats for troubled economic times. In large cities from Buenos Aires to Monterrey, law enforcement agencies are carrying out "class cleansing." They are exterminating children. In Guatemala City in 1990, for example, National Police officers kicked to death 13-year-old Nahaman Carmona on a city street, in plain sight of witnesses. Some 100 street children accompanied Carmona's body to the cemetery where he was buried under a gravestone that reads, "All I wanted was to be a child, but they wouldn't let me."

While violence against street children is widespread, the phenomenon takes on monstrous proportions in Brazil, where youngsters are regularly beaten, tortured and killed. According to a recent investigation by the Brazilian Congress, from 1990 to 1993 4,611 children—3,781 of them black—were murdered in Brazil, and the rate is rising. At least three children a day are killed, and others disappear; in October 1990, a common grave containing the bodies of 560 children was discovered in a São Paulo cemetery.

Although a growing number of children are killed by other young people in turf wars over drugs, the dirty work is usually carried out by death squads using skills acquired during military rule in the 1960s and 1970s. A congressional study revealed that in Rio de Janeiro alone at least 180 different death squads operate. Fifteen of these groups target children exclusively and work "under the protection of the police and justice system," according to Congresswoman Rita Camata. The investigation named 103 people—including lawyers, police and former police officers—involved in death squads that murder children.

The killers often are funded by businesspeople eager to "clean up" commercial areas. Street people, particularly children, are seen as a nuisance by merchants. Though many street children work shining shoes, cleaning windshields, collecting cardboard or selling gum, some simply beg and some occasionally pick pockets, steal purses, filch merchandise and terrify tourists. The public, worried about security and egged on by a sensationalist and elite-controlled media, often supports the violence.

Down the street from the theater showing *Batman*, Antonio Barbosa directs a government-run agency that provides food, medical care and counseling for youngsters on the streets of Recife, statistically the most dangerous city in Brazil for street children. Barbosa says that some local businesses have "torture rooms" where security goons beat up street children to frighten them. He has provided local authorities with testimonies of children who have passed through the torture rooms, but he says that nothing has been done. According to Rafael Indlenkofer, a German working with street kids in Recife, "Some of the torture practiced here makes the activities of the German SS look innocuous."

The assassins ironically call themselves *justicieros*: those who do justice. Many are police officers moonlighting to augment their meager salaries. According to Juan Rodríguez, a streetwise 19-year-old shoeshiner in São Bernardo do Campo, "killing children means no more to the *justicieros* than stepping on an ant," he slams his foot down hard on the sidewalk to illustrate. "They want the poor cleaned off the streets," Rodríguez says, "but they don't understand that they can kill one of us and there's always another to take that one's place."

Rodríguez has lost two brothers to the street violence. When I asked him what other friends have been killed on the streets, he looked into the distance and slowly recited: "Andres, Leandro, Wilson, Juanito, Marcos..." The list was long.

Although a few of the *justicieros* have been caught and jailed, they are not the cause of the problem. The killers often come from the same overcrowded slums as their victims; their families barely survive on police salaries that are low and constantly losing value due to inflation. They kill for a living, and most believe the public is behind them. According to Hélio Saboya, head of the Justice Department in Rio and a former human-rights activist, "It is impossible to have a good police officer in a rotten country."

In Saboya's rotten country, the killing of street children is not an aberration but rather a symptom, a natural part of a capitalist system developed to its extremes. The death squads help control excess population breeding in the miserable *favelas* that surround the business centers of Brazilian cities. It is savage capitalism's final solution to the problem of class. The killers of Patricio da Silva Hilario stated it clearly. In May 1989 this nine-year-old boy who made a living selling fruit outside a Rio supermarket was found strangled in a doorway. A note left on his body proclaimed, "I killed you because you didn't study or produce anything."

Blaming the victims is in vogue in Brazil these days. According to Fernando Altemeyer, a parish priest in São Mateus, a suburb of São Paulo, "There is an entire ideology built around these children, that they are at fault for what is happening in the economy, and that in order for society to recover and prosper, they must die."

Yet it is not the poor who are at fault for Brazil's troubles. It is the greedy rich. After 20 years under military dictatorship, Brazil emerged in the 1980s as one of the world's top ten economies, a success story among Third World nations. Yet the alleged economic miracle benefited the few at the expense of the many. At the beginning of the 1980s the richest 1 percent of the country's 150 million people controlled 12 percent of the wealth; by decade's end it controlled 16 percent. The richest 10 percent of the population received 45 percent of the nation's wealth in 1980; by 1990 it received 53.2 percent. While the wealthy grew wealthier, the poor got even poorer, and by 1990 the poorest 10 percent of the population received only 0.6 percent of the country's income. The poorer 50 percent of the population received only 3.5 percent of national income.

This increasing concentration of wealth means that the fancy restaurants along Rio's beaches are full of customers but the streets outside are full of half-naked children and adolescents. They come from the 54 percent of Brazilian families who earn less than $35 a month—families torn by poverty, alcoholism and violence, families whose children turn to the streets for food, money and affection. About 4 million of Brazil's 31 million school-age children have never attended classes. Understaffing and overcrowding drive away many who do start school; 15 million of the 27 million who start school drop out before the end of their fourth year.

Almost a third of Brazilian children suffer from stunted growth, and social scientists here have identified a whole new race of dwarfs growing up in the teeming *favelas*. The endemic hunger and malnutrition they suffer are not natural in this land of abundance: They are fabricated, induced by policies and laws dating from the beginning of colonization when land and labor were concentrated to generate wealth in international markets, not to feed the majority. Such policies still reign. During the two decades of the U.S.-backed military dictatorship beginning in 1964, billions of dollars in loans were acquired to develop huge, capital-intensive industries focused on export. Such "development" benefited the wealthy almost exclusively. As a result, Brazil today owes First World lenders $120 billion, the largest foreign debt in the Third World. The government has slashed social spending in order to keep up the interest payments of $8 billion a year.

In the mid-1980s Brazilian street kids and the people who work with them recognized that the government had no financial interest nor moral capacity to address the children's problems. Facing both neglect and violent death, those who live on the streets decided to take matters into their own hands and in 1985 they organized the National Movement of Street Children. Accompanied by social workers and educators, the youngsters themselves led the new organization, which rapidly spread to almost all of Brazil's urban centers.

The children's insurgency moved quickly to change the legal foundation of their oppression. They launched an attack on legal codes dating from the dictatorship, in which a distinction was made between "minors" and "children." In class-specific Brazilian parlance, according to Cardinal Paulo Evaristo Arns, "a rich person's son or daughter is called a child; a poor person's, a minor." A newspaper headline from the early 1980s in Belém proclaimed, "Minor Attacks Child"—"minor" meaning a poor, thieving, suspicious kid who had no rights. Following a campaign of pressure by the children, in 1988 the Brazilian congress rewrote the constitution's description of children's rights, doing away with the distinction.

Constitutional changes notwithstanding, the government bureaucracy has done little to help the street kids. A spurt of rhetoric by Fernando Collor de Mello, a master of gesture politics who promised in his presidential campaign to make life better for the "shirtless ones," was not matched with significant action once Collor took office. Corrupt and lacking vision, the network of government agencies remains staffed by social workers educated in the ethos of the old laws and interested primarily in protecting turf and keeping their jobs amid constant budget cuts. According to Walmer do Nascimento, a National Movement activist in Rio, only one dollar of every 20 makes its way through government institutions to the children. The bureaucratic machine consumes most of the resources allotted to children's issues.

So the youth pressed for more change. In 1990—shortly after 800 street children occupied Congress in October, 1989—Congress adopted the Statute on Children and Adolescents (ECA). The ECA guarantees the children's rights to adequate housing, education, health care, and special protection. It recognizes that all of society, not just the government must take responsibility for street children, and it places child-welfare policy in the hands of grassroots councils rather than giant governmental institutions. Municipalities supposedly will receive federal funds for children's programs only if they implement the ECA's demands.

Many of the changes demanded by the ECA have yet to be realized. Ironically, one of the ECA's immediate effects—placing tight restrictions on juvenile arrests—has made kids more attractive prey for drug lords looking for couriers and paid assassins. But beyond that the ECA's track record is mixed. A lot depends upon the creativity and will of local leaders.

In São Bernardo do Campo, a sprawling industrial city on the outskirts of São Paulo, progressive church leaders and city officials—the latter elected on the slate of the leftist Workers' Party—have worked well together to make the ECA work for the children. The first step toward implementing the ECA in São Bernardo was a public forum held at Methodist University. The forum elected a council that includes six representatives of non-governmental organizations working with street children. The council chose Onésimo Genari, a Methodist pastor, to be its coordinator.

The group quickly closed down the local children's prison; Genari says the cement beds and crowded, dirty environment were something "right out of a Charles Dickens novel." Closing the prison broke with the tradition of throwing innocent young children in with hardened adolescent criminals, which in effect created an academy for delinquency. Now when a child is detained by the police, he or she is taken first to an educator, who makes a recommendation to a judge. During the process, the child is allowed to have parents and an attorney present—which wasn't permitted previously.

Genari insists that street kids be part of the council's decision-making. He recalls a conversion experience that happened while he was working with youth who had run afoul of the law. He realized that the phenomenon of street children was a structural problem, not something coincidental or accidental. He decided that well-meaning outsiders could do nothing for the youngsters without children themselves having a key role in decision making.

That issue sets the work of many church organizations off from government agencies and others who work with street children. As many as 10 million poor children spend a good portion of their time on Brazil's streets these days. Hundreds if not thousands of governmental agencies and NGOs spend millions of dollars a year to house, feed, counsel and protect the children. International attention in recent years has stimulated a burgeoning industry; it is a cause célèbre and big bucks are available. Yet there are many ways of working with the children. Government programs tend to be staffed by bureaucrats who claim to know best what the children need. Church-sponsored programs are often paternalistic, with starry-eyed volunteers giving children a bath and teaching them table manners. Such approaches tend to reinforce the children's dependency.

There are many exceptions, fortunately, including church workers who have risked their lives to work with and defend the children. And there are those who approach the children with humility. In Recife, for example, a group of young middle-class Christians concerned about the children on the street gather late each evening on the Rua da Palma to sit and chat with them. Mary Ruth Lemos, a Baptist, says her group saw that while many groups work with the youngsters during the day, few educators or social workers are around at night. So they decided to sit with the children and listen during the lonely and often dangerous night hours. They promised themselves that they would devise no program nor look for funding for at least a year; first they wanted to learn from the children what's important to them. Lemos claims that people who show up with preconceived notions of how to help the kids are part of the problem. They might as well pretend to be Batman.

In São Bernardo, Genari and other Methodists work with the children in a way that's designed to empower them rather than take care of them. In partnership with the National Movement, church workers sponsor a variety of artistic activities, from street theater to dance, for both children on the streets and those in the *favelas* at risk of ending up there. According to pastoral worker Sandra Corrêa, the project seeks to "create a space where children can fantasize, where they can envision a different future."

Holney Mendes, a young Methodist pastor assigned to the streets of São Bernardo, meets regularly with children to practice the *capoeira*, a combination of dance and martial arts that came to Brazil with black slaves. A method of resisting slavery, it was banned at one point in Brazil's history and remains a symbol of resistance to oppression. The church workers promote it as a tool of organization and education. "It requires discipline," says Mendes, "something not found on the street. It gets rid of aggressiveness and passivity. It's a survival tool."

Capoeira is a marginalized dance for marginalized people. Street children often have no possessions besides their bodies, so it encourages them to value their bodies and use them for self-expression. Yet middle-class Brazilians, long schooled to disparage black culture, are often frightened by *capoeira* as if it were some sort of consummate mugging technique. One evening in São Bernardo I was looking for a *capoeira* session and ended up by mistake at the wrong Methodist church. I asked a man in the back of the sanctuary where the *capoeira* group was meeting. He stared at me as if I were crazy. "This is a church," he announced firmly.

The Methodists also work with a group of street children who shine shoes in the city's plaza. Mendes helped them form a cooperative; he tutors them on how to manage their money and make decisions democratically. Group members pool their resources to buy supplies; they save money and learn the benefits of working together. "We're not interested in giving these kids charity," says Mendes. "We want to become partners with them in changing their lives and changing the society that abandoned them." In effect both union organizer and pastor, Mendes also works with groups of youngsters who watch cars in parking areas or carry out bags of produce at the local market. In group sessions the children analyze common problems and determine collective approaches to solving them. Last year, for example, the youngsters in the market set a minimum fee per bag that consumers must pay or else carry their own bags of bananas and cabbage. Every week the children meet to air any problems that may have emerged at work.

Mendes says the time has come for those working with children to move from paternalism to political activism. He and other pastoral workers in São Bernardo began meetings for the mothers of street children, encouraging the women to organize and face the problems they and their children confront. It's not easy work, but Mendes insists it will foster change in the long run.

With funding from abroad, including money from the National Council of Churches (U.S.), the Methodists give scholarships to children who show academic promise; the recipients make a commitment both to study and to give back a certain amount of time to helping other children organize. And since September 1987, when six children from Mendes's project were massacred while sleeping in a city market, the ministry has provided the funds to relocate children who became targets for local *justicieros*.

While it's long been socially acceptable to provide charity for children in the street, working to change the structures that oppress children is not allowed by Brazil's ruling elite. Several church activists in São Bernardo have been threatened. One received a note stating, "Whoever defends a thief is also a thief and deserves a coffin and a black candle."

[Editors' note: For a detailed 1994 report on violence against children in Brazil, entitled *Final Justice: Police and Death Squad Homicides of Adolescents in Brazil*, contact Human Rights Watch, 485 Fifth Ave., New York, NY 10017 (212)972-8400.]

26

In Brazil, Sterilizing Women Is the Method of Choice

Jon Christensen

A spectacular decline in Brazil's birth rate has provoked praise from international family-planning agencies and anger and controversy at home. The reason: In recent years, female sterilization has become the most popular form of birth control in Brazil and the principal factor behind a steady decline in the country's rate of population growth since the late 1970s.

Every year, more than 300,000 Brazilian women have their fallopian tubes tied, according to statistics from the Ministry of Health. Nationwide, health officials estimate that 27 percent of married women between the ages of 15 and 44 have undergone tubal ligation.

Some feminists put the estimate even higher, at four out of ten women. In parts of the Amazon and in such poor northeastern states as Maranhão, they say the figure runs as high as 75 percent.

The picture has changed dramatically since the mid-1960s, when the ruling military encouraged big families and only 5 percent of couples used contraceptives. Now two-thirds use some form of contraception.

Changing values and the devastating collapse of the Brazilian "economic miracle" of the 1970s have made women turn in ever greater numbers to ways of limiting family size. And, in the absence of adequate health care and family-planning options, many of them have chosen the fail-safe method, tubal ligation.

But not without raising a storm of controversy.

In what remains the world's largest Catholic country, the Church officially opposes any form of birth control other than abstinence and the rhythm method. The Brazilian Catholic Bishops Conference branded the number of sterilizations performed in public hospitals "scandalous." Roughly half are performed in public clinics, in most cases on women during Cesarean deliveries.

"The reduction in the number of births does not solve the growing level of misery in the population," the bishops warned in a pastoral document. More than half of Brazil's 140 million people live in poverty; forty million are thought to live in "absolute misery" without adequate food, shelter, or health care.

Some feminists charge that the First World is more interested in limiting Third World populations than in helping to eliminate their poverty. "They want to end poverty by preventing the poor from being born," says Eloni Bonotto, president of the São Luis Women's Union.

Many feminists argue that an "ideology of control" rather than "choice" has dominated international family-planning efforts in Brazil.

Maria Berenice Godinho Delgado, coordinator of the Single Workers' Central (CUT) commission on women workers, claims that the International Monetary Fund has demanded reductions in Brazil's birth rate in exchange for renegotiation of its $115 billion debt. IMF officials deny the charge.

"Nonetheless," says Carmen Barroso, a feminist health researcher at the Chagas Foundation in São Paulo, "the IMF has been important in crushing the country and subtracting real income from people through structural adjustments. Women can't feed their children because of the policies of the IMF and that leads them to limit their births with desperate moves."

The relatively high female sterilization rate in Brazil compares to a rate of only 8 percent in neighboring Peru; in the United States, it is 17 percent; in China, where there are official birth-control incentives, 24 percent. There is no parallel trend toward sterilization of Brazilian men; only 0.8 percent have been sterilized.

In contrast to countries where incentives and coercion have driven women to sterilization, Barroso says poverty and a lack of choice have determined the trend in Brazil.

"Coercion is institutionalized," she says. "It is not done against women's will. But their will has no choice."

Eloni Bonotto was fired from her job as an anesthetist at the largest hospital in São Luis, the capital of the state of Maranhão, because she refused to participate in sterilizations. "I tried to tell the women that it was not the first option but the last," she says. "The doctors said I was bad for business."

Like many other Brazilian feminists, Bonotto pins the blame for the high rate of sterilization on the absence of effective government-sponsored family-planning programs. Into the vacuum, she says, rush private organizations that receive millions of dollars and contraceptives donated from the United States and Europe. From clinics and family-planning posts throughout Brazil, she says, 135 different private agencies distribute free or low-cost contraceptives and encourage women to be sterilized.

Figures from the United Nations Population Division, which tracks international funding of family-planning efforts, indicate that about $46 million has been channeled from U.N. and nongovernmental sources to Brazilian agencies, both government and private, for a wide range of activities in recent years.

The largest of the private agencies, the Brazilian Society for Family Well-Being, or BEMFAM, has forty-four family planning posts in São Luis alone and more than 2,500 nationwide. BEMFAM posts offer information on family planning, birth control, and prevention of sexually transmitted diseases. The posts also distribute free birth-control pills and other contraceptives at minimal cost and will refer women to clinics that perform sterilizations.

Many critics charge that women workers are being pressured to undergo sterilization in order to find and keep jobs. Union officials report that the guarantee of a 120-day maternity leave in the 1988 constitution has led many businesses and industries to request proof of sterilization, pregnancy tests, and signed resignation letters that are kept on file for use if an employee becomes pregnant.

Kleber Gomes, president of the São Luis Shopworkers Union, says most of the stores in the capital discriminate against female employees in one or more of these ways. However, he does not believe the employers' practices cause the high rate of sterilization.

"It's necessity," says Gomes. "Our social conditions and limited family incomes lead to sterilization."

Brazil suffered stagnant per-capita income—and declining real income for much of the population—throughout the 1980s. On the periphery of big cities such as São Luis, the poor simply can no longer afford to have more children.

Some poor women save for nine months to pay for a tubal ligation at the end of a pregnancy. Others submit to Caesarean deliveries, which are paid for by the public health system, in order to undergo sterilization, which is not covered. Waiting lists for the operation are reported at many clinics.

Thousands of independent women's groups, such as the São Luis Women's Union, have sprouted up around the country in recent years. Many are organizing self-help clinics in poor neighborhoods to provide women with alternatives.

The government should not be let off the hook, however, feminists argue. The National Women's Rights Council calls for family planning to be part of a comprehensive public health program aimed at women. Public health services should provide access to all the reversible forms of contraception, the Council says, as well as the medical assistance necessary for each type.

That Brazilian feminists now recognize the need for family planning is a departure from the 1960s, says Carmen Barroso. Back then, feminists were part of an anti-birth-control coalition that included everyone from conservative generals, who sought a population boom to occupy the Amazon, to the progressive wing of the Catholic Church, which became the principal arena for popular organizing during the dictatorship. In such a politically charged atmosphere, the government has been reluctant to do much about family planning.

'We have to accept part of the blame because we were against population control and not in favor of anything before," says Barroso.

In Brazil, another factor has contributed to demographic change.

More households have television sets than have running water. Nearly everyone has been steadily bombarded with the insistent modern cultural message that small families are better and enjoy a higher standard of living.

In her new job as a public-health educator in the poor neighborhoods surrounding São Luis, Eloni Bonotto seeks to inform young women of family-planning alternatives and discourage them from jumping to the conclusion that sterilization is the answer. But she constantly runs up against the strength of a communications network that has probably done more to popularize sterilization than even television in Brazil—word of mouth passed from woman to woman, mother to daughter.

On a recent visit to the Guardian Angel slum, Bonotto met with Euzamar Perreira Santos, who grew up the eldest in a family of eight children. After giving birth to her second child recently, the twenty-three-year-old woman joined the legion of young Brazilian women opting for sterilization, a legion that includes her mother and a sister.

Sitting in the bare living room of her rough brick house, Santos wonders what alternative she had. "To have another child year after year, a house filled with kids and misery, and us unable to feed and clothe them well?"

Santos learned about sterilization when her mother had her tubes tied after bearing her eighth child. Santos says if she had known about all the alternatives, she might not have chosen sterilization at such a young age.

But she doesn't feel any regrets. She says if she wants more children she'll adopt, but only after she finishes raising the two children she has borne.

"A lot of women in this neighborhood have so many kids they give them away like dogs," she says. "Last week a girl offered me two kids. I said I couldn't take them. I'm already struggling to raise these two."

27

In Live-and-Let-Live Land, Gay People Are Slain

James Brooke

A Brazilian paradox—tolerance of homosexuality and violence against homosexuals—has been highlighted by the granting of political asylum in the United States to a Brazilian homosexual on grounds that he would be persecuted if returned home.

The ruling in July 1993 by a San Francisco immigration judge, Philip Leadbetter, represented the first time that a homosexual had won asylum in the United States on the ground that homosexuals were a persecuted social group in the country of origin, said Julie Dorf, executive director of the international Gay and Lesbian Human Rights Commission, a private group in San Francisco. Marcelo Tenorio, a 30-year-old house painter, told the judge that he had left Brazil after he had been stabbed and badly beaten outside a gay bar on a Rio beach front in 1989. A Brazilian gay rights campaigner who testified in favor of Mr. Tenorio's request said 1,200 homosexuals had been slain in Brazil since 1980.

But Brazil is also renowned for its tolerance of gay life. Transvestite shows, where many of the performers are gay, are considered family entertainment, and transvestites play an integral part of Rio's Carnival. Caetano Veloso and Gilberto Gil, two of Brazil's most famous singers, openly flaunt their bisexuality and wear dresses in public.

Rio's gay bars and gay Carnival balls have long attracted tourists from Europe, the United States and Brazil's more conservative South American neighbors.

'A Very Ambiguous Opinion'

"Brazil displays a very ambiguous opinion about homosexuality," said Luiz Mott, president of the Gay Group of Bahia, Brazil's oldest and most prominent gay rights group. "On one hand it is a nation with a very exuberant gay culture, exporting transvestites to Italy and France, attracting tourists for Carnival. On the other hand, one homosexual is murdered in Brazil every five days." Relying on newspaper reports Mr. Mott's group tabulated 1,200 killings of homosexuals since 1980, and Mr. Mott believes the real number is twice as high. Of the recorded killings, only ten percent led to arrests, he said.

David L. Harrad, a spokesman for the Dignity Group, a gay rights group in Curitiba, in southern Brazil, said: "In Curitiba, we have had 20 murders of homosexuals over the last 10 years and only one was solved. The one that was solved was only cleared up because the family paid the police to keep on the case."

"More people practice homosexuality in Brazil than in most countries, but very few people reveal their condition," said Mr. Harrad, a Briton. "People have a great fear of revealing their homosexuality for fear of machismo."

In Rio de Janeiro, 38 killings of homosexuals were recorded in the first half of 1993 alone, according to the Atoba Group, a gay rights group. Most of the suspected killers are male prostitutes. In a recurring scenario, a young street hustler goes home with an older man, has sex, kills the man, then loots his apartment.

Mr. Mott's group has identified 12 "extermination groups," including a São Paulo skinhead group with T-shirts reading "Death to Homosexuals." But the government and some mainstream newspapers say homosexuals are not victims of organized attacks.

"Judge Tricked: Gay Wins Asylum in U.S.A. With Lie About Brazil," was the headline of an article about the San Francisco court ruling in *Veja*, the nation's largest-selling news weekly.

"There is no conspiracy or evidence that could indicate an organized practice," *Veja* wrote of the killing of homosexuals here. "In the hands of the noisy American pink lobby, Tenorio's cause became a festival of demagoguery—and of Brazil-bashing."

Since there are no separate statistics on the killing of homosexuals, whether they are disproportionately victims cannot be
proved. But the sometimes sordid circumstances of the deaths attract a lot of attention.

In one of 1993's most shocking killings, Renildo Jose
dos Santos, a town councilman in Alagoas State, was kidnapped,
tortured and decapitated in early March.

Six weeks earlier, Mr. Santos had revealed his bisexuality in a
radio interview in his town, Coqueiro Seco. The council immediately voted to bar him from office. When the councilman started to
receive death threats, the Gay Group of Bahia tried to win political
asylum for him in Canada. Before a response came, Mr. Santos
was kidnapped and killed. After his severed head was discovered
in an adjoining state, five men, including the town's mayor, were
arrested.

March Draws Only 100

Gay campaigners say they hope that the United States asylum
case will stir Brazilian public opinion to call for an end to impunity in gay killings. In September 1993 representatives of 38 gay
groups met in São Paulo to devise a strategy to lobby Brazil's Congress. But Brazil's gay rights movement suffers from a lack of foot
soldiers. A gay pride march on a Rio beach in June 1993 drew only
100 people.

"Brazil's gay movement is relatively weak and disorganized, in
part because there are no laws prohibiting homosexuality to organize around," said Richard Parker, an American anthropologist who
works with AIDS prevention groups here. Brazil de-criminalized
most homosexual acts in 1823.

In a 1993 *DataFolha* poll, 44 percent of respondents nationwide said they "totally agreed" that "homosexuals should be accepted like anyone else."

"In the United States, friendship networks of gay men are largely
gay men," continued Mr. Parker who has written two books on

Brazilian sexuality. "Here in Brazil, their lives are much more integrated with their families; their friendships tend to be much more mixed."

But the impunity enjoyed by those who kill homosexuals appears to stem from the closeted nature of gay activity here. "In many cases, the families don't want to expose themselves to ridicule," Parker said of killings of gay men that go unsolved.

28

Women-Run Police Stations Fight the Odds

Thais Corral

A teacher invited two homeless girls to his place; he showed them a pornographic videotape, then raped them. It's just the kind of crime that might have gone unpunished in Brazil prior to 1985, when many acts of violence against women and girls were not even registered as crimes.

Until the advent of women's police stations, that is. The result of a successful feminist lobbying effort, the first of these *delegacias da mulher* opened in downtown São Paulo in August 1985. Staffed entirely by women police officers, the *delegacias* were intended to do what regular police stations did not. They would record crimes against women like sexual assault and domestic violence, and offer victims emotional support and the chance to prosecute abusers. In its first year, the São Paulo *delegacia* served 2,038 women. By 1988, it was helping 7,000.

There are now approximately 18 *delegacias* all over Brazil (and some in other Latin American nations). From January 1991 to August 1992, they registered 205,000 attacks on women, with a daily average of 337 incidents. These unprecedented statistics have helped bring violence against women before the public eye.

Maria dos Anjos Canardella, chief of a *delegacia* on the outskirts of Rio de Janeiro, is proud of her station's achievements— among them solving the 1992 rape of the homeless girls. Her investigation sent the man to jail; he hanged himself before he could be tried. But a lack of institutional support hampers the *delegacias*' best efforts. "We need an administrative structure that is more supportive of our work," says Canardella. Due to inadequate government funding, her officers can't always get police cars that run, and they have to pool their money to buy paper or mail a letter. In addition, there are only three shelters for domestic abuse survivors in all of Brazil. "The fact that women have to return home to their husbands after having gone to the women's police station most often means risking their lives," says Rita Andrea, a cofounder of the antiviolence group *SOS Mulher*.

The biggest obstacle to protecting women in Brazil is the country's legal structure, which allows—and therefore promotes—violence against women. Despite a 1991 appeals court ruling to the contrary, men are still routinely acquitted for killing or beating wives or lovers as a "defense of honor." And, under a 1940 penal code still in effect, crimes against "dishonest" women are punished less severely than those against "honest" (read married or virginal) women.

Both of these legal weapons were used against Maria Celsa da Conceição. On Valentine's Day 1987 in Porto Velho, Celsa broke up with her boyfriend, Domingos Savio Lemos. Enraged, he doused her with rubbing alcohol and set her afire. She barely survived. At Savio's trial, officials seemingly ignored the evidence *delegacia* officers had collected. Savio told the judge that Celsa had another lover while she dated him; therefore his honor had been impugned. Even the prosecutor said Celsa's "bad moral behavior" cast doubt on her credibility. Savio was acquitted.

So while women may flock to the *delegacias* for help, they seldom get justice. A *delegacia* chief told Americas Watch that in 1990, more than 2,000 battery and sexual assault cases were registered at her station, but she didn't know of a single one resulting in prosecution. Feminists continue to fight to change the laws. A coalition of groups is now lobbying to establish violence against women as a human rights issue in Brazil. They're also pushing Congress to rewrite the penal code.

29

Brazil's Black Consciousness Movement

John Burdick

On May 11, 1988, two days before the hundredth anniversary of the abolition of Brazilian slavery, 5,000 people marched under a punishing sun through downtown Rio de Janeiro. At the head of the march, Frei Davi, the fiery leader of Rio de Janeiro's Commission of Black Religious, Seminarians, and Priests, bellowed through a megaphone: "They say the good white masters gave us our freedom! Nonsense!" The true importance of the anniversary, he thundered, was that it reminded Brazilian blacks that they had yet to be liberated. "One hundred years without abolition!" the crowd chanted. "We are still enslaved! Racial democracy is a lie!"

Brazil's black consciousness movement, a loosely linked collection of nearly 600 organizations, is now active in almost every state in the country.[1] Their goal: to teach the younger generation of *negros* that their history and the very terms they use to describe themselves have been distorted by whites.[2] These organizations include lay associations established by the Catholic Church, university-associated research centers, state-sponsored agencies, tightly run political bodies, and informal clusters of activists.

The Pastoral of the *Negro* in Duque de Caxias, a Rio suburb, was established by the progressive bishop Dom Mauro Morelli in 1986 and is now led by two priests and a dozen activists who organize workshops, disseminate literature, and run discussion groups.[3] The aim, as one organizer put it, is "to get *negros* to think differently about themselves." The first step is to teach that abolition was not a gift of the master; the second, to convince all those who call themselves "*mulato*" or "*moreno*" (brown) to call themselves "*negro*" (black) instead. As another explained, "We see that for every 100 *negros*, 70 reject their identity. So we must convince the *negro* to reject the ideology of 'whitening.' And the way to start is for him to call himself a *negro*."

Some organizations present racism as primarily a cultural problem, to be solved through the development of black identity, based on the rediscovery of one's slave and African "roots." In São Paulo, for instance, the Afro-Brazilian Research Dance Company offers training in samba music, an art form derivative of African rhythms. Similarly, São Paulo's Center of Negro Culture and Art has tried to promote black consciousness through classes in *capoeira*, an Afro-Brazilian martial art.[4]

Other black consciousness organizations, however, including the São Paulo-based Group of Black Women, the Group Nzinga, and the Group of Unity and Black Consciousness, believe the struggle against racism must seek to change economic, social and political structures. By far the largest (and, as it happens, oldest) of the more explicitly political groups is the São Paulo-based Unified Negro Movement (MNU), founded in 1978, with roughly 6,000 members today.[5] The MNU is currently the closest the black movement comes to having a national organization. MNU's platform embraces socialism, and states that blacks constitute an underclass whose labor maintains the wealth and power of the white elite.

MNU's activists do not deny the value of raising consciousness about "roots." Their priority, however, is contemporary racial politics. They have demonstrated against police violence and fought in the courts for the enforcement of existing laws against discrimination in the workplace. They also provide logistical support to struggles for better health care, and support the rights of prostitutes, battered women and street children. During the writing of Brazil's current constitution in 1986-1988, MNU activists were instrumental in calling for a National Convention of Blacks for the Constitution, which promoted debates on the constitutional process in hundreds of towns and cities.[6] Along with the direct pressure of Carlos Alberto Oliveira and Benedita da Silva, two black congresspeople elected in 1986, the grassroots debates undoubtedly helped bring about the inclusion of a constitutional amendment which outlawed racial discrimination.[7]

The vocal presence of groups like the MNU has persuaded a number of political parties, from left to center, to place anti-racist planks in their platforms and create commissions on racial issues, as well as to nominate blacks to run for office. In 1982 São Paulo's governor, Franco Montoro of the centrist Brazilian Democratic Movement Party (PMDB), created the Council for the Participation and Development of the Black Community. His equally centrist successor, Orestes Quercia, appointed several blacks to highly visible posts, and set up an office to eliminate racist hiring practices. Similarly, the desire to steal MNU's thunder prompted the federal government in 1986 to create "Palmares National Park" in Alagoas state, commemorating the great seventeenth-century community of runaway slaves.

At first glance such gestures appear to be garden-variety co-optation; but they offer the first (admittedly limited and tentative) state-sanctioned acknowledgment that "racial democracy" is a myth. The new agencies also use their position inside the government to gain access to important resources. They have pressured the state census bureau in São Paulo to gather data on black employment, income and education, to publicize racial issues, and to disseminate information about blacks in newspapers, booklets and videotapes. In 1987 São Paulo's Council for Black Participation ran Project Zumbi, an extensive program of lectures, concerts, exhibits, and public debates publicizing the historical importance of the leader of Palmares.

Despite the willingness of mainstream political parties to carry black favor, in 1982 only two out of the 54 black candidates who ran in São Paulo were elected, and currently there are only a handful of blacks in Congress. Because of this, as well as to avoid dilution of their message, many black militants have called for distance from white-dominated parties; indeed, in 1982 the MNU adopted this position formally [8]

Still, many negro activists continue to seek alliances with progressive parties, such as the Workers Party (PT), led by Luís Inácio Lula da Silva. The PT succeeded in sending two *negros* to the Constituent Assembly, including the only black woman ever elected to national office, Benedita da Silva. [In October 1994, Benedita was elected to the Senate. See Chapter 36.] Black militants are, however, wary of the PT's tendency to regard racial discrimination as the result of class oppression. In 1982, for example, the party published a pamphlet in which it denounced racism primarily as a device to maintain an army of cheap reserve labor.

Put off by this kind of analysis (which they regard as denying the primacy and specificity of the race issue), many black leaders have been attracted instead to Leonel Brizola's social democratic, populist Democratic Worker's Party (PDT), which lacks the sectarianism of the Left and has one of the best-oiled patronage machines in the country. As governor of Rio de Janeiro, Brizola placed blacks in prominent positions and, in a gesture that earned him the undying affection of Rio's (mainly black) domestic workers, he prohibited employers from requiring maids to use separate stairwells and elevators. Soon thereafter, MNU firebrand Abdias do Nascimento went to Brasilia as a congressman on the PDT ticket, as did black singer Agnaldo Timoteo.

The black movement is currently far from being the mass political phenomenon to which its militants aspire. "Ninety percent of all *negros* in Brazil," Frei Davi told me, "don't acknowledge their blackness; they want to forget their slave past. That is what we're up against." Even optimistic observers concede the movement has a fairly narrow social base. Recent estimates place the number of black organizers throughout Brazil at no more than 3,000. These in turn are estimated to have only about 25,000 active followers, out of an Afro-Brazilian population that the movement estimates at over 70 million.[9] The large number of organizations is a bit misleading. In Goiás state, for example, the movement musters no more than a few dozen activists. And the 5,000 marchers who protested the centennial of abolition are less impressive when compared to the 20,000 Brizola can muster at a moment's notice, or the half million that gathered in Rio to call for direct presidential elections in 1984.

Black consciousness groups are composed primarily of professionals, intellectuals, and upwardly mobile students, a pattern that has characterized the movement from the start.[10] In the late 1960s, the dictatorship's policy of subsidizing private universities allowed an unprecedented number of young blacks and *mulatos* to enter college. By the early 1970s, they faced the bitter realization that even a college degree could not outweigh the color of their skin on the job market.[11] Among these students were many, such as well-known activist and journalist Hamilton Cardoso, who turned their frustration into an organized challenge to the myth of racial democracy and its underlying institutional racism.[12]

Middle-class blacks who see racial politics as their primary concern sometimes find themselves talking past black workers for whom race occupies a secondary (though important) place. "The guy came here all hot," one young black worker told me about the visit to his town of an MNU militant. "'You must assume your black identity,' he said. OK, fine. I assumed it, long ago. What does that get me? Does that help feed my family?" Undoubtedly such sentiments help explain why the few black candidates in São Paulo elected in 1982 and 1986 did not run on race-based platforms, but rather emphasized working-class issues.[13]

Typically, the audiences for the movement's "culturalist" activities are students, professionals, journalists and middle-class artists, rather than the art form's usual consumers — the inhabitants of the *favelas* or urban periphery. In Rio de Janeiro, the Institute of Research on Black Culture produces video documentaries on Afro-Brazilian religion and recreates the musical instruments and songs of the slave quarters, then shows these at its downtown headquarters and at art galleries. The way the Instituto Senghor in Porto Alegre exhorts Afro-Brazilians not to forget their ancestry is by publishing "African" poetry read primarily by university students.

Not surprisingly, the little systematic evidence available suggests that the working class is largely unaware of the movement. In one study of working-class, black voters, a majority had no opinion about the black consciousness movement, many had not even heard of its existence, and 90 percent could not name a contemporary black political figure.[14]

Not only is the leadership of the black movement primarily middle-class; it also appears to be dominated by Afro-Brazilians with comparatively light skin.[15] In the town of Duque de Caxias, among the 24 activists I knew, no fewer than 20 admitted that before becoming involved in the movement, they had identified themselves not as *negro* or *preto* (black), but as *mulato* or *moreno* (brown).[16] Confronted with this fact, they cheerfully accepted it, explaining that their about-face was simply proof of the movement's success in raising consciousness.

Both the causes of the *mulato* monopoly on leadership and the tensions inherent in it are evident in the *negro* organization led by the progressive Catholic Church.[17] *Mulatos*, given greater opportunities than their darker-skinned brothers and sisters, achieve institutional positions in the Church, but then often find themselves treated as second-class citizens. Mariana, a nun who used to call herself *morena*, explained, "I thought that by becoming a nun I could wipe away that blemish. But I found out that no one would let me forget it. Who do you think made coffee for visitors? That disgusted me."

Translating this disgust into action, Mariana joined Frei Davi in his Commission. Already literate, educated and well-placed institutionally, Mariana "returned" to her "black identity" in the role of leader. Her return is typical of *mulatos* who, discriminated against in the white world, try to resolve the ambiguity of their status by embracing black identity while insisting on being compensated with a higher status in the black realm.

My own research showed that *mulato* leadership was one reason that very few dark blacks participated in Catholic consciousness-raising programs near Rio. One dark-skinned black told me, "Look, *mulatos* have always tried to run away from us. How could they have our culture? They want to use what we have. They don't know what they are." Another commented, "They say they are *negros*, but they aren't. They haven't suffered.... *Mulatos* still think they are better than us. They think the black man still needs to look to them as masters."

Poor and working-class blacks are not immune to the myth of racial democracy, reinforced as it is by schoolbooks, the media, and state-sponsored rituals. But the relative scarcity of working-class *negros* in the contemporary black consciousness movement does not mean such people have little "consciousness." An extraordinary variety of popular cultural practices among the black working class keep an alternative, subversive interpretation of Brazilian history and race relations alive.

In the early 1970s, large numbers of young, uneducated, underemployed youths living in Rio de Janeiro's *favelas* began crowding into all-night clubs to dance to the music of James Brown, Isaac Hayes, and Aretha Franklin. They filled movie houses to see films like "Wattstax," "Claudine," "Superfly," and "Shaft."[18] Within a few years, the phenomenon had developed its own lexicon of English-language phrases such as "soul" and "black-power kids," as well as its own paraphernalia of colorful clothes and elaborate handshakes.

Though many dismissed this "soul" movement as simply cultural imperialism, it revealed acute disillusionment with elements of traditional Afro-Brazilian culture.[19] Young blacks felt keenly what scholars had observed for some time: that traditional practices of the black community such as samba and *capoeira* had been co-opted by white society.[20] Soul music, on the other hand, was perceived as the incontrovertible patrimony of North American blacks.

Anything suggesting that blacks in Brazil might have something in common with angry North American blacks could not fail to be a highly charged political phenomenon. The "soul" movement thus struck at the very heart of the myth of racial democracy, by proclaiming a transnational "pan-black" community of suffering, symbolized by the youths' clenched-fist black power salutes.

Religion is another vehicle for black consciousness. Umbanda is, along with pentecostalism, one of the fastest-growing religions in Brazil today.[21] In literally thousands of small ritual centers throughout the country, blacks, *mulatos* and whites come together to become possessed by, and seek advice from, a range of distinctively Brazilian spirits, including deceased slaves and Indians.

The most well-known version of Umbanda situates the slave at the bottom, beneath the Indian and white in the hierarchy of spirits.[22] But this version is adhered to mainly by whites and *mulatos*. Blacks in Umbanda worship a spirit unrecognized by either whites or *mulatos*: Zumbi, one of the chiefs of Palmares, the great maroon society that survived for almost a century in the backlands of Alagoas, until it was finally destroyed by the Portuguese in 1697.[23]

Catholicism, too, provides *negros* with martyrs and saints, including Anastasia, an eighteenth-century Brazilian slave, not yet canonized, who enjoys a large following among older black women. As recounted by these elderly *negras*, the jealous wife of a slave owner unjustly accused the virgin slave Anastasia of seducing her husband, and forced her to wear a face-iron for the rest of her life. Anastasia's legend embodies a sharp critique of the master class, and stands as a popular rebuttal to claims that Brazilian slave owners were kindly and paternal.

The music, dance and lyrics of samba are rich with the history and experience of Afro-Brazilians. In the shantytowns of large Brazilian cities, on Saturday afternoons and evenings, one often encounters small groups of young men under the awnings of corner bars, beating a drum, singing and dancing a sliding four-step. The music the men are singing is samba, and the small gathering is most likely a delegation from a far larger group, known as a samba "school," that organizes a major parade during carnival. Thousands of *favela*-dwellers are members of these schools, rehearsing and practicing year-round the sambas they perform during the last Tuesday before Lent.

The music and its accompanying dance originated in slaves' melodic calls to African gods, asking them to descend into spirit mediums.[24] In classic samba, a circle of people sing and clap their hands, while someone in the center improvises quatrains about everyday life. These improvisations provide the vehicle for subtle, ironic commentaries on race relations and society in general.[25] Even under the military dictatorship, the samba schools commented on hyper-inflation, police violence, corruption, low wages and the foreign debt.

The black consciousness movement is contributing in important ways to the cause of racial justice in Brazil. Still, Frei Davi's claim that "we are casting light into all the dark corners of Brazil" seems overstated. The important question may not be the accuracy of the claim, but whether the casting of light should ever be one way. Many leaders of the black movement have already begun to realize that profound change in the racial status quo will occur only when they allow the masses to shed a little light on them.

Footnotes

1. For a tabulation, see Caetana Damaceno, Micenio Santos and Sonia Giacomini (comps.), *Catologo de Entidades de Movimento Negro no Brasil* (Rio de Janeiro, 1988).

2. Whenever possible I have substituted the Brazilian term *"negro"* for "black" because of its special political connotation. In general, Brazilians distinguish three racial categories: *branco* (white), *mulato*, and *negro* (or *preto*). The black consciousness movement, however, has politicized *"negro"* by making it include both *"mulatos"* and those who have always called themselves *negro* (i.e.. dark-skinned blacks).

3. "Pastorals" are educational or missionary programs carried out under the auspices of the Catholic Church.

4. In this remarkable art form opponents pair off inside a circle of singers and drummers, and throw themselves at each other in a tightly choreographed mock battle. Spinning, jumping, and using closely controlled kicks, *capoeiristas* score points and audience approval by demonstrating acrobatic agility, grace, and the ability to come within a hair's breadth of their opponent's face and mid-section, without touching either. *Capoeira* has usually been interpreted as rooted in the way slaves, deprived of weapons by their masters, would settle scores among themselves.

5. Lelia Gonzalez, "The Unified Black Movement: A New Stage in Black Mobilization," in Pierre-Michel Fontaine, *Race, Class and Power in Brazil* (Los Angeles: UCLA, 1985), pp. 120-134.

6. George Reid Andrews, *Blacks and Whites in São Paulo, Brazil, 1888-1988* (Madison: University of Wisconsin Press, 1991), p. 185.

7. It should be noted, however, that Brazil still lacks a coherent body of legal precedent for dealing with race discrimination. The constitutional amendment is a symbolic gesture, part of an ongoing process of legitimating racial issues.

8. Andrews, *Blacks and Whites*, pp. 195, 323.

9. Joel Rufino, "IPCN e Cacique de Ramos: Dois exemplos de movimento *negro* na cidade do Rio de Janeiro," *Comunicações do ISER*, vol. 7, # 28 (1988), p. 6.

10. Jorge, a black militant in Rio, openly acknowledged to me that movement leaders throughout the city are "mainly educated people, teachers, lawyers and all." My own experience confirmed this: all the meetings I attended were led by people with at least some professional training or college education. Other observers report the same pattern in Rio, São Paulo and elsewhere. See Michael

Mitchell, "Blacks and the *Abertura Democratica*," in Fontaine, *Race, Class and Power* ; Gonzalez, "The Unified"; and ibid. See also I.K. Sundiata, "Late Twentieth-Century Patterns of Race Relations in Brazil and the United States," *Phylon* No. 47 (1987), pp. 62-76.

11. Pierre-Michel Fontaine, "Transnational Relations and Racial Mobilization: Emerging Black Movements in Brazil," in John F. Stack (ed.), *Ethnic Minorities in a Transnational World* (Westport: Greenwood Press, 1981), p. 145.

12. See Hamilton Cardoso, "Limites do confronto racial e aspectos da experiencia negra do Brasil—reflexões," in Hamilton Cardoso and Emir Sader (eds.), *Movimentos sociais na transicao democratica* (São Paulo: Cortez, 1987), pp. 82-104.

13. Ana Lucia Valente, *Politica e relações raciais: Os negros e as eleições paulistas de 1982* (São Paulo, 1986), p. 139.

14. Ibid., p. 139. As Andrews points out, "neither the black movement nor the party organizations responsible for turning out the black vote had succeeded in making contact with these individuals." Andrews, *Blacks and Whites,* p. 197.

15. This, too, is not new: black consciousness movements in Brazil have historically been led by *mulatos*. See, for example, Fernandes, *The Negro in Brazilian Society* (New York: Columbia University Press, 1969, p. 208; and Pierre-Michel Fontaine, "Research in the Political Economy of Afro-Latin America," *Latin America Research Review,* No. 15 (1980).

16. This pattern was not limited to this area. Visits to meetings of various black organizations in Rio confirmed my impression that the majority of the leaders and militants were not dark-skinned blacks, but rather people who had once identified themselves as mulato.

17. On the race issue in the Catholic Church, see Caetana Damaceno, "Cantando por Subir," (Ph.D. diss.), Universidade Federal de Rio de Janeiro, 1990; also Flavio Lenz, "Tres Versões da Fraternidade," *Comunicacoes do ISER* (1988); and John Burdick, "Observações sobre a Campanha da Fraternidade de 1988 na Baixada Fluminense," *Comunicações do ISER* No. 40 (1991).

18. Lauro Cavalcanti, "Black-Breque. Estudo de um Grupo Soul em relacão a Adeptos do Samba," *Comunicacoes do ISER* No. 28 (1988).

19. Ibid.; Mitchell, "Blacks and the *Abertura,*" 1985; Fontaine, "Transnational Relations," 1981; and James H. Kennedy, "Political Liberalization, Black Consciousness, and recent Afro-Brazilian Literature," *Phylon,* Vol. 47, No. 3 (1986).

20. Thus *feijoada,* originally slave food, has been emptied of its history and transformed into the national dish; *carnaval,* originally the popular expression of black street groups, has become a tourist showcase for beautiful mulatas and a rite of national communion and unity.

21. On the growth of Umbanda, see Diana Brown, *Umbanda: The Politics of Religion in Urban Brazil* (Ann Arbor: University of Michigan Press, 1986).

22. Many have denounced Umbanda as a form of racial assimilation. This view is systematically propounded in Renato Ortiz, *A Morte Branca do Feiticeiro Negro* (Petropolis: Vozes, 1978); Roger Bastide, *The African Religions of Brazil* (Baltimore: Johns Hopkins University Press, 1978); Brown, *Umbanda.*

23. R. K. Kent, "Palmares: An African State in Brazil," in Richard Price (ed.), *Maroon Societies* (Baltimore: Johns Hopkins University Press, 1979).

24. Muniz Sodre, *Samba, o Dono do Corpo* (Codecri, 1979).

25. A good discussion of samba as a form of cultural resistance may be found in Muniz Sodre, *O Terreiro e a Cidade* (Petropolis: Vozes 1988). See also Z. Moore, "Reflections on Blacks in Contemporary Brazilian Popular Culture in the 1980s," *Studies in Latin American Popular Culture,* No.7 (1988).

30

Pastoral Agents Movement Raises Black Awareness

Ken Serbin

Like Christ washing the feet of the apostles, Mauro Sergio Alexandre wipes clean the shoes and souls of 20th-century Brazilians.

For a few bucks a day, Mauro the shoe-shiner, who wears a rosary around his neck, and his nine-year-old son, David, stoop before others from dawn to dusk in the plaza by the cathedral in South America's largest city, São Paulo. Or they may earn a little money selling old newspapers and cardboard they haul in a large, homemade cart. Later, laid on its side with a piece of carpet over the opening, the cart becomes their bed. Like that of millions of other black Brazilians who wax shoes, sweep streets, iron clothes or do any number of other jobs for pennies, their day of sacrifice ends with uncertainty about the next.

Last December, Mauro discovered something that would drag him beyond the naked neoslavery of Brazilian capitalism to the way of the cross of the black and poor. While taking David for a walk on his day off, Mauro came upon the corpse of a 14-year-old boy who had been strangled and left in a pool of water.

Revolted at the injustice, Mauro told the police. But as is often the case with dark skin, instead of reaping the blessings of justice, Mauro spent a night in jail, where a cop who didn't like "black witchcraft" made him take off his rosary.

Four men and a woman tortured Mauro for two hours, trying to force out information about the crime or perhaps a confession. Hung on the infamous "parrot's perch," his limbs tied, body crouched and soles of his feet exposed to beatings from a club, he caught glimpses of his tormentors from behind a blindfold. The woman applied electric shocks to his toes and fingers.

Freed but summoned by the police again, Mauro returned with a lawyer from the São Paulo archdiocese's center for human rights. There was no torture, but he had to sign a charge of vagrancy that could later help put him back in jail. Mauro has filed no complaint about the abuse; he remembers that another victim who denounced police brutality has since disappeared from the plaza.

As Mauro tells his story, two policemen pass by escorting eight brown and black men to a wall for a frisking. Six go free because their identity cards are in order. The remaining two climb into the police wagon. An officer calls one a "thief" because he was carrying a broken watch. The other, the darkest of the eight, did not have identification.

Mauro, David and the other blacks in the plaza are symbols of Brazil's blacks. Their situations are typical of blacks across the country and emphasize the need for activists of Black Pastoral Agents, the movement of lay militants, priests and nuns that has become a leading force among the fledgling black-consciousness groups in Brazil.

According to 1980 government statistics, less than six percent of Brazil's population, now close to 150 million, is "black" and about 38 percent "*mulatto*." However, these numbers are a serious underestimation to the casual observer and ironic in light of frequent police discrimination against dark-skinned people.

For Pastoral Agents, the figures are a manipulation by census officials and the dominant white ruling class to make Brazilian society less "black" by reinforcing the ideology of *embranquecimento*, the "whitening process." In reality, says Pastoral Agents, which is trying to persuade the government to change its census-taking methods, about 60 percent of Brazilians are black. The size of the black population is central to Pastoral Agents and its sister groups because it is directly linked to the ideas of negritude (blackness or black cultural assertiveness) and *consciencia negra* (black consciousness), two of the pillars the movement is using to lift the black population to racial and economic equality.

"Nobody has negritude at birth. It's difficult to find somebody who's secure in his black consciousness," said Father Luiz Fernando Oliveira, a recently ordained black priest in the city's large and impoverished eastern zone. The fight against "invisibility, the fact that people don't appear because they are black— this is what leads us to work on black consciousness."

In the struggle for equality, Pastoral Agents envelops a wide range of issues that directly affect blacks and often touch other groups among Brazil's poor, such as problems of the landless and the homeless, health and jobs. Specific concerns with respect to blacks include racial violence, the condition of black children and the nurture of *quilombos*, the organizational nuclei of Pastoral Agents that adopted the word for the colonial Afro-Brazilian runaway slave colonies. Silva estimates at 500 the number of Brazil's *quilombos.*

The religious roots of this movement are similar to those of the North American civil-rights and South African antiapartheid movements. The fight for black equality in Brazil is increasingly important, and at times delicate, for the Catholic hierarchy.

Black Pastoral Agents sprang from a National Conference of the Bishops of Brazil task force on blacks which was created at the suggestion of a group of black Catholics to help prepare for the historic 1979 general assembly of Latin American bishops in Puebla.

At the time, about 200 black groups already existed in Brazil, but not one had the participation of black Catholics, because the church was not teaching blacks to become active, said Father David Raimundo Santos, a black Franciscan and one of Pastoral Agents' key leaders.

The majority of bishops sympathize with the black movement within the church, "but those that in fact involve themselves in this work are relatively few," Silva said. "We are the church, but we survive in autonomy. The question should be: Could the church survive without us? Because here in Brazil, the majority of the church is black."

Oliveira said, "The church, even on the local level, still hasn't expressed solidarity. There is black expression in the church only because the blacks are there." There is no department in the church to take care of the pastoral work with blacks, as there is with CIMI, he added, referring to the Indigenous Missionary Council.

"Whenever there is a manifestation of black culture, there is still fear," Oliveira continued. "It's not passive expression. We still have to conquer our own space."

That fear has reached the Vatican, which in the early 1980s intervened in what Pastoral Agents sees as a key area of Afro-Brazilian expression—the liturgy—by slapping a prohibition on *Missa dos Quilombos*, the "Mass of the *Quilombos*." Progressive bishops, including black Bishop Jose Maria Pires, joined with Milton Nascimento, one of Brazil's most brilliant composers and singers and also black, to hold the Mass, which has African rhythms and themes throughout. A commercial record of the Mass was also produced.

Despite Rome's frown, the Mass continued to be celebrated, and the evolution of the Afro-Brazilian Mass continued throughout the 1980s. "We waited awhile to let the bad climate pass," said Oliveira. "Only the people are capable of barring something."

Some black priests and bishops began adapting their Masses to more popular rhythms and celebrating with an altar made up of a cloth placed on the floor in the middle of a circle of dancing worshipers. In 1986 the Commission of Black Religious, Priests and Seminarians of Rio de Janeiro sent a letter to the Vatican requesting the creation of the Afro-Brazilian Catholic rite.

In a surprise move in February of 1990, the Vatican allowed Brazil's Bishops to start the official paperwork for initiating the rite. Representatives from the Bishops and Brazil's movement of black priests and bishops will join to draft a proposal to Rome. "For us, this authorization represents the restitution of a sacred right that was denied for more than 500 years," said Santos. "We believe this is one of the ways that the Vatican found to ask for forgiveness from the black people."

Oliveira also said the move by Rome was positive but added, "They (the Vatican) saw that there is value in what is happening.

It's something that isn't happening within the church. They want to be a conduit. They see that we're on the move, but without dialogue with the hierarchy. They want contact. It's a warning, too."

Control has also come from within the Brazilian church. In the mid-1980s, black Catholics pushed hard for the Bishop's annual Lenten fraternity campaign to adopt the theme of black suffering in Brazil for 1988, the 100th anniversary of the emancipation of Brazil's slaves. However, the manual for the campaign underwent ten revisions before publication and was watered down for its historical analysis of slavery, recalled Oliveira. The songs which blacks most wanted for the manual's liturgical section were left out, bringing criticism from black Catholic activists.

Blacks are also seeking to gain strength in the church by increasing their vocations. Santos and others are critical of the paltry number of blacks in the clergy: Brazil has only 230 blacks among its more than 13,000 priests and only seven black bishops among the more than 300. Black vocations are growing he said, but many have trouble adjusting to a European-style priestly and religious formation seemingly intolerant of black culture.

31

The Role of Liberation Theology:
An Interview with Alvaro Barreiro

James S. Torrens

lvaro Barreiro, S.J., is a professor of theology at Centro de Estudos Superiores, Belo Horizonte, Brazil, and author of Basic Ecclesial Communities: the Evangelization of the Poor *(Orbis Books, 1982). He was interviewed by James S. Torrens, S.J., associate editor of* America, *who translated this text.*

Father Barreiro, how would you sum up your special interests, or concentration, as a theologian?

As a pastoral theologian in Brazil, I have had to focus on the "marginalized" of our country and of our planet. This fits remarkably with what I find in that early, programmatic discourse of Jesus at the synagogue of Nazareth (Lk. 14:16-30), where He tells us that those with emergency needs: lack of food, housing, work, schools or hospitals—in short, the poor, have priority. What we now call the preferential option for the poor belongs to the very marrow of the Gospel of the Kingdom as proclaimed by Jesus. A German author wrote a book which he entitled *Jesus in schlechter Gesellschaft* ("Jesus in Bad Company"), noting how Jesus surrounded himself with people not much esteemed, those on the edge economically, sociologically, religiously.

The church has been launching what it calls a "new evangelization." What are the challenges this process has to face in Latin America?

How to announce the Gospel as good news, as splendid news, in a continent of terrifying social injustice, of monstrous structural inequity—that is a huge and persistent challenge. Paradoxically, a second ranks right along with it, the challenge of modernity. How to announce the Gospel to the men and women, old and young, of the middle classes in Latin America, not very numerous admittedly, and to the handful in the upper classes—those marked by the phenomenon called "modernity," whose world is industrial, urban, pluralistic and individualistic.

A leading Brazilian economist, Edmar Bacha, has called Brazil "Belínda," an amalgam of Belgium and India. A small consumer society, with people living just as well as one does these days in Belgium, exists amid an India, a mass of "pariahs," as a minister of our military government called them 15 years ago. At that time, 30 million lived at the edges of our producer and consumer society, without even the basics. By now the number has probably jumped to 50 million.

The abyss between the rich and poor keeps widening even as the scandal of misery grows in Latin America, with modernity and urbanization playing their parts. When the movement of the Christian Base Communities began, 70 percent were urban. The percentages may differ elsewhere in Latin America, but the general trend is to the city, where the new arrivals are subject to every hustler and huckster. They are propelled from rural religiosity, with its processions, novenas, patronal feasts and family prayer, into an anonymous arena, conflictive and violent.

Pedro Arrupe [1907-91: Superior General of the Society of Jesus, 1965-83] used to say that we have to preach the Gospel to "the marginalized of below and the marginalized of above." I don't think the freeing of the poor is possible without the participation of the middle classes—the political and entrepreneurial people, the liberal professionals, the intellectuals. The poor have to claim their rights, be politicized in the good sense of the word, as the subjects of their own liberation, and this is a slow process. But they need the collaboration, the help, the mediation of the classes with more political know-how, more technical resources. There are Christians, after all, among the middle and upper classes.

Jesus takes His starting point, remember, from the Pentateuch, the books of the Law in the Old Testament, which mark out the poor, the widow, the orphan for special consideration. As the Israelites went from a nomadic society to a more sedentary one, taking up agriculture and then commerce, the number of poor increased. The prophets kept announcing and urging the justice of God on their behalf.

Jesus is not a simpleton when saying, "Blessed are the poor." Especially in the Beatitudes according to St. Luke, with their trace of Isaiah, Jesus is saying, Rejoice, you who are poor, because with the coming of the kingdom of God, you will no longer hunger, you won't be afflicted any more.

At the center of the theology of liberation is a commitment of the church: the poor man has to stop being poor, because his condition does not correspond to the plan, the love, the mercy, the tenderness of God. We have to keep hoping that this project, this utopia, will come to realization in Latin America, as it has in some other regions, because if not, what outcries, struggles, demands are in store!

I often ponder what gospel we will announce when the poor are no longer poor. What are the Beatitudes to mean to the middle classes, people who have their basic needs fulfilled? Our own country is far from that state, however, and the Gospel thus offers a head-on challenge to our urban and secularized sectors. Two months ago on television I saw the president of the International Monetary Fund, I think it was, say that the money spent on armaments should, in the new world situation, be spent to help the countries of the East and of the South. Why deem that impossible? This church, which is Catholic and universal, has to announce among all countries the needs of justice in our world.

What you seem to be calling for is not just a new strategy but a major change within people, a change in how each of us thinks and reacts.

In the mid-1980's, Pope John Paul II and the bishops of Latin America launched a renewal process for the Americas under the

title *la Nueva Evangelización*, "the New Evangelization," thus
marking it off from the old colonial style. The New Evangelization
underlines the Gospel as being truly good news, because it announces the arrival of the kingdom of God—of the justice, tenderness and mercy of God—as the realization of God's dream from
all eternity for the men and women of this earth. What has to be
new, the Pope has said on various occasions, is our fervor, ardor,
fire, since there is no greater fire or light than in Jesus of the Gospel. Discovery of this news and warming ourselves at its fire require a conversion, as the New Evangelization insists, starting from
the Pope on down to the most remote Basic Christian Community
in the tropical forest, or on Brazilian shores, or in the Chilean and
Peruvian Andes.

To grasp this notion of "conversion," consider the two shortest
parables in the Gospels, the parable of the hidden treasure and that
of the pearl of great price (Mt. 13:44-46). The man who sells all
else to buy what he has discovered does so with joy, on the run,
because nothing is comparable or able to compete with that treasure or that precious pearl, the gospel of the kingdom as announced
by Jesus. Conversion has to begin with what St. Ignatius calls an
internal knowledge of Jesus, the fascination that leads to deepening friendship, intimacy, even passionate love. Only on the basis
of such knowledge and such love will any "following" of Jesus be
possible or any "service" of the kingdom of God.

The Jesus of the Gospels is a mystic, passing the night in prayer
to his *Abba*, confiding in him at the crisis of the agony and on the
cross, yet a committed person too, a man of *praxis*, full of concern
for the poor, the needy. How true this has been also of the great
religious founders and reformers—Ignatius, Teresa of Avila,
Catherine of Siena, Charles de Foucauld—they were mystics too.
The same may be said of some outstanding bishops today, champi-
ons of the poor, like Oscar Romero, a martyr, but also Dom Helder
Cámara and Dom Pedro Casaldáliga, who dedicate hours daily to
prayer. And it can be said, of course, of such servants of the poor as
Mother Teresa of Calcutta.

The action of Jesus, His commitment to His brothers, unfolds necessarily from his experience of God. The two things are insepa-rable. José González Faus develops the above theme in a little book, a series of talks he gave in Saragoza, Spain, entitled *Acceso a Jesús* *("Access to Jesus")*. Faus emphasizes the polarity "*Abba*-kingdom" in Jesus. The kingdom Jesus announces is the kingdom of the warm-hearted Father, not one achieved by intrahistoric forces that deny or overlook God. And the *Abba* whom Jesus reveals to us is the *Abba* of the kingdom, the kingdom of justice and of mercy.

Conversion, then, implies a personal experience of the love of God, a conviction that He knows me by my name, loves me and says "you're mine." The prophet Isaiah, for one, prepared us to believe this. Karl Rahner, S.J., has said that the Christian of the future will either be a mystic—someone with experience of the tenderness, the mercy, the pardon of God—or not a Christian at all. But according to the New Testament there is no personal faith that is not also communitarian, the faith of disciples as a body, a community. The people of Latin America accept this communitarian dimension naturally; it fits into their tradition of popular celebra-tions, as it does also with the African and the indigenous peoples. But for men and women marked with the spirit of modernity, the stamp of individualism, what can possibly make the communitarian living of one's faith acceptable and practicable? It comes down to example and contact. Evangelization won't be possible without evangelizing communities.

Communities of this sort, in Brazil, are more than just a concept or a pious hope, I understand, but an impressive force.

Yes. We are speaking, of course, of the Christian Base Commu-nities (*Comunidades Eclesiais de Base)*—the CEBs. The CEBs, numbering in the tens of thousands in Brazil, are a model of evan-gelization for Latin America, thanks to the joyful welcome they give the Gospel, their way of living it out together and their wit-ness to it. Members of these communities, traveling to other parts of Brazil and the continent, set right to work, even on the periph-ery of the huge cities, forming new communities.

The church that makes itself seen in the base communities re-sembles the church in Corinth, as described by Paul, people without prestige or any human power. Dom Luis, formerly Bishop of Vitoria in Brazil and now of Campina Grande, a pioneer of the Christian Base Communities, loves to repeat that a CEB is often born with few people or resources, little preparation and very little noise. But their own members attest to a change away from passivity and from the belief that only other people count and that one must take one's orders and derive one's well-being from them, to a genuine initiative and freedom.

Most of these communities begin as Bible groups. The discovery of the word of God is their most fundamental experience. They subsequently start gathering for adult education courses, meeting of mother and young people about specific problems, community projects and health work, even sports and recreation. They cultivate a desire for learning and for a relationship with God. They practice a care of the sick, a spirit of unassuming service, forgiveness of offenses and public reconciliation. They certainly denounce injustices, but in a nonviolent spirit. Remember that even Jesus, announcing the Beatitudes (according to Lk: 6: 20-26), adds a matching series of condemnations for those who act otherwise.

Children receive the faith in the bosom of such a community, not as something merely doctrinal, but as something lived. The preparation for sacraments is always treated as a privileged moment of evangelization. In fact, a catechesis stemming from the Gospels—a reading of the Gospel and the local news jointly— goes on continually. This marks off the CEBs as very different from the evangelistic groups called "the sects," including Afro-Brazilian spiritist cults. The latter are not preoccupied with looking at life today, with labor politics, for instance, or a structural analysis of society so as to transform it according to God's plans.

The Christian Base Communities are not a panacea for all of Latin America; many problems and possibilities lie outside the reach of such groupings. Still, it is a new form of being a church, and it evangelizes the larger church, which has not perhaps been living this way but is now put to the question. Experience has shown bishops and priests and other pastoral ministers that to live with the poor of these communities is to rediscover a series of Gospel values they have never lived out, or have kept in the penumbra: simplicity, a sense of solidarity, attention to the worst off, a disposition to share all one has, a determination to fight injustice.

The CEBs witness to the Gospel even unto martyrdom. They are communities of martyrs. The theologian Hans Urs von Balthasar, not exactly a liberation theologian, has written that one cannot be a Christian without saying very sincerely, in his heart or in face of real danger, I am ready for martyrdom. The Christians of the *Comunidades* do not formulate their readiness that way, but in moments of truth, knowing the risk, they live it.

You are really speaking about a new spirituality?

Yes, in discussing the base communities and our own need for conversion, we indeed accept a new spirituality. All evangelization has to be spiritual in the sense of impelled, dynamized by the Spirit of Jesus. Jesus went forth under the impulse of the Spirit, anointed (hence His title "the Christ") to announce the good news. The church is a creature of the Spirit, which renews it in a continuing Pentecost, as it does the face of the earth. The Spirit breathes freely but also incarnates, brings the body of Christ to birth within structures, gifts and limitations. Consider the *Epiklesis*, the pair of invocations of the Holy Spirit over the Eucharist. Through the first, the bread and wine transform to the body and blood of Christ; through the second, all of us who communicate can declare ourselves the body of Christ.

In the sharing of the Holy Spirit, the poor of the communities often find new insights into the Gospel, new commitments, new charisma, new ministries and new forms for living out their Christian communion. Karl Rahner, S.J., once wrote an article, "Who Goes in Fear of the Holy Spirit?" The conservatives do, Rahner said, in trying to program the Spirit from curias or central offices. When things do not come out as this programming has foreseen, they get very unquiet and nervous. Progressives also fear the Holy Spirit, worried that changes will not come fast enough and according to plan. Only the saints have no fear of the Holy Spirit and let themselves be borne ahead, they know not where. Jerome Nadal, S.J., was led to this comment by the *Autobiography* of St. Ignatius:

"He was gently carried, he knew not where."

You have discussed the base community as you have seen it in Brazil, and in the context of Latin America. In closing, would you have some application to the church at large?

The base communities, participating actively in the New Evangelization, tell us something about the relation between the universal church and the particular. They shed some light on the problem of inculturation. The French theologian H.M. Legrands, O.P., disciple of Yves Congar, O.P., makes a statement at first glance shocking but true: "Because it is Catholic, the church has to be particular." The early church, born among the many languages of Pentecost, knew how to inculturate itself in a very nonuniform Mediterranean world. Hence that great diversity of theology, church practices and the broad span of liturgies: Alexandrian, Antiochean, Roman, North African, Egyptian Coptic, Milanese, Mozarabic.

By the law of evangelization, the church is called on to speak all languages, if we understand "language" as a vehicle of culture, a tradition, a manner of being, of facing life. The church taking flesh in all cultures is thus forever new. In Latin America, Catholic liturgy and forms of living the faith will thus be marked by Native American and Afro-American culture, with characteristics of the various locales, such as the Brazilian, Caribbean, North American. When we have to decide, for example, on an Afro-Brazilian Catholic ritual, why such sharp criticism, so much fear, such slowing down? This is not a task we can complete from one day to another, but it doesn't have to take centuries!

For a paradigm of the Gospel being inculturated in a whole new environment, consider, finally, the story of the appearance of the Blessed Virgin Mary to the Indian Juan Diego on the hill of Tepeyac in Mexico. The language, the symbols through which the Virgin Mother transmits her message are symbols and language from the world of Aztec culture. This is what makes Our Lady of Guadalupe so prized throughout Latin America; she is a carrier of the Word "ever old and ever new."

32

Activists Take on AIDS

Elizabeth Station

Several times each hour on prime-time television, the Brazilian government's latest and flashiest AIDS advertisement punctuates the commercials between *telenovelas*, rock videos and news programs. "Use condoms with unknown partners, from beginning to end," counsels singer Caetano Veloso in a quick, tight close-up. "There's no medicine for AIDS, but it can be combated through prevention," adds a well-known soap opera star. And in its final seconds, the government delivers the real message to those who hope the government might do something about AIDS besides run commercials. "Don't wait for the authorities to act!" warns Jo Soares, a late night talk-show host, "The solution depends on us alone."

A growing number of activists have taken such advice to heart. Nearly 40 new organizations have sprung up in response to the AIDS epidemic. "With AIDS, it has become clear that [this government has] no real commitment to the health of the Brazilian people," says sociologist Herbert de Souza, the founder of the country's most prominent non-governmental organization which deals with AIDS. "This is a political issue for which all of us must take responsibility." For some, taking responsibility means providing services to the sick; for others, defending their civil rights. But most conclude it means pushing the government to act.

As a country, Brazil has the third highest incidence of AIDS cases worldwide. Although official statistics place the number of people with AIDS at around 7,000, doctors, academics and activists say the figure is at least twice that high and may be doubling every ten months. Perhaps 500,000 Brazilians carry the HIV virus.

When AIDS first appeared here in 1983, most Brazilians with the disease were young, gay, educated white men from the big city. Many tried to dismiss it as a *doença do desviado da Zona Sul*, an affliction that would only befall "queers" from the affluent and touristy southern neighborhoods of Rio de Janeiro. But today more and more heterosexuals, women, poor people, drug users, small-town residents and children are joining the ranks of those who are ill or dying from the disease.

According to Dr. Mauro Schechter, who heads AIDS research at the Federal University of Rio de Janeiro, in 1985 the ratio of men to women with AIDS in Brazil was thirty to one; three years later, it was eight to one. Schechter also says that around 70 percent of Brazilians with AIDS in 1985 held university degrees; by 1989 the figure was closer to 30 percent. In 1985, 72 percent of the country's AIDS cases lived in Rio de Janeiro and São Paulo; by 1988 it had dropped to just under half.

The number of Brazilians with the disease suddenly skyrocketed in 1986. In that year Herbert de Souza, a hemophiliac, founded the Brazilian Inter-Disciplinary AIDS Association (ABIA). ABIA's early "safe sex" materials targeted middle-class gays, and were reminiscent of literature which circulates on the streets of New York or San Francisco. Now, ABIA produces frank, explicit videotapes for use with street kids and construction workers, and distributes pamphlets equipped with free condoms to sailors and dock workers. The group also sends speakers to Rio de Janeiro slums, schools and workplaces.

Alarmed at the fact that 10 to 20 percent of AIDS cases originate from contaminated blood transfusions, ABIA activists also lobbied hard to insert a clause in the country's new constitution prohibiting the commercialization of blood and its derivatives. They were successful, but most blood still comes from unscrupulous private banks that do not screen for malaria, Chagas' disease, syphilis, hepatitis or AIDS. Activists complain that only wealthy patients can get a pure transfusion, yet nothing guarantees purity. De Souza himself is HIV-positive; two of his brothers, also hemophiliacs, died of AIDS in 1988.

Varig's Surprise

"People with AIDS are the best means to disseminate correct information about AIDS," says Herbert Daniel, a writer, gay activist and ex-guerrilla leader who, like de Souza, spent most of the 1970s in exile. He discovered he had AIDS earlier this year, and has since joined with ABIA to found "*Pela VIDDA*" (For the Valorization, Integration and Dignity of People with AIDS), the only group in Latin America which organizes people who have the disease to demand their civil rights.

Pela VIDDA held its first public demonstration in August, picketing the downtown Rio de Janeiro offices of Varig airlines for administering AIDS tests to prospective employees without the applicants' knowledge or consent. Worse yet, charged *Pela VIDDA*, when those who tested positive returned to see if they would be hired, they were told they had the AIDS virus—and no job. A Varig spokesman admitted the allegations were true, and insisted that the testing would continue.

Though illegal, it is common for public and private hospitals to deny treatment to AIDS patients, alleging lack of space and specialization to deal with the disease. Even when an emergency AIDS patient is admitted, staff members may refuse to go anywhere near him. Insurance companies have summarily bumped clients when it is revealed they have AIDS. People with AIDS or the HIV virus are frequently fired from their jobs and are often abandoned by their families.

One objective of the Varig protest was to fight the notion that *aidéticos*—as people with AIDS are called in Brazil—are social deviants on the verge of an inevitable, gruesome and somehow deserved death. "Ever since I found out I had AIDS, I repeat constantly that I am alive and I'm a citizen. I have no deficiency that immunizes me against my civil rights," says Daniel, who rejects the term *aidético* as dehumanizing. Zeca Nogueira, a founding member of *Pela VIDDA* who recently lost his lover to the disease, agrees. "We aren't people dying of AIDS; we aren't victims of AIDS," Nogueira explains. "We're people living with AIDS. This is really a political problem and we have to fight it politically."

Private Initiative

Not all activists see political struggle as an appropriate response to the AIDS crisis. Three years ago, Ubiratan da Costa e Silva began to take strangers with AIDS who had nowhere else to go into his São Paulo home. He now manages a group of 27 volunteers who make house-calls to over 80 patients throughout the city. "It's not easy to keep this work up," admits the interior decorator-turned-activist, pointing to the tall metal shelf in his dining room which is piled with bottles of antibiotics, AIDS education materials, food and medical books. "Until yesterday, there was a piano there." (He sold it to raise money for the project.) Raffles, book sales, donations and da Costa e Silva's own savings have underwritten most of the AIDS work he coordinates. "The responsibility is ours too; it's not only up to the government," he says.

Transvestite Brenda Lee is the owner of a house in an Italian district of São Paulo known as "The Palace of Princesses," where for years transvestites shared expenses and household tasks while they weren't out on the streets. The city's press discovered the house in 1984 after a group of thugs, probably police, went on a shooting spree that left several transvestite prostitutes dead. Brenda then told reporters from a popular TV news program that she would take in any prostitute or transvestite who needed protection—including those who had AIDS. "I said having AIDS isn't any worse than getting gunned down in the street," Brenda recalls. Within days, she had opened her doors to several patients whose families refused to care for them.

The house has been a full-fledged AIDS clinic since October 1988, when the São Paulo state Secretary of Health, in an unusual collaboration, agreed to cover most of the expenses that Brenda previously struggled to pay on her own. The house now provides food, medicine and shelter for transvestites, homeless gays and anyone else with AIDS referred by the state health department. Nurses, maids and most of the 24 patients under Brenda Lee's roof usually go about their daily routine in drag. "When a family won't accept them because of prejudice, they come here," says Veronesa, a transvestite nurse's assistant who has worked at the house for about a year. "These people are abandoned," adds Brenda. "It's terrible—we don't have room for all the patients."

Brenda Lee and da Costa e Silva are quick to distance themselves from "leftists who blame the government for everything." They believe that private initiatives are the best hope for stopping AIDS in Brazil. "I'm different from everyone," shrugs Brenda. "I hear everyone complaining about the government, (but) I've learned that in general, the community is never satisfied with the government. If they all worked as hard as I did, there wouldn't be any problem," she says.

One of Many Disasters

Herbert Daniel is one of the few gay activists working on AIDS to openly, and proudly, admit his homosexuality. The gay rights movement was tiny and fragmented before AIDS hit the country, and it is hard to tell whether the disease has helped or hurt its growth. As in the United States and Europe, in Brazil a few gay leaders have been able to win mainstream recognition and respect for their activities on behalf of people with the illness. But only one gay organization, located in the poor northwest suburbs of Rio de Janeiro, is openly attempting to address AIDS from a gay perspective. The group, Atoba, distributes 6,000 condoms a month in plazas and gay bars, along with flyers which read, "Homosexuality is not an illness! It's not a crime, it's not a sin, nor a punishment! Find out about and defend your rights."

By most estimates, Brazil is at least five years behind the United States and Europe in terms of its response to AIDS. Only a few AIDS groups have secured funding from foreign foundations or national agencies. Volunteer organizations like the Support Group for the Prevention of AIDS (GAPA), which has chapters in 12 Brazilian cities, run hospices, distribute food and medicine, make hospital visits and provide patients and their families with counseling services. Members of Protestant and Catholic churches also visit and provide material aid to the sick, although the Catholic rank-and-file complain that the church hierarchy has been slow in responding to the crisis. A Rio de Janeiro-based group, Religious

Support Against AIDS (ARCA), is attempting to form an ecumenical front which includes Catholic, Protestant and Jewish volunteers, as well as practitioners of the Afro-Brazilian religions Candomble and Umbanda.

Meanwhile, financially strapped public hospitals, which treat 80 to 90 percent of AIDS cases, bear most of the burden. Available beds fall far short of the total needed; drugs like AZT are either unavailable or prohibitively expensive. Federal funds for AIDS research and lab equipment have been drastically slashed as part of a general cut in spending on health and social services, and training programs for hospital personnel are still inadequate. "I'm absolutely certain that if I were a construction worker," says Herbert Daniel, "I'd already be dead."

Dealing with AIDS on a day-to-day basis has led doctors, nurses, social workers and hospital administrators to join the movement to demand a more vigorous government response to the epidemic. According to Dr. Ranulfo Cardoso, the director of ABIA's health education program, "It doesn't matter how many hospices we open—the AIDS issue is one for the government to face."

Though he urges individuals to join the fight, Cardoso points out that civil society can't clean up blood banks, import AZT and create public hospital beds unless these are also official priorities.

Health professionals also point out that, while serious, the AIDS epidemic is only one of many disasters resulting from Brazil's failure to invest in public health over the years. One in three people has no access to health services, and public hospitals suffer chronic shortages of funds, beds, drugs, ambulance services, lab equipment and staff. Ministry of Health statistics show that preventable and treatable illnesses like malaria, yellow fever and dengue still run rampant. Over 2,000 Brazilians die of syphilis and gonorrhea each year, making these diseases bigger killers than AIDS.

AIDS activists have picked up on the Green Party slogan, "All Brazil is a high-risk group," from rubber tappers to homosexuals to people attempting to live on the minimum wage. According to Herbert Daniel, people with AIDS must join forces with those fighting to obtain housing, education, decent wages and human rights.

As Daniel has written, "My problem, like thousands of other people with this disease, is not to ask for easier conditions for death but to demand a better quality of life. A problem, by the way, which is common to almost all Brazilians."

33

Fighting for the Soul of Brazil

John Powers

*I*t may seem odd to begin a section on the Workers Party with
an article from the campaign trail, considering that Lula lost
his bid for the presidency in the October 1994 elections. Yet this
chapter—in addition to being a good read—provides insights into
the character of Lula that show why he and the PT will remain
potent political forces for the Left.

There are places you only visit when you're running for office
or writing about someone who is. Such a place is Roraima (pro-
nounced Roe-RYE-mah), the Brazilian state known to the outside
world, if it is known at all, for being home to the last of the Stone
Age tribes, most famously the Yanomami. Although its capital, Boa
Vista, affects an elegant modernity—wide, untrafficked boulevards
shoot like rays from an archshaped city center—it's still a ram-
bunctious gold-boom town filled with bars, brothels and starving
children whom the authorities don't bother their heads about. Boa
Vista is so far off the beaten track that even people who live a
thousand miles up the Amazon think of this city as the middle of
nowhere. On a clear day, you can see Guyana.

During the flight in, I'd been talking about the city with an af-
fable professor of tropical diseases, who said, "Its name means
'beautiful view'."

"And is it beautiful?"

He laughed sadly. "If you don't look at the city."

A photographer broke in, shaking his head. "Roraima is a place
for *garimpeiros*—prospectors. There are hundreds of billions of

dollars' worth of minerals here. Everybody who comes here is digging for something."

He smiled, proud of his own little joke; just a few rows behind us sat Luis Inácio Lula da Silva, known by everyone simply as Lula, the charismatic socialist [who in mid-1994, at the time this was written, was favored to become Brazil's next president]. Lula was heading to Roraima as part of his nationwide *Caravana da Cidadania*, or Citizenship Caravan, a euphemistic term for a pre-campaign swing; he was prospecting for votes.

And what was I looking for in following him to a backwater where miners still massacre Indians? Nothing less than the future of Latin American politics. Lula's rise from a peasant's shack to the threshold of the presidential palace is one of the great political stories of our time—a personal odyssey every bit as brave and historic as those made by Lech Walesa and Vaclav Havel.

It was coming up on midnight when we finally saw lights, gaudy as Vegas after the black canopy of rain forest that had stretched below us for the last hour. The landing gear touched down, and before the door swung open, a lovely, eerie singing rose from the night:

Lu-la-lahhh.

Lu-la-lahhh.

It was Lula's theme song, a musical phrase as famous in Brazil as any bossa nova. The second-floor observation deck was filled with hundreds of Lula supporters, nearly all of them under 25, singing and laughing draped over the parapet, waving every kind of banner and sign. Four-letter placards exclaiming "Lula!" Red-and-white banners bearing the initials PT, for *Partido dos Trabalhadores*, the Workers' Party. And, of course, signs reading *"Feliz* 1994"— happy, because 1994 is the year they will get to elect Lula.

When Lula emerged from the plane, he raised his fist and the crowd roared. They smelled a winner. As the PT vans drove us to the hotel, the kids hot-rodded alongside, honking and waving banners and shrieking into the night. The air was thick with the scent of burning rubber, soon to be replaced by the scent of gunpowder as people set off one Roman candle after another, tinting the treetops pink. Lula shook dozens of hands, laughing and calling his admirers *companheiro* before finally going inside. The *petistas* (as the PT's followers are known) lingered in the driveway, setting off firecrackers and periodically breaking into a chant: "Olê, olê, olê, olá, Lu-la, Lu-LAH!"

And in the exhausting heat, which even after midnight wrapped itself around us like a barber's towel, I marveled at the passions raised by this short, hairy 48 year-old man whose thick neck, powerful torso and spindly legs give him the physique of a cartoon bull. Squeezed into a cheap tan sport coat that would be fashionable nowhere, he had none of the shimmering charisma of JFK or Gorby. But the crowd didn't mind his lack of patrician style. That's part of what they loved about him.

He is one of them, a son of the peasantry poised to become a new kind of president: a socialist, a democrat and a worker. If he wins, Lula will be South America's first elected president to come from the dispossessed classes. Like the Chiapas uprising or the voting-out of the neoliberals in Venezuela, Lula's ascent challenges the official post-Cold War story line in which everyone is rushing to embrace market capitalism. ("I defend private property," he says, "but for everybody. We cannot allow one man to own 25 million acres when others are starving.") Old-school communism may be dead, but the conditions that fostered it are still thriving, especially in Brazil, a country permanently on the verge of a nervous breakdown.

The prototype of the new Latin American leftist, Lula shatters all the cliches about wild-eyed revolutionaries. He's not a *caudillo*. He's not a guerrilla with bandoleers crisscrossing his chest. He's not even reflexively anti-American. (He has always opposed Soviet-style communism.) His party boasts some of Brazil's leading congressmen and mayors. It brings together tens of millions of supporters in a coalition of unionists, peasant farmers, rubber tappers, intellectuals, progressive priests, left-wing millionaires, activists and militants.

"The more democracy there is in Brazil," Lula says, "the better our chances of winning." That's why, the morning after our arrival in Boa Vista, the Citizenship Caravan drove two hours through dusty savannah punctuated by cashew trees and cracking, gray termite hills that resemble avant-garde sculptures. Our destination was the Maloca do Bismarck, central meeting place for the Macuxi tribe, whose members have no idea how such a Teutonic name was applied to this collection of open-air huts roofed with leaves from the *naja* plant.

Outside the main hut, scabby-kneed kids ran around in T-shirts adorned with peculiar misspellings ("Vacatign Time!") and sneaker logos unknown to the industrialized West. Inside, the village elders reported on the state of the tribe then turned the rally over to Lula, who rose and talked about the things he always talks about: better health care and education, the social cost of corruption, the egregiously unfair distribution of wealth, the absolute need for land reform. But all politics is local politics, and the Macuxi were listening for what he said about Indians. They unleashed their most vigorous nods when Lula said that he would support their right to their lands "without vacillation."

It was a good speech, and Lula held his audience easily, flaunting all the charisma I'd missed the previous night. Using no notes, he started softly, his gravelly bass voice working against his deliberateness, a slight lisp comporting oddly with his coiled physicality. As he went on, his tempo quickened, and he worked himself up, not hammy but focused, like Brando burrowing into an especially tasty scene. His finger jabbed, his hand made small circles (you noticed the missing little finger of his left hand, lost in a machine press) and, as a flush brightened his skin, his eyes became the smoldering black coals of a thousand romance novels. He's not a person you want glaring at you. Lula spoke with the angry, barrelhouse directness of one who cut his teeth addressing the hard men in São Paulo union halls. By the end of the speech, he had reached the point I recognized from the television clips, when his impatience for change surrounds him like a white-hot aura.

Angry, impatient, direct—was this the way to win an election in a country that prides itself on tropical good humor? I mentioned this to the professor on the airplane, Marcus Barros, who is also president of the Amazonian chapter of the PT. His eyes lost their smile, and he put his hand on my shoulder. "You have to understand. We've been waiting all our lives for this election. Now is the chance to change the history of this country. The same people have been running Brazil for the last 500 years. It finally has to stop."

The world's fifth largest country in population (152 million) and area (slightly smaller than the United States), Brazil has the surreal expansiveness of a country that embraces the Amazon rain forest and the hardscrabble northeastern *sertão*, the Girl from Ipanema and the ugly sprawl of São Paulo with its umpteen million people. Such a vast, swirling country is impossible to get a handle on; there are just too many stories. Small wonder that many commentators fall into the cliché of treating Brazil as the real life version of its *telenovelas*, the nighttime soaps watched by everyone from millionaires to slum dwellers in the *favelas*.

Of course, there is something delirious about the place. In São Paulo, people were laughing at the black-comic refinements of the latest corruption scandal. Explaining how he'd made $51 million from an $80,000-a-year job, Congressman João Alves got on the tube, clasped his hands and insisted he'd done nothing wrong: God had helped him win the lottery 24,000 times. After a few days of such hijinks, I began to understand Charles de Gaulle's remark "Brazil is not a serious country."

It all depends on what you mean by serious. There are 40 million Brazilians in absolute poverty, another 60 million living in squalor even though many of them have jobs. There are millions of homeless children, the *abandonados*, and they are routinely murdered in the streets of Rio de Janeiro, often by policemen and paramilitary thugs paid by local businessmen. The minimum wage buys less than it did in 1940, and the distribution of income is far worse than India's. The inflation rate—2,751 percent a year in early 1994—makes simply buying one's groceries a brain teaser, and crime has reached the point where the middle class sequesters itself in bunker-like enclaves, protected by armed sentries, while the poor crowd into some of the world's most dangerous slums. Even the legendary beaches are being destroyed. The vast majority of

Brazilians live from hand to mouth, without money or power or hope.

The seeds of this catastrophe were planted centuries ago. Since the days of Portuguese control, Brazil's ruling elite has been notorious for its cruelty and greed. But the current mess has its immediate roots in the 1964 coup d'etat, when President João Goulart, a moderate reformer, was ousted by the military in the name of "order" and anticommunism, with the support of President Lyndon B. Johnson's Administration. For the first 15 years of the diadem, the dictatorship, the Brazilian economy expanded by leaps and bounds, but most of the new wealth went to the elite and the emerging middle class. Brazil was becoming what they call "Belindia": a prosperous population the size of Belgium's, surrounded by masses living in the misery one associates with India. In 1972, President General Emilio Garrastazu Medici described the situation memorably: "The economy is going well, the people not so well."

Although many brave souls stood up to the dictatorship, the military cracked down brutally. Even today, everyone you meet knows someone who was bullied, jailed, tortured or driven into exile. As happened in the communist bloc, the Brazilian generals lost their grip when the economy began collapsing and people began publicly challenging their authority. Perhaps the boldest of these challenges came in the late 1970s, from the São Paulo auto workers, whose union was led by the fiery young Lula.

Under duress, the generals announced the *abertura*, a gradual political opening, and in 1989, Brazil had its first direct presidential elections in a quarter of a century. But in the absence of a sturdy democratic tradition, the 1989 campaign had a frantic, almost demented quality. Months into the campaign, the country was shaken by the entry of a new candidate, Silvio Santos, a TV variety-show host whose sweaty hucksterism made one yearn for the self effacing sincerity of Jerry Lewis in mid-telethon. Santos promptly shot to the top of the polls and might well have won, had the courts not ruled that he'd filed improperly for the race. "After the dictatorship, we did not know how to have a politics," explains Andri Petry, a senior political editor at *Veja*, the Brazilian equivalent of Time magazine. "There were too many parties. Sometimes one man was a party. The people did not know how to understand a campaign, and the press did not know how to report it. That is how Collor won."

Petry is referring to Fernando Collor de Mello, the little-known governor of Alagoas who narrowly defeated Lula for the presidency. Collor's campaign cast him as a young handsome outsider who wanted to go to Brasília to fire overpaid bureaucrats ("maharajahs") and clean up corruption; a famous photo showed him with his pockets pulled out, demonstrating their honest emptiness. In fact, the crazy-eyed governor was a multimillionaire scion of the ruling class (his father once shot a man to death on the Senate floor but was never charged) and ran for president as the Menendez boys might buy a car. After taking office, Collor spent a year dazzling everyone with his vigor, he did karate, drove racing cars, jogged in T-shirts emblazoned with catch phrases about the Amazon. President George Bush compared him to Indiana Jones, an embarrassing move, as it turned out. Enraged by a family squabble, Fernando's own brother Pedro went to the press and announced that President Collor had been peddling influence to the tune of tens of millions of dollars. Collor was impeached in 1992 but, true to the traditions of Brazilian justice, has never been charged with any crime.

Collor's dishonesty left the public shocked. The cynicism kicked in last October when it was revealed that nearly 20 members of the congressional budget committee had used their positions to make themselves rich. They stole $200 million of federal money earmarked for charities. They pocketed millions in kickbacks from construction projects. They siphoned off millions meant for health care and education—this in a land where most adults have only a grade school education, and schoolteachers make barely $100 a month.

These high-octane scandals, plus scores of routine ones, have shaken public faith in politicians; a few idiots have begun making pleas for the good old days of the dictatorship. But according to *Veja*'s Petry, such scandals have a positive side: "It is good for us to get over our illusions. Before, we thought it was only the generals who were the problem. Then we thought it was only Collor. Now we see that the corruption is all through the elite. We see the connections between the business elite and the political elite that we did not know before. We are no longer naive, and this is a good thing."

It's certainly good for the PT, which has been at the forefront of investigating the congressional scandal—none of its 37 members were accused. It has been even better for Lula himself. Before the scandal broke, he had been assailed for claiming that the Congress was filled with *picaretas*, chiselers. Now, Lula's claims as a truth teller are stronger than ever and his personal honesty even more of an asset. He's a worker who's never moved in the circles where big deals are cut and million-dollar bribes exchange hands. The PT pays him a salary of $24,000 a year, he lives in São Bernardo do Campo, an industrial suburb of São Paulo.

"Lula's a known quantity," says Petry. "He's been famous since the late 1970s, and everybody knows he hasn't become rich. Even people who hate him know he is not a thief."

"Here's a classic story for you." The speaker is Adrian Cooper, an expatriate documentary filmmaker who's been filming Lula on and off since the late 1970s. "A couple of months ago, I was flying back from Belo Horizonte (Brazil's fourth largest city), and I ran into Lula in the airport. He was all alone in a coffee-stained white suit, carrying his battered old bag, waiting for his flight home on Tam, a domestic airline with mostly prop planes. We went for a drink in the bar, and I remember thinking how amazing it was that this guy was probably going to be the president of Brazil next year, and here he was flying in his stained suit in an economy seat on a second-rate airline. It's so extraordinary, the difference that separates him from a man like Paulo Maluf (the mayor of São Paulo), who would always take a Lear jet or fly first-class—he'd never rub shoulders with the masses. But then, that's Lula."

It's certainly the Lula of the public image, a man invariably described by his supporters as *um brasileiro típico*, an ordinary Brazilian man. Of course, such a characterization is more than a little disingenuous: How many perfectly ordinary men have the talent and drive to approach the presidency of the world's fifth biggest country? Still, it's true that, like a much greater Jesse Jackson—greater because he is less vain and more accomplished—Lula is as much a metaphor as a man. He's lived a life that encapsulates the mythic trajectory of his whole country. To understand his rise is to understand Brazil.

Luis Inácio da Silva was born in 1945 in the farming town of Garanhuns, in the perpetually poor northeastern state of Pernambuco; the youngest of nine children, he was given the nickname Lula (which was later officially added to his name for electoral purposes). Shortly after his birth, his father, Aristide, moved to the southern city of Santos, where jobs were more plentiful. When Lula was seven, Aristide returned to Pernambuco, put his family on the back of a truck and took them down south, a 13-day journey of 1,800 miles. In making this journey from the rural north to the urban south—the great symbolic journey of modern Brazil—Lula joined in a migration made by 30 million of his compatriots since the end of World War II.

The family lived in a shantytown where Lula sold peanuts on the street and dreamed, like all Brazilian boys, of becoming a soccer star; at 11, he quit school to work in a laundry. When he was 13, he landed a job in a factory that made nuts and bolts, working a machine press from 7 in the morning to 7 at night. It may sound dreadful, but for a boy of Lula's background, this entry into the labor elite was an achievement comparable to a Kentucky coal miner's son getting a degree from Harvard.

At the time of the 1964 coup, Lula was working for Industrias Villares, a heavy goods producer in São Bernardo do Campo. And despite the heated protestations of his brother Jose, a militant Communist, he was vehemently antiunion. Lula didn't so much as enter the union hall until 1967. Once he did go inside, however, he quickly became one of the union's leaders. By 1972, the year he married his current wife, Marisa Leticia (his first wife died of hepatitis), he was elected to the governing board of the São Bernardo Metalworkers Union. Within three years, he'd been elected union president, winning more than 90 percent of the votes from its 140,000 metalworkers. At 30, Lula already led the largest union in South America.

Despite his position, he remained largely apolitical—"a common union leader," he now says. All this changed when, in 1975, the military arrested his brother for being a "subversive." Rather than backing off, Lula was galvanized. By 1978, he was leading the Metalworkers Union in a labor action against the Scania truck company, the first full-fledged Brazilian strike in ten years. Scania was forced to negotiate a pay raise for the workers, who at the time were making 60 cents an hour (compared to $8.65 in the United States). This success led to a series of more ambitious strikes that became a test of the government's authority. Lula became a household name, famous for his skill at rallying his troops, less known for softening their militant stridency.

Cooper remembers "going to a football stadium filled with 80,000 metalworkers, all of whom desperately wanted to keep on with the action. Lula got up before them and explained why they shouldn't—how it would be pushing beyond their strength and lead to disaster. Nobody in the stadium wanted to hear that—they all wanted to keep striking—but he eventually persuaded them with the clarity of his logic and the passion of his speech. By the end, the whole stadium was chanting 'Lu-lah, Lu-lah, Lu-lah.' I've never seen anything like it."

Unwilling to negotiate with Lula, the government sentenced him to 3 $1/_2$ years in prison on trumped-up "national security" charges. But the political winds had changed, and Lula's conviction was overturned on appeal. Back in the streets, he was free to take his next step in the creation of a workers party, the PT.

"I realized it was necessary in 1978," Lula says, "when I went to Congress to talk to the representatives. And I learned that of 480 representatives, only two were from trade unions. I asked myself, 'How can the Congress approve laws for the workers if all the representatives there represent the businessmen?' So we decided to create our own political organization." He snorts a laugh. "If I'd known that doing it would be so difficult, I possibly never would have tried."

It is always difficult to know exactly when something new has entered the world, but the creation of the Workers' Party on Feb. 10, 1980, may have been one of those moments. "The PT established itself as the first political party in the country's history that was not formed at the behest of the elite." So say Ken Silverstein and Emir Sader in *Without Fear of Being Happy*, the best book in English on Lula and the PT. Their words are echoed by professor Jorge G. Castañeda, whose "Utopia Unarmed: The Latin American Left After the Cold War" sees the PT in an even larger context. "Lula's PT is a harbinger," he tells me from his office in Mexico City. "It may well be the new Latin American populism—in the good sense of the term."

It took the PT years to expand its influence. In 1982, Lula ran for the governorship of São Paulo state with the slogan "A Brazilian Like You"— a phrase designed to attack the traditional authority of the elites. But at this point, the ordinary Brazilian was still so filled with a sense of inferiority that the slogan backfired: It was taken to mean, "A loser like you." Paunchy, kinky-haired and un-grammatical, Lula lacked the sable elegance that the masses associated with a real governor. Despite such setbacks, the party continued to water the grassroots, winning important mayorships and enlisting the fervent support of top agrarian reformers, prominent Roman Catholic priests (including the famous liberation theologian Leonardo Boff) and rainforest activists such as the late Chico Mendes.

By the presidential election of 1989, the PT was ready to explode. After months of campaigning, the election came down to two men: the underdog, Lula, and the overwhelming favorite, Collor. It was a campaign to make the Clinton-Bush contest seem dignified. Although Collor, as a governor, had ended taxes on sugar companies that then backed his candidacy to the tune of $12 million, the campaign centered on increasingly shrill charges against the PT's candidate. Lula, it was claimed, owned a JVC stereo; this proved he wasn't really a worker. Lula, it was claimed, would force middle-class families to give rooms in their homes to PT workers.

Lula, it was claimed, was antidemocratic—this despite his leading role in the democracy movement and Collor's own voluminous silence during the dictatorship.

Still, Lula whittled away at his opponent's lead, promising land reform and a higher minimum wage and calling down wrath on the corrupt elite. The race was a dead heat when Collor pulled a stunt that could have come from a *telenovela*. Days before the election, he arranged for Lula's ex-mistress, Miriam Cordeiro, to hold a press conference and accuse Lula of offering her money to abort the fetus that was to become their daughter Lurian (he has four children with his wife). All the evidence rebuts these charges—Lula acknowledges paternity, Lurian's a PT activist, Cordeiro suddenly came into a lot of money—but the attack threw Lula into a funk. He performed feebly in the last presidential debate, and specially edited lowlights of his performance were replayed over and over by TV Globo, the pro-Collor network watched by 70 percent of the population.

In the end, Collor won, 35 million votes to 31 million—a triumph soon to be sullied by the man who enjoyed it. Yet even as the election showed that the PT had not fully arrived, it established Lula, only 44 years old, as the national alternative to the traditional political elite. The past 5 years have diminished neither his stature nor his savvy at wooing the middle class: His grammar is better, his beard more neatly trimmed, his suits more likely to be Italian. In mid-1994 polls that had him running against every possible candidate at once, Lula invariably received 30 percent to 32 percent of the vote, more than twice the share of the nearest opponent. He was, if anything, more popular than ever, both personally and as the embodiment of his party.

"He's an ordinary Brazilian guy, and that's his appeal," said Ricardo Kotscho, a shrewd, witty ex-journalist whose official title of press secretary masks a more profound role as Lula's buddy, confidant and jester. "Usually your Brazilian politicians are from the elite, the political elite or the cultural elite. Lula's the first one who comes from the people, and he already has much more than he ever dreamed of. So now he feels responsibility to do something about the injustice in Brazil. It's not that he's a saint. He's not. He's a man, *um Brasileiro típico*. If Lula was free to do whatever he wanted, it would be fishing, soccer, women and parties. And that's why people like him."

Of course, not everyone likes Lula, or he wouldn't have lost the 1989 election. Late one smoggy afternoon, I stopped by São Paulo's City Hall to talk to the mayor, Paulo Maluf, who has twice run for president as the candidate of the Social Democratic Party, which was created by the dictatorship. Maluf is a dapper, funny man whose penchant for deliberate, cheerful buffoonishness—his hoarse voice and full cheeks recall a thousand sendups of Don Vito Corleone—can't hide his enormous shrewdness. Although coy about whether he would again seek the presidency, he was straightforward when it came to Lula and the PT. He couldn't imagine why anyone would vote for them.

"Lula's probably good at many things, but for being president" —he wrinkled his brow ironically—"he has no more experience than the average people. He never worked in business, private or public. He never was a director of a free enterprise or public enterprise. He never was a mayor. He never was on a city council. He never was a secretary of transportation or anything else. He never was a minister." Maluf rubbed his thumb along a desk the length of a shuffleboard court and gazed happily around his huge office with its scale-model version of a new public-works project. The problem, he said, isn't merely Lula himself: It's the limitations of his ideology.

"The ideas of the left are old-fashioned. Don't pay the public debt, don't pay the national debt, complete control of the banks this was a speech that was good 50 years ago. That's the reason they're not going to win the election. The PT was the government for four years in the city of São Paulo, and they lost the next election because of mismanagement."

This view of Lula is shared by the elite and much of the middle class. Some of their disdain is mere snobbery toward any man with a working-class style and little formal education. But their main objection is economic. The PT wants to limit the size of landhold-ings, stop privatization of state industries, maintain trade barriers and find ways to redistribute wealth. These economic proposals will cost his opponents money and diminish their power. They also run counter to the neoliberal orthodoxies of the West. There's con-siderable off-the-record nervousness about what a leftist govern-ment in Brasília might do to the spread of free-market policies in South America. At the same time, most international financiers and U.S. State Department experts think that it's too early to be sure how radically Lula would actually govern. As one Latin American financial expert told me, "Reform governments have a way of com-ing back toward the middle."

Brazil's economic elite isn't nearly so sanguine. The daily pa-pers are filled with business leaders arguing that a Lula presidency will lead to stagnation, the ruination of trade, the end of luxury imports, capital fleeing the country. To reassure them, Lula has had 54 meetings with businessmen's groups to let them see firsthand that he's not *o bicho-papão*, the bogeyman. In Boa Vista, I sat in on one such session with the Commercial Association of Roraima (lo-cated over a bridal shop) and was startled at how well he eventually got along with these small-city entrepreneurs, who clearly couldn't stand his economic plan. "I liked him," a store-owner said after-ward. "I'm against him, but I liked him."

This seems to be the general attitude, whether in Roraima or São Paulo. The businessmen he meets plan to oppose him tooth and claw, but they respect his personal honesty and willingness to negotiate: They think he's a man you can do business with. What scares them is that Lula, who stands at both the figurative and ideo-logical center of the PT, often cannot control his party's radical left wing, whose dogmatic zeal has gotten them dubbed "Shiites." It's this group that leads many middle-class Brazilians to fear that Lula's election will destroy the country's cruel but functioning balance, unloosing an even crueler chaos onto the land.

Although the presidential campaign won't hit its stride for sev-eral more months, Lula and the PT are expecting nonstop attacks between now and October, especially because the political right is floundering. All its potential candidates of national stature have been discredited; the right can't even field a dazzling unknown because Collor discredited that kind of dark horse.

Their opponents' current disarray hasn't lulled the PT into a false sense of confidence. Its leaders know that anything is possible in Brazilian politics and that it would not be easy to defeat another left-of-center candidate, such as Finance Minister Fernando Henrique Cardoso. Whoever Lula's opponent, he will be backed by the most powerful men in Brazil: baronial landowners who buy the votes of their peasant workers with shoes or food; right-wing politicians such as Ballia's Gov. Antonio Carlos Magalhães, who are expert at manipulating the government bureaucracy; corporate magnates like Roberto Marinho, owner of the Globo media empire, whose support of Collor is widely believed to have swung the last election.

Every politician in the world gripes about the media, but in Lula's case the complaints are often justified. Headlines accuse Lula of crimes that the stories beneath them do not mention, much less justify. News programs trumpet every charge against him, even unsubstantiated smears by his political enemies. Last November, a small-firm union boss named Oswaldo Cruz Jr. accused the PT of taking illegal campaign contributions from the Central Workers Union; over the next weeks, the papers never stopped implying that Lula was just as corrupt as any other politician. The story eventually petered out. Then in early January, Oswaldo was murdered. For the next week, the media were filled with insinuations that Lula had ordered him assassinated. TV Globo's nightly news show devoted seven or eight minutes each night to the crime and its possible links to Lula. Wishful thinking, as it turned out: The confessed murderer had killed Oswaldo in the course of a personal argument.

Lula has no illusion that he can win over the media, and it's unlikely that he would want to even if he could: He has a bracing blue-collar contempt for politicians who tart up their images for television. Yet virtues have a way of becoming vices, and Lula's hostility to image making might hurt his electoral chances in a country that gets its news from TV.

Nothing captures the ambiguities of his relationship to the image-making process better than a brief exchange that occurred at Roraima's Lake Caracarana, where the Citizenship Caravan stopped for a few minutes after meeting the Macuxi tribe. Relaxed for the first time that day, Lula rolled up his blue jeans and walked into the lake. Roberto, the photographer from *Veja*, was snapping away, happy to catch Lula in his red T-shirt against a picturesque background—the big-city socialist grooving on nature. Noticing a woman doing her wash in the water, he suggested that Lula go over and help her. Lula shook his head.

"Go on," said Roberto. "It will make a great shot."

"No," Lula said. "I don't want to bother her. I don't want to turn everybody I meet into part of my campaign."

Back in the van, Roberto couldn't stop talking about the strangeness of a politician who would pass up a photo op. "As a man, I respect him for not wanting to bother the woman. He's a good guy. I voted for him. But as a photographer"—he shook his head sadly—"he just doesn't know how to give you any good pictures."

In the 30 years since Theodore White and Norman Mailer transformed how journalists write about politicians, it's become impossible to cover any presidential hopeful without asking, "What's driving this man to seek the big prize? What gives him the fire in his belly?"

Unable to get these answers while talking to him on the fly, I waited around São Paulo for days, hoping for the in-depth personal interview that would show me the real Lula. I finally got my audience with the candidate in his airy office atop a small office building off the Rua Pousa Alegre.

From the moment he stood to greet me, his body tight as a cramped muscle, I knew he was in a dark mood. He'd been fighting with a São Paulo newspaper and obviously didn't care what somebody would write about him in Los Angeles.

When I began by saying I wanted to ask about the past, he glowered at his press secretary. He'd answered these questions a thou-

sand times before. I persevered, but his eyes took on the half-va-
cant look I recognized from American politicians he was talking
by rote. He listened to my questions as if they contained fishhooks.
Lula may be an unconventional politician, but he's still a politician, and he used my questions to score his own points—parrying
perceived criticisms, attacking the media, insisting that the campaign was completely under control.

His impatience filled the room, and I suddenly got the slightest
whiff of something I've seen in Jesse Jackson, a sense of entitle-
ment, as though the world owes him the presidency because he's
come so much further than the other candidates and cares so much
more deeply than they do. In that moment, I felt sure I understood
what was driving Lula to seek office: the rage of a man who was
raised hungry, faced the humiliations of powerlessness, battled for
everything he'd gotten and now feels that he spends his life being
slandered by the very men who grew rich from the fruits of his
labor.

Yet even as I was struck by his ill temper, I knew better than to
think it was the whole story. It's one of the small-minded habits of
our time that we are always looking for unsavory private motives
to explain compassionate political behavior, as if a consuming desire for justice or passionate solidarity with the poor couldn't possibly be enough to make anybody do anything except write a small,
tax-exempt check. To say that Lula is driven simply by anger is to
diminish the man by mistaking moral indignation for personal resentment; if anger is his goad, it is not his goal. I remembered how,
during the Roraima caravan, he'd been mauled by his public: strangers wanting a handshake, reporters asking about allegations from
his political enemies, PT workers vying for his gaze, seeking the
benediction of one whose potential power makes him a source of
good luck. I could see in his eyes that he wanted to flee—he was
beat—but he kept right on with his task.

His situation reminded me of something I'd heard about the Amazon. It seems that when you need to lead cattle across a river where
there may be piranha, you always throw in one ox first so that the
fish will attack it and the others can cross safely; the term for this

first ox is *boi da piranha*, and in an odd way, that's how Lula struck me on that trip to Roraima: a man who was letting himself be devoured to help his comrades get across.

Of course, there are those who say that the piranha won't really start biting until Lula wins the Oct. 3 election. That's when he will learn what Solidarity learned in Poland and the Sandinistas in Nicaragua: Nothing can destroy you more exquisitely than the expectations you create. In fact, a small version of this has already happened to the PT: When Luiza Erundina was elected mayor of São Paulo in 1988, her achievement fell so far below the dreams she had excited that the PT's next candidate for mayor was defeated.

"Luiza Erundina did not satisfy the expectations that were created," says *Utopia Unarmed*'s Castaneda. "She didn't make a revolution. All she was, in a sense, was a good, honest, decent, somewhat progressive mayor. That doesn't sound like much. On the other hand, having honest, decent, somewhat progressive mayors in countries like ours is not something we're used to.

"And the same will probably be true if Lula is president. The expectations will be too high. The best that can be hoped is that he be honest, decent and somewhat progressive in the face of so many problems that no one president could solve them. That would be enough."

But his defeat would be a crushing disappointment for the Latin American left and, in particular, his followers in Brazil. It wouldn't be enough for them that Lula had proven to be their Jesse Jackson, the underclass hero who gives the best speeches but never wins the top prize.

One Saturday, I had lunch with Luis Tenorio de Oliveira Lima, a prominent São Paulo psychoanalyst, and asked him if he could explain Lula's place in the national psyche. He smiled, perhaps at my curious American way of putting the question.

"I would answer this way. There have always been two Brazils: a Brazil where people have many things, and a Brazil where people have nothing. For a long time, these two Brazils looked at one another through a pane of glass. They did not really touch, but they saw each other, and they could communicate. Over the last 30 years or so, the country has grown more fragmented, and the glass has grown much darker. When the haves and have-nots look at each other now, they see only their own reflections and their own dark fantasies of the other. They can no longer communicate but only know fear and hatred. The country functions, but it is . . ."

"Psychotic?"

He nodded: "Lula is the one man who can stand where the glass has always been and communicate with both sides. He can talk to both the poor and the powerful as their equal. He is the only politician since the 1920s with the potential to start the two Brazils talking again."

"And do you think he'll be able to do it?"

"I'm too old to have hope in anything." He cocked his head. "Of course, that doesn't mean I wouldn't vote for him."

34

Interview with Luiz Inácio Lula da Silva

James Bruce

L uiz Inácio "Lula" da Silva, the eighth child of migrants to São Paulo from Brazil's Northeast, began his career as a machinist. As president of the São Bernardo metalworkers' union from 1975 to 1980, he led the first major labor strike during the military government. In 1980 he was elected president of the Workers Party, and he served a term as a federal deputy. He was interviewed in São Paulo by veteran journalist and North-South Magazine correspondent James Bruce.

Like the reasonably priced, utilitarian, "popular" model cars launched in Brazil through an accord among industry, unions and government, Luiz Inácio "Lula" da Silva promises more mileage for the fuel available since he lost the 1989 Brazilian presidential election to Fernando Collor de Mello. The winner of 31 million votes in the 1989 elections, Lula was still going strong in mid-1994. From when preference polls for the 1994 election began appearing prematurely in 1993, Lula consistently led with 25 percent to 30 percent of the votes. In the October 1994 elections Lula placed second to Fernando Henrique Cardoso.

The *Partido dos Trabalhadores* (or PT, as the party is known) has become one of Brazil's most broadly distributed social phenomena. Membership includes factory workers, university faculty intellectuals, rural field hands and public functionaries. Enthusiasm at party rallies recalls heated soccer matches. The geographic dispersion is reflected in Lula's support throughout the country. Party habitats range from the grimy ABCD industrial satellite cities ringing São Paulo, where the red star was born in the late 1970s, to dusty towns in the Northeast visited by Lula during a 1993 pilgrimage back to his migrant origins.

PT watchers thought they saw fissures developing when the party elements most to the left began challenging leadership positions. Dissidents questioned party compromises and their candidate's growing taste for suits, neckties, and luncheons with business leaders. PT stalwarts—including Lula—insisted the row was merely another facet of party democracy. In an ideological shift to the left, leftists and extreme leftists won 12 of the 21 executive committee seats during the Eighth National Party Conference, held in June 1993 in Brasília. At the conference, Lula agreed to accept a second term as party president after it became evident that his was the only name with broad enough appeal to unite all the factions.

Lula, visibly tired from the conference proceedings, talked to us about Brazil, himself, the 1989 election, the government of president Itamar Franco and the political party which—despite any signs of internal dissent—he insists is even better prepared now to wage a presidential campaign and provide the basis for a national government.

The world has changed a lot since 1989 when you and Fernando Collor de Mello were the final candidates for president. Collor served almost three years of the five-year term to which he was elected, then resigned during impeachment proceedings. In what ways have you—or have you not—changed since that 1989 campaign? How has Brazil changed?

Beginning with Brazil, I think the country has changed for the worse. I think that the outcome of the presidential election with the selection of Fernando Collor as president was decidedly a disaster for Brazil. Social indicators show that the situation has gotten worse, whether in industrial development, economic growth or the quality of life.

Speaking for my own part, I also have changed. Today I am more conscious of Brazilian problems and feel more mature about how to resolve them. I have also changed because I have a stronger political party today than I had in 1989. These changes mean we have a more realistic view of Brazil today, we have a more realistic view of Latin America, a more realistic view of Brazil with respect to the relationship between it and other countries. We are convinced today that it is possible to resolve Brazil's problems with effective measures beginning with domestic problems. In short, I think there have been changes, changes in all the world, and I think Brazilian society changed, too, because I think it lost a lot with the outcome of the 1989 election.

What is your assessment of President Itamar Franco's government?

Brazil's situation is delicate from the economic viewpoint, from the political viewpoint and from the social viewpoint. We are in a politically delicate situation, specifically because President Itamar has shown himself incapable of governing Brazil. He has no project; he lost the chance to put together a great cabinet (he put together a club for his friends—a cabinet incompetent even by Brazilian standards of the day); he has no plan for the economy. Franco has no proposal for industrial development or for the agrarian situation. So Brazil's situation from the political viewpoint is very debilitated exactly because the executive power is weak and the National Congress is highly conservative. We hope that by getting more progressive legislators elected to the National Congress we can make what is called the Brazilian political class return to credibility.

From the economic viewpoint Brazil's situation today is extremely delicate. Our economy is stagnant. We don't have the capacity to produce what we did ten years ago. There is tremendous unemployment in Brazil. Just in metropolitan São Paulo 1.3 million workers are unemployed. These jobs can't be filled either because of modernization or because of imports. We have yet another grave economic question in the lack of credibility. Brazilian businessmen prefer to invest their savings in speculation rather than invest in Brazilian production. Brazil has no credibility to attract new money and the state has no capacity to invest. Just to give you an idea, during the first four months of 1993 the Brazilian government's investments were zero. It couldn't invest anything.

Besides all this, 50 percent of Brazilian companies do not pay their income taxes. For every dollar collected there is another dollar's worth of tax evasion. So the economic situation is delicate. The situation is delicate from the viewpoint of salaries. Brazil has only 30 million workers officially registered for labor benefits and even among them salaries are really low. Just to give you an idea, metalworkers who are the best organized class that we have considering the pay of metalworkers in the São Paulo satellite city of São Bernardo do Campo in December—their purchasing power in 1993 was 50 percent of what it was in 1985. It has dropped 50 percent in eight years!

From the social viewpoint Brazil's situation is even more delicate. We have 70 million Brazilians living below the poverty line, that is people who earn less than two minimum salaries a month. The monthly minimum salary today is worth around US$70; and we have 70 million Brazilians earning less than US$150 a month. Among those 70 million, 32 million are indigent. Can you imagine those who earn a quarter of a minimum salary—something less than US$20—a month? We have a public health system that has failed. We have no agrarian reform. So our social situation is very delicate. This really hits home when you see that more than 70 percent of the Brazilian population does not have an adequate sewer system. We have to resolve basic problems like education and public health. Brazil has no experience with agrarian reform; it has no agricultural policy to help the small- and medium-sized producer. And we have 32 million Brazilians going hungry.

What does Brazil need to get on the right track?

First of all I think there is hope. I think Brazil is viable. It has conditions to develop. Brazil has a good industrial base, a good business structure and a good intellectual base. Now it is important to understand that the crisis is political. And because it is political it is a crisis of credibility. Brazil needs three components to begin growing again: (1) credibility abroad (2) credibility at home and (3) financial credibility. The state must resume its power to collect taxes so that Brazilian companies have confidence in Brazil and invest in the productive sector. There must be a synchronization among the social actors that form part of the Brazilian political scenario.

I am convinced that we can resolve Brazil's problems. Renegotiate the problem of the foreign debt . . . extend the profile of the internal debt . . . give the state greater investment capacity . . . avoid state building of pharaonic projects that are not priority projects for the populace . . . convince Brazilian capitalists to trust in Brazil and to invest their money within Brazil. It is necessary to establish agreements with labor through industrial sector associations which can negotiate wages and prices and begin to reduce inflation in Brazil.

Would the administration of a President Lula and the Workers Party continue the recent privatization of public companies, selling those companies to private investors, or would state companies have a different destination under your orientation?

For us in the Workers Party, privatization and stabilization are questions of principle. It is a strategic issue. I think the state must maintain control of the companies considered strategic for national development. I would block the current privatization system because I would like to give a chance to the honest democratic state. Instead of privatizing its companies, I would like to democratize those companies, changing the concept of state enterprise to public enterprise, creating mechanisms through which civil society could have access to the administration of these companies.

The Lower House of Congress recently approved a new patent law, which was then sent to the Senate. What is your position about the protection of intellectual property?

I think Brazil, a poor and developing country, is subordinated to the interests of the big powers. I think we have to have a patent law that is first in our own interest. After that we can discuss the interests of the other nations. I favor a patent law that preserves national sovereignty.

What is the role of foreign capital—of foreign investment— in Brazil today?

I think that foreign capital will always be welcome in Brazil. I think it is necessary. The economy is internationalized, and it is humanly impossible for any country to close itself to foreign capital. But it is necessary to establish correct rules so that the entrance of foreign capital does not signify the closing of Brazilian companies. It is necessary to create conditions for Brazilian companies to develop, conditions to have strong domestic capital without prohibiting the entrance of foreign capital.

It seems that the whole world is racing to form regional trade blocs, like the European Common Market and the North American Free Trade Agreement. Would the Southern Cone Market (Mercosur) have your backing to continue integrating beyond the goals already set for 1995?

I favor the opening of frontiers as long as we take care to establish a certain equality among the countries. For example, I am very much in favor of Mercosur, but it is necessary that the workers join in elaborating the project and consecrating this integration process. I think that we have to see a cultural opening, too. I think Brazil can open up to the world so long as Brazil has the conditions to be competitive, because if Brazil opens to the modern world without competitiveness we are going to wind up importing a lot and exporting little because our productive capacity is less than that of the developed world.

That's why I favor the Mercosur experience. It is an important experience not only with Argentina, Paraguay and Uruguay but with all of South America. We must have this opening and integration process to take advantage of the good things that each country has and to put an end to the bad things in each country.

What position should the Brazilian government adopt with respect to the North American Free Trade Agreement (NAFTA)?

I do not know NAFTA very well. I have been talking to the political opposition in Mexico, and they think Mexico is not benefiting much with this accord. There are protests from Mexican comrades that for every dollar the United States invests in Mexico, Mexico has to buy four dollars worth of American goods. I think that is very grim. It is an accord that favors whoever is rich and not whoever is poor. Also, there is the problem of so much unemployment in the United States, which was one of the reasons for Clinton's election.

I think this kind of accord between nations cannot always be seen only from the economic viewpoint. It is necessary also to look at it from the social and the political viewpoint. Normally, whoever makes these accords only represents capital and never represents the workers. It is necessary to use representatives of the workers in elaborating these accords so that social interests can be placed on an equal footing. An accord that may be good economically for General Motors must also be good for the workers of General Motors.

Do you perceive the future of the country in terms of international leadership? Is that a viable goal for Brazil? Should it participate more actively in hemispheric and international organizations like the Organization of American States and the United Nations?

I defend the idea that Brazil should have a greater international presence. It is necessary to change the correlation of forces, as much for the United Nations as for the Organization of American States. Brazil needs to have a greater presence because it is a big country, an economically viable country, a country that has an important political presence on the continent. I think that it is necessary to put an end to the veto power of the wealthy countries in the United Nations. The United Nations needs to be democratized.

At the time of this interview (October 1993), the leadership of the Workers Party is debating whether the party can maintain its ideals in favor of reforms and at the same time administer a country. The PT moderates—identified with you, José Genoino, Aloisio Mercadante and Luis Gushiken—insist there are only three questions that divide the party: (1) the policy of alliances for the 1994 election, (2) the character of your government program, and (3) the candidate's profile. For readers outside Brazil who are trying to follow and understand political developments in Brazil, how would you summarize your own position on those three points?

First, the Brazilian press is very uncomfortable with the PT. In truth, that which appears to be division for the Brazilian press and for the U.S. is democracy. Going into a national party congress, we are discussing various things, and it is logical that there are various positions. I have talked with all the currents of thought in the PT, and I see that the disagreements about political alliances with other parties are minor. I think we will be able to approve a correct political alliance policy because all the currents of thought—be they more to the left or to the right—know that the PT needs alliances to win elections and govern Brazil.

Second, with respect to the nature of a PT government program, everybody knows that the PT must have a more populist, democratic nature. Hence, we have to affirm in the program the political necessity of a policy of income distribution, and of agrarian reform, the need to make the poorest sectors of the population our priority and NOT to wait. It is necessary to distribute now because, if in the decade of the 1970s the governments said that we needed to grow to distribute the wealth, today we say that we need to distribute to grow. We need to create a consumer society. One does not yet exist.

Third, the nature of a government program will be no problem. We will reach an accord for that. We are going to mount a government looking toward the social questions. We think that the rich sectors of society have to pay for the distribution of income in Brazil. I'm going to give you a graphic example. In Brazil, the poorest 50 percent of the people get by with only ten percent of the national wealth and the wealthiest ten percent have 50 percent of the national wealth. Income is very badly distributed in Brazil. So a PT government program will aim at addressing these injustices.

There is going to be no problem of a political party split. The PT is going to come out of the encounter very much more unified and with more competency to win the elections.

Critics say that only one thing unites a divided PT today: the determination to maintain Luiz Inácio Lula da Silva as party president. Assuming that extends also to the desire to see Lula as the party's presidential candidate again and to win the

office this time, is that enough to hold the party together during a political campaign and during the subsequent government?

I am certain that the party will be united during the entire presidential campaign. I did not want to be a candidate to be president of the PT, because I think it is possible to project new leadership through the party. I had appeals from all the comrades to continue in the party presidency, but I really did not want to continue. I am disposed to be a candidate for the presidency of the republic for the PT, I am disposed to make political alliances, I am disposed to win and to govern this country. I think that Brazil needs the experience of the PT in power, of a democratic experience, of a popular experience in order for it to get on the road to development.

I think that for the foreign press that comes to Brazil, that has so much contact with the Brazilian press, that sees the PT occupying so much space in that press with its internal problems, it is important to say to the readers that the PT makes people uncomfortable because the PT today is undeniably the biggest leftist party in the world. There has never been, throughout the history of the world, any other party like the PT—any party that has the social extension that the PT has in Brazil. I think that this greatness of the PT, this dimension of the PT, this involvement of the PT in the social movement is what makes the PT so irritating to the conservative sectors of our country.

It is the best organized—the most extensively distributed through the social strata—and the only party in Brazil that functions like a real political party. That makes our critics uncomfortable, and we like that.

35

Brazil's Workers' Party:
Socialism as Radical Democracy

Margaret E. Keck

The Workers Party (PT) of Brazil is the most important new political party to form on the Left in Latin America in the last quarter of a century.[1] When the PT was founded in 1979, structural conditions in Brazil—egregious and growing inequality coupled with a significant increase in the size of the working class— may have appeared propitious for the formation of a mass-based party espousing radical forms of democracy and socialism, but political conditions were decidedly not.[2] Leftist ideologies and organizations worldwide were in crisis, and Brazil, a country long known for elitist politics, was in the midst of a cautious, 16-year transition from military rule.

Yet in 1989, as pieces of the Berlin Wall were being sold for souvenirs on German streets, the Workers Party candidate came within six percentage points of winning the first direct presidential elections in Brazil in almost 30 years. The PT's success is due to its unusually rich reinterpretation of the importance of socialism to democracy and vice versa. By insisting on the right of the excluded to speak with their own voices and in their own names, the PT broadened Brazil's traditionally narrow conception of democracy. At the same time, this commitment to broadening democracy became a foundation of the party's notion of socialism. Therein lies the party's significance, and its testimony to the possibility of continued vitality on the Left.

Of course the PT is not immune to the worldwide crisis of the

Left. At the end of November 1991, the party held its first congress to promote far-reaching debates on "Socialism: Conception and Paths to Building It" and "Conception and Practice of Party Building and Party Activity." The idea was to re-ground and refound the party on the basis of a critical examination of its first decade.[3]

The party's search for a definition of socialism is a process of "theorizing its practice."[4] At the congress, the crux of the debate concerned whether winning political office and governing should be central to the PT's strategic vision, or merely tactical steps in a broader project of social change, in which primary emphasis would go to movement-building. Radical leftist factions of the party interpreted increased stress on political institutions and elections as reformist, as an abandonment of the working class and of the PT's mission. The party's majority faction, *Articulação*, viewed this emphasis instead as an effective use of available political opportunities. While for most of the 1980s, PT discourse stressed its *movimentista* side, an increasingly self-confident party emerged from the first congress determined to shed its sectarian image and build a broader network of electoral alliances with other parties on the Left.

When one looks back on the Brazilian democratic transition, what stand out are the elements of continuity: the remarkable ability of traditional elites to conserve their positions of dominance in the system, and the permeability and gradual blurring of the boundary between supporters and opponents of the military regime.[5] A vivid illustration was President José Sarney (1985-1990). After splitting with his pro-military party over its choice of presidential candidate, Sarney was elected vice president in indirect elections on a ticket headed by conservative opposition leader Tancredo Neves. When Neves died before taking office, Sarney became Brazil's first civilian president since 1964 as a new member of the PMDB, the largest party to emerge from the antiauthoritarian opposition. Sarney was not alone in his odyssey; a considerable number of PMDB federal deputies elected in 1986 were former members of the pro-military party.

But continuity was not the essential characteristic of the political mood in Brazil in the 1970s. The liberalization initiated by military president Ernesto Geisel in 1973-1974 allowed social and political organizing to flower. The PMDB's predecessor, the Brazilian Democratic Movement (MDB)—the legal opposition party whose establishment the military government had promoted in 1965—began in the 1974 elections to behave like a real opposition, with startling success.

A variety of neighborhood organizations and other social movements emerged out of grassroots Catholic associations and base communities. The Cost of Living Movement gathered over a million signatures for a petition to the president. The Amnesty Movement organized nationally and internationally to free political prisoners and lobby for the return of exiles. Press censorship was gradually lifted. Students mobilized on campuses (initially meeting heavy repression) and eventually reconstituted their state and national organizations. And at the end of the decade, Brazilian unions, widely believed to be under the thumb of state corporatist structures, rocked the country with a series of strikes beginning in the automobile-producing suburbs of São Paulo.

In 1977, leftist intellectuals, politicians and political activists began to discuss what kinds of political parties might best address the needs of Brazil's poor. In a parallel process, trade unionists began to talk about the need for a party in which workers could speak with their own voices; past experience had taught skepticism about elite-led parties that claimed to represent their interests. The 1978-1979 strikes, which catapulted labor leaders like Luiz Inácio "Lula" da Silva to national prominence, made it clear that workers were not seeking to be represented, but to represent themselves.

The decision in late 1979 to form a Workers Party was greeted with some ambivalence among the Left. Differences over the extent of real opportunities afforded by the democratic transition and over the centrality of the working class in bringing about change led most of the prominent progressives in the MDB (such as Fernando Henrique Cardoso and Almino Afonso in São Paulo) and a number of trade unionists to remain in an MDB successor. Some of the most bitter anti-PT invective of the early to mid-1980s came from this group.

Those who chose to stay with the MDB understood the importance of new social movements and the new unionism but were convinced that a partisan appeal on the basis of class was sectarian and would not address the diversity of political identities in Brazilian society. They also recognized that the military's willingness to leave power was contingent at best, and would require delicate negotiations. The PT's radicalism threatened to upset the apple cart.

Much of the PT's early discourse linked the party's class base to the industrial proletariat of São Paulo's ABCD region, center of the Brazilian auto industry and detonator of the strike waves of the late 1970s.[6] This linkage was personified in Lula, the party's first president and best known leader, who was president of the São Bernardo and Diadema Metalworkers Union and linchpin of the strike movement. But this rather narrow conception of class, which focused heavily on urban factory workers and their unions, was always somewhat at odds with the party's real base. The "new unionism" contained an important white-collar component, especially bank workers and teachers. In addition, from the outset the PT appealed to "workers" not only on the basis of their workplace and union experience, but also on the basis of their involvement in a broad spectrum of social organizations in poor neighborhoods.

Over time, the PT's conception of class came to center on forms of self-organization rather than on structural position. This shift owed something to the broadening constituency of the unions associated with the party: their growing influence among farmworkers and landless peasants, as well as the astronomical growth of white-collar unionism in the 1980s. It also owed a great deal to the identification of neighborhood and other non-workplace struggles as working class struggles, an identity forged in the streets during the last years of the military regime.

In fighting for the right of workers and the poor to speak with their own voices, the PT often seemed to identify class struggle with the struggle for citizenship. From its founding, the party was conceived as a legal political party that would compete within the system on an equal footing. To become legal was a deliberate and crucial decision whose logic structured the party's evolving view of political institutions. The party could have chosen (and with a less Herculean effort, given the serious logistical difficulties posed by the military's legal code) to remain outside the political system as a party of resistance.[7] Instead, it chose to pursue both the institutional and the societal routes. Party organizers believed that by remaining rooted in civil society the PT would eventually win elections, because those it sought to represent were a majority. By winning public office, the PT would improve the lot of the majority. And by strengthening the autonomous capacity of movements in society, the party would help foster a rupture with the status quo.

The party's first electoral campaign in 1982 was euphoric. Lula's candidacy for governor of São Paulo rallied tens of thousands, leaving many PT members convinced of victory on the eve of the elections. Instead, Lula placed fourth out of five candidates, and only in São Paulo and the Amazonian state of Acre did the PT win more than 3 percent of the vote. It elected eight federal deputies, and only two mayors nationwide.[8] After three years of organizing the party and a year of intense campaigning, PT stalwarts saw these results as a stunning defeat.

Subsequently, institutional and electoral concerns became distinctly secondary to strengthening unions and social movements. Many believed that the party's early focus on the 1982 elections represented a deviation from its real goals.[9] This perspective was reinforced by the involvement of the party's top leadership in founding and building the CUT labor federation (*Central Unica dos Trabalhadores*) during this period.[10]

Even so, the party did not desist from electoral activity, and its relatively greater success in the 1985 mayoral elections in state capitals and the 1986 legislative elections helped bring the institutional side of the party's identity back into the equation. The Congress elected in 1986 doubled as a constituent assembly. PT deputies wrote sections of Brazil's new constitution and grew increasingly adept at bargaining and coalition-building in Congress.[11] The party also actively participated in the presentation of popular amendments to the draft constitution, a process made possible largely by a PT initiative.

When the party won mayoral elections in some of Brazil's largest cities in 1988 (including São Paulo), and Lula came close to winning the presidency in 1989, those elements in PT discourse that downplayed institutional activity appeared increasingly at odds with the party's real evolution. If real change was to come from below, from social movements and organizations in civil society, what was the proper role of the party in government?

To say that government should work with and be responsive to the organized population was one thing, but to do it was quite another story. The party's municipal platform proposed governing via popular councils (*conselhos populares*)—comprised of representatives of a wide variety of local social movements who would establish priorities for PT administrations. This experiment in broadening grassroots participation in government and building popular power left unresolved such questions as whether the councils would be consultative or deliberative, how they would be chosen, and what their relationship would be to elected parliamentary bodies like municipal councils.

While some issue-specific consultative councils have played an important role in PT-governed municipalities (for example, the health councils in São Paulo), the popular council proposal foundered on three counts: the difficulties in organizing them, their inability to prioritize demands and consider the needs of the population as a whole, and the recognition that organizing them from above amounted to corporatism under another name. The relationship between direct and representative democracy, a problem that has perplexed socialists for generations, remains squarely on the agenda. The entire question of the state's role in social change cries out for more serious reflection.

The PT has always aspired to be internally democratic, to ensure a substantial degree of participation by its over 600,000 members. Prior to party conventions (whose composition is dictated by party law), the PT holds pre-conventions with broader participation, which are intended to be the real decision-making arenas.

Grassroots activity is supposed to take place in party nuclei organized in neighborhoods or workplaces—a conception which owes
as much to Catholic base communities as it does to the traditional
Leninist cells. The nuclei are intended to stimulate active participation and to provide links between the party and local social movements. In practice, the number of stable nuclei has been far fewer
than the party would like; many exist only in pre-electoral periods
to take part in candidate selection, or at other times in response to
specific controversies. In spite of these and other limitations (fragility of the party press and intra-party communications, for example, particularly during the early and mid-1980s), participation
is extraordinarily high by Brazilian standards.

The PT is generally perceived as highly factionalized. From the
beginning, it contained a number of Trotskyist and Marxist-Leninist
organizations (Socialist Convergence is probably the best known)
whose independent existence was illegal under the military regime,
and who joined the PT to enhance their influence. Some were groups
formed out of the student movement in the 1970s; others resulted
from earlier splits in Communist, Maoist, or Fourth International
parties. Their activists were important human resources in the lo-
gistically difficult organizational phase of the party, and in some
regions they were initially the dominant force in the PT. While
condemning these factions' dual allegiance and their commonly
held view of the PT as a mere tactical expedient, party leaders like
Lula believed that as the party developed, the problem would resolve itself. They expected these organizations either to assimilate
or to leave. Some did eventually decide to disband as independent
organizations; others continued to act on two fronts.

In 1983 much of the PT leadership formed a faction of its own,
Articulação. The idea was to stake out a middle ground between
the vanguardism of the leftist organizations and the reformism of
those who eschewed movement-building, a center that could attract a majority of the membership. *Articulação* espoused partici-
patory democracy and a rather diffuse conception of socialism. The
institutional corollary to the formation of *Articulacão* was a rule
change providing for proportional representation in party directive

organs. Although it made factionalism more visible, this change was arguably a much more democratic solution than the previous system of informal negotiations leading to a single slate. Nonetheless, the existence of well-organized, intensely ideological minorities in the party, whose primary allegiance was not to the PT, remained a problem.[12]

The conflict came to a head in April 1986, when a group of former members of the PCBR (Revolutionary Brazilian Communist Party), claiming to be PT members, were caught robbing a bank in the northeastern city of Salvador, ostensibly to garner funds for the Nicaraguan revolution. Although the perpetrators were immediately expelled from the party, the media went to town with the story. The PT's fourth national meeting the following month called for a national debate on the issue of parties within the party, and the ensuing process of regulating factional behavior stretched over the rest of the decade. By July 1990, ten internal groupings were recognized as legitimate PT factions, and statutory limits were placed on their autonomy.[13]

Regulating factional behavior contributed to internal democracy by rendering the organizational bases of internal disputes more evident. Yet the increased visibility of factions led some to complain that party debates were dominated by factional positions, and that the only way to participate was to belong to a faction. It is hard to evaluate the weight of this complaint: factions always played an important role in party debates, and structuring debate in such a large organization is bound to privilege aggregate positions. For the party congress held at the end of 1991, the debate on socialism and democracy was carried out prior to the congress with the publication of position papers, each of which had to be signed by at least 100 party members. While some of these represented factional positions, others were ad hoc groupings. At the congress itself, the *Articulação* position clearly dominated, receiving around 70 percent of the delegate votes.

By a wide variety of measures, the Workers Party has been remarkably successful. The party has become increasingly institutionalized. Internal communications, while still somewhat precarious, have improved enormously. Internal elections are held regularly and new leaders have emerged from the ranks. While Lula remains the key party leader, two others have held the post of president. The CUT labor federation, with which the PT has close ties, is by far the largest such organization in Brazil, and the PT has a striking presence in a wide variety of social movements, including "new" ones like the ecology movement and urban movements around housing and social services. The PT's influence in rural areas, in rural unions and in the landless movement is growing.

The PT has grown well beyond its initial base in São Paulo to become a genuinely national party. It governs three state capitals and a number of other major cities. Lula came within a hair of being elected president in 1989. The party's congressional delegations have approximately doubled with each election, and in 1990 the PT elected its first senator, Eduardo Suplicy from São Paulo. PT federal deputies were elected in eleven states, and state assembly members on PT tickets (including coalitions) won in all but two.[14]

The PT is, however, still very much an outsider in the Brazilian political game, and not only because it is on the Left. More than ten years after its founding, the PT remains an institutional anomaly: it is a programmatic party among non-programmatic, catchall parties; its congressional representatives respect party discipline while other legislators rarely follow the party line; and it has a rich and conflictive internal party life while most parties are coalitions of notables. In a system where political decision-making continues to rely on elite backroom deals, the party calls for openness and accountability to party organizations and to society at large.

The November 1991 party congress did not resolve the problems inherent in asking what it means to be socialist at the end of the twentieth century. Nor did it do what leftist elites outside the PT and Trotskyist factions in the party respectively praised or condemned it for—declare itself social democratic. But the congress did come closer to defining what socialism is not. Although the PT never espoused a dictatorship of the proletariat, the 1991 congress explicitly repudiated that notion, and restated its commitment to a mixed economy. These two positions, along with tighter restrictions on internal factions, are likely to exacerbate conflict between the party's majority and its more ideological leftist members. And the congress voted to require that 30 percent of the positions in party directive organs be filled by women—in response to the embarrassingly large gap between the party's stated commitment to women's equality and the derisory number of women in the party leadership.

Essentially, the congress reaffirmed the path the party has followed throughout its history: a trajectory in which a logic of means, whose core value has always been the extension of democracy, remains in a dynamic tension with a logic of ends, socialism, a society without exploiters or exploited. The party claims that socialism will be defined more clearly in the course of popular struggle during a prolonged period of accumulating forces. Competing for political office and exercising political power are an inherent part of this process. Socialism for the PT is inseparable from a radical form of democracy. In Brazil, as nearly everywhere in Latin America, democracy remains a revolutionary demand.

A decade may be a long life for a Brazilian party, but it is a short time in world-historical terms. Nonetheless, since 1980 the Workers Party has brought hundreds of new actors into politics. It has created new constituencies that expect political leaders to be responsible and accountable. And it has insisted that the capacity to participate politically comes not from status or specialized learning, but from the experience of everyday life. The PT has had a marked impact on the new generation. Its strongest support is among the young, and the party may be playing a crucial role in socializing youth into a radically revised vision of what politics is about.

The PT's future depends on its ability to convince substantial numbers of Brazilians of the feasibility of the kinds of social change and the kind of democracy it promotes. The party's greatest electoral successes, in 1988 and 1989, reflected its ability to channel a massive protest vote against the status quo. Repeated governmental failures and prolonged economic stagnation of the kind that Brazil has seen over the last decade do not, however, necessarily produce a more politicized population. On the contrary, much recent evidence shows the result to be civic burnout, and a loss of belief that change is possible. This spreading anomie is dangerous not only for the PT, but also for Brazilian democracy.

The challenge for the PT, as for the Left in general, is to discover ways to renew one of the oldest arguments of the Left: that social equality, or attending to the needs of the least favored, is in the interest of society as a whole. Reclaiming this fundamental dimension, while shedding the accumulated baggage of failed experiments with models that produced new forms of inequality in the name of socialism, is extraordinarily difficult. The party approaches this challenge with a significant advantage, having recognized and learned from its own experience that the effort to rethink socialism is inextricably linked to the effort to broaden and deepen democracy.

Footnotes

1. This did not occur in other countries experiencing democratic transitions around the same time as Brazil, most importantly because of the different treatment accorded political parties and elections. In Brazil preexisting parties were abolished and replaced with new ones that, however artificial, did compete in regular elections over a 15-year period. In other countries where partisan activity was banned, preexisting (and long-standing) political identities may have been frozen. In Brazil such identities, in any case of shorter duration, were at least to some extent reorganized. In addition, Brazil is the only country where the industrial working class as a percentage of the economically active population actually grew (and substantially so) under the military regime; in the other countries in question this sector shrank. As Brazil's military regime was winding down, new industrial workers and increasingly organized elements of the growing service sector were politically "available" in a sense that was unique in Latin America in the 1980s.
2. Most of the ideas presented in this article are discussed in much greater depth and detail in Margaret E. Keck, *The Workers' Party and Democratization in Brazil* (New Haven: Yale University Press, 1992).
3. Though party leaders called this their first congress, to emphasize its importance for the party's self-definition, it was the PT's eighth national meeting.
4. Emir Sader, ed., *E Agora PT: caráter e identidade* (São Paulo: Brasiliense, 1989), p. 8.
5. On the first point see Frances Hagopian, "Democracy by Undemocratic Means? Elites, Political Pacts, and Regime Transition in Brazil," *Comparative Political Studies* Vol. 23, No. 2 (July 1990), and her forthcoming book from Cambridge University Press; on the second see especially Guillermo O'Donnell, "Challenges to Democratization in Brazil," *World Policy Journal,* Vol. 5, No. 2 (Spring 1988).
6. ABCD refers to the Santo André, São Bernardo do Campo, São Caetano, and

Diadema; the region also includes the smaller cities of Mauá, Rio Grande da Serra, and Ribeirão Pires.
7. For a discussion of the legalization process, see Margaret E. Keck, *The Workers' Party and Democratization in Brazil,* ch. 5.
8. Of the federal deputies elected, six were from São Paulo and one each from Rio de Janeiro and Minas Gerais. The mayors were in Diadema, São Paulo, and Santa Quitéria in the interior of the state of Maranhão; the mayor of the latter left the PT early in his term.
9. This widespread attitude goes a long way toward explaining tensions between the party organization and the legislators it elected in 1982. It also explains the party's delay in attempting to adjudicate conflict between the local party organization and the elected PT administration in Diadema, São Paulo, over whether a PT mayor ought to be primarily responsible to (or indeed an instrument of) the local party organization (in choice of personnel and policy) or to the city as a whole. The conflict was exacerbated by three factors: a) the mayor, Gilson Menezes, was elected by a small margin in a three-way split of the city vote; b) there were bitter factional differences between the mayor, the leaders of the local party organization, and the PT representatives on the municipal council (who were in any case a minority of the council); and c) as Diadema was the only significant municipality the PT won, what happened there held implications for the party well beyond the municipality.
10. The literal translation of the CUT—Single Workers' Central—is not very satisfactory, as the CUT was not the only central labor confederation formed at this time. For a discussion of the formation of labor confederations, see Margaret E. Keck, "The New Unionism in the Brazilian Transition," in Alfred Stepan (ed.), *Democratizing Brazil* (New York: Oxford University Press, 1989).
11. In fact, the PT was the only party to present a complete constitutional draft. This was published as Fábio Konder Comparato, *Muda Brasil* (São Paulo: Brasiliense, 1986).
12. As long as these leftist organizations remained illegal, however, those who wanted to discuss their activities openly were constrained by the argument that to do so was akin to denouncing them to the police. The main communist parties were legalized in 1985, opening the way for the others. Nonetheless, the process remains somewhat difficult (though less so than when the PT was legalized), and unless these parties want to run candidates on their own slate, there is not much incentive to become "legal." Although they are no longer illegal, one might call them a-legal since "legality" for parties is structured around electoral participation.
13. The resolution passed at the party's fifth national meeting held that, "the PT will not allow the existence within it of organizations which have: their own policies regarding the PT's general policies; their own leadership; their own public presence; their own discipline, implying inevitably a double allegiance; parallel and closed structures; their own organic and institutionalized systems of financing; regular public news organs." ("A Reglamentação das Tendencias: PT: Partido estratégico rumo ao socialismo," resolution approved at the Fifth National Meeting, published in *PT Boletim Nacional,* No. 33 (Nov. 1987-Jan. 1988).
14. For the numbers of federal and state deputies elected in 1982, 1986, and 1990, see Keck, *The Workers' Party and Democratization in Brazil,* pp. 163-64.

36

Black, Female and Favelada:
An Interview with Benedita da Silva

Michael Shellenberger

B*enedita da Silva became* "Senadora Benedita" *on October 3, 1994. As the first female and black senator in the history of Brazil, Benedita has vowed to back social programs and economic investment to improve the conditions of Rio de Janeiro's majority.*

I left in Portuguese the words "favela" *and* "favelado," *often translated as* "slum" *and* "slum-dweller," *to avoid the negative connotation these words have in English. In addition, I left* "morro," *the hills upon which* favelas *in Rio are built, in its original Portuguese. The interview was conducted on September 18, 1994, at the studio where Benedita records her television and radio spots.*

The Voice of the *Morro*

When I was growing up I learned that there were two ways to effect change: education and political action. Because my family didn't have the means for me to study after elementary school, I developed a political consciousness at a young age on the streets and as a domestic servant. I did everything I could to avoid starving to death. By the age of 16 I was already politically active, doing important community work.

After years of hard work, I helped build the Workers Party (PT) in the early 1980s. The Party provided a voice for the poor, the illiterate and me, so that in 1982 I was elected as City Councilperson for Rio de Janeiro. My slogan was "Black, Female and *Favelada* in Defense of the Citizens." I worked for the oppressed: women, blacks, children, the poor, the *favelados* and the workers. In 1986 I was elected Federal Deputy, the first black woman elected Federal Deputy in the history of Brazil.

When Brazil adopted its new constitution in 1989, we fought and succeeded in introducing a series of laws to benefit women, blacks, Indians and minorities. Then a new era began in 1990. After four years as federal deputy, struggling for the rights of the *morro*, of the *favelados* who live on the hills surrounding Rio, I realized that we had to fight for adequate housing and property rights without playing with the emotions of the *favelados* who had been thrown around time and time again by various city governments. I became the voice of the *morro* in the congress.

In 1990 I was reelected with a mandate to raise the status of the oppressed to become full citizens. We began to push for laws in the congress to regulate domestic labor and create governmental agencies to combat racism. We created commissions in Brazil and in the United Nations to investigate the killing of street children in Brazil. I was vice-president of a congressional commission that investigated child prostitution and the illegal adoption of children within Brazil.

I also pursued commissions to investigate the mass sterilization of Brazilian women. Though we defend the right to family planning for both women and men, we are deeply opposed to the sterilization that is pushed on young women at the age of 17 or 20 years old. As it turns out, many of these women don't even know they are being sterilized.

Above all else in our legislative work, we have been committed to pressuring the executive branch to enforce laws already on the books.

The Crisis and Its Alternatives

Rio de Janeiro is in an utterly miserable state. We have extreme poverty and a violence that foreign tourists don't experience. People know we have bandits in the *favelas*, but they don't know that there is another kind of violence. It's the violence of a society without housing, health care, education, jobs or programs to care for the kids on the street. There are 32 million hungry people in our country. We have entire families of unemployed workers living below the freeways. There are children on the streets who have to sell their bodies to feed themselves and their brothers and sisters.

This situation cannot continue. We want international investment, we want to open up to the world market. The question is: what kind of market will it be if there isn't a social return to eliminate poverty and hunger?

We need a determined government with clean hands, a government that understands and shares the same interests of the people. Brazil needs a president like Lula. We can no longer go on believing that economic growth alone will bring about change. We need social investment too, and Lula will bring both.

Popular Movements

Allying themselves with the PT was the best move our popular movements ever made. Before the PT, community leaders were used simply as vote-getters by the elites and their political parties. During the dictatorship, popular movement leaders were isolated and without room to create their own political representation. We didn't have the power to raise our voices and demand our rights.

The PT represents a big political school with a guaranteed space for popular movements. The space is guaranteed because the popular movements built the party for themselves. As a result, there isn't discrimination within the party between middle-class, unionized workers and workers in the lowest class of Brazilian society. The very structure of the party ensures that these constituencies are heard from within the legislative, judicial and executive branches.

The women's movement is the most important social movement for me. It provided the backing that made my first bid for office in 1982 successful. We've contributed a great deal to the struggle in the workplace, against domestic violence, the rights of domestic workers, single women and for the rights of children. We are the majority of the population, and our movement is providing a new vision for Brazilian society. We are fighting to ensure that our differences aren't transformed into inequalities. And, I want to add, the PT is the only party where we women won a battle that requires that at least 30 percent of party leadership must be women.

The history of the black movement in Brazil has two different phases: before and after the military dictatorship. Though it started out as a struggle to preserve our cultural values, the movement became highly political and eventually left a strong influence on most political parties, especially progressive parties.

It is now understood that our current capitalist system came out of slavery, making the black movement decidedly political. And though the black movement is nonpartisan, it plays a strong role in political debates and is in favor of party platforms that prioritize the racial question.

The PT is the best example of a party that prioritizes the black movement. Of all the country's political parties, the PT has the largest number of black members and black leadership. The PT has fought for representation of blacks in the congress and has, through me, elected the first black woman senator in the history of Brazil.

Left-wing parties and progressive movements have historically given more attention to the black movement. So, just as Brazil's first black federal deputy belonged to the Communist Party and came from the *favelas* of Rio, as Brazil's first black senator, I was elected from the *favelas* of Rio and belong to the Workers Party.

Building Support Internationally

What will my role as a Senator mean? First, I will work to create a system of lobbying in Brazil where interests other than big business can be represented politically. We want to include representation for women, blacks and children in defining national policy.

Second, I want to work toward the development of Rio de Janeiro by bringing in support from the international business community to achieve better commercial relations between Rio and the rest of the world. We would specifically like to create more exchange between black businesspeople in the U.S. and here in Rio.

We have followed the anti-racist struggle in the U.S. for years, a struggle that is famous throughout the world. I want to call on support from the North American black, women's and solidarity movements to assist in our struggle against racism and sexism and for the lives of our children.

I want to be part of an international campaign that mobilizes resources for these people. People don't realize how unjust it is to live without potable water or a sewage system, to live somewhere without any protection from crime. We have so much labor simply halted in the *favelas*. If the government had the sensibility to seek an international policy that would lure international support to simply put needed materials in the hands of a *favelado*, he or she would build a home with dignity. Our goal is to ensure that the government provides the technical assistance and resources to build these homes.

I can't leave this world without having made a strong difference providing housing, water and sewage systems to the millions of *favelados* in Rio de Janeiro. I want to see *favela* children smiling and playing, blacks and whites hand-in-hand, and a people unashamed of saying where they live.

37

Interview with Marco Aurélio Garcia

Michael Shellenberger

M arco Aurélio Garcia is the International Relations Secretary for the Workers Party (PT) and professor at Unicamp University in Campinas, São Paulo. Garcia coordinated the drafting of the PT's 1994 Government Program and sits on the PT's National Executive Committee. Garcia is one of the party's most influential intellectuals and a key advisor to Lula. He gave us the interview on September 5, 1994, at the national PT headquarters in São Paulo.

At a moment in history when powerful capitalist interests reign supreme throughout the world, how do you explain the strength of the PT, a socialist party?

Before the military coup in 1964, grassroots movements were organizing for the structured reform of banking, agriculture and other sectors. These movements realized that the national economy was experiencing a major crisis and began to mobilize. The 1964 military coup that overthrew President Goulart—who had links to some of the grassroots movements—frustrated these reform efforts.

On coming to power, the military regime attacked the previous political system. It suppressed all the political parties and allowed only two of its own creation. As the traditional political arena was destroyed, it allowed space for traditional outsiders, including the working classes, to form their own political representation.

As economic growth exacerbated class divisions, social movements began to make demands. Civil society confronted the economic crisis and popular movements began to form. In both the cities and the countryside the working class became increasingly powerful and thus difficult for the state to control. The combination of popular movements with working class militancy provided the conditions to found the PT in 1980.

In contrast to the military dictatorships in Argentina, Chile and other countries, in Brazil the military generals didn't implement a liberal economic program. On the contrary, the generals enormously reinforced the power of the state (that included political repression) in conjunction with international and national capital to create the conditions for a massive expansion of the Brazilian economy during the 1970s. It was the time of the so-called "Brazilian miracle" where the economy grew at a rate of 10-12 percent a year. All of this had an important social effect: The working class grew to four times its 1964 size and the number of small and medium-sized businesses expanded.

How is the PT's model for governing Brazil different from the neoliberal project, specifically as represented by Fernando Henrique Cardoso?

The fundamental issue in Brazil today is the existence of 60 million people who are excluded from society, the production process and the market. Our model of development is essentially aimed at these 60 million excluded people. We seek to include these people in national development through the creation of a mass, internal market that would offer food, clothing, housing, water and sewage systems, health care, transportation and education. The creation of this market would have a powerful ripple effect on the larger economy, spurring the development of infrastructure, capital goods, durable goods and even more sophisticated economic sectors. This is no simple distributive model. On the contrary, this is a model that would transform the Brazilian economy from an economy of scale into an internationally competitive economy.

Our model is fundamentally different than Fernando Henrique's model. Fernando Henrique's model is basically the same as ex-President Collor's: Open up the economy totally, so that competitive sectors survive while others perish. The result is a strong de-industrialization of a country that built, in the last 60 years, a respectable industrial base, the tenth largest in the world.

We realize that the fundamental problem in Brazil is that Brazil's concentration of wealth created the conditions for economic paralysis. In contrast, Fernando Henrique opts for a purely monetarist solution to inflation, one that seeks to reproduce in Brazil the IMF's traditional recipe already implemented in Eastern Europe, Mexico and Argentina. It is a recipe with extraordinarily recessive effects on the credit sector.

In a country with the poverty and underdevelopment of Brazil, the IMF is creating an explosive situation. Fernando Henrique is proposing a model of growth similar to that proposed by Delfim Neto [a supply-side government economist during the military dictatorship—Ed.]. "First let's make the cake, and then we'll distribute it."

They think they can resolve social problems through compensatory programs, similar to what President Salinas did with Solidarity in Mexico. But we know that these programs made no real gains against growing misery and social unrest. The proof can be found in Chiapas.

But beyond whatever is written in the political platforms it's important to remember who will implement the policy. When you look at the coalition of forces accompanying Fernando Henrique you'll find the traditional right-wing bloc of politicians without any incentive to reform government policy.

How does the U.S. fit into the PT's vision?

Of course we hope to have positive relations with the United States. In May 1994, President Clinton was asked by a Brazilian journalist what the U.S. would do if Cardenas in Mexico or Lula in Brazil were elected. Clinton said that the U.S. would respect each country's electoral choice. This is a normal response. But, at the same time, we realize that throughout its history the U.S. has interfered in the internal politics of many countries.

U.S.-Brazil relations have been tense in the past, not so much for ideological reasons but rather because Brazil has an industrial sector that can often compete with the USA. This is a trend that is likely to grow. Nevertheless, with good diplomacy, we are confident that we will have totally normal relations with the USA.

How does the PT view pressure by the Clinton administration to privatize state industries?

For us, privatization isn't a question of principle. We are concerned when we hear certain discussions about privatization that tend to be purely ideological, without taking into consideration particular government economic projects.

There are sectors of Brazilian state industry that could be privatized quite easily. However, we identify three key state sectors that should not be privatized. First, the petroleum sector is, until other sources of energy are found, of strategic importance to our country. As such, we can't turn it over to private control, especially given that its vertical structure doesn't facilitate its being divided up. The petroleum industry must remain more or less intact.

The two other strategic sectors are energy and telecommunications. But given their particular structures, joint ventures in both of these sectors are possible.

During his 1989 presidential campaign, Lula had a much stronger line regarding Brazil's external debt, going so far as to call for a moratorium on interest payments. In the 1994 campaign we heard almost nothing. What happened?

The answer is simple: the foreign debt had a much larger impact on the national economy in 1989 than it does today. International interest rates have fallen considerably and anti-debt forces in the Third World have weakened in the absence of a national government pushing the movement forward. In addition, various countries made bilateral negotiations with the U.S. that reduced the debt burden and made it less of a structural problem.

We continue to believe that the Brazilian government signed a bad agreement in 1993 to reduce the debt. Still, we understand that the moment has changed and that the debt itself has changed. If elected, we intend to reopen debt negotiations with foreign lenders (especially North American ones) and with multilateral lending institutions. As far as the rest of the debt, owed to the Paris Club [representing private banks], we intend to seek out the concessions similar to those given to other debtor nations. Other countries, such as Poland, have received a reduction of their debt by more than 50 percent under the pretext of supporting democracy in those countries. We feel strongly that the Paris Club should make the same contribution to democracy in Brazil.

How do you feel about the advice James Carville, a key advisor to President Clinton with a 24 hour access to the White House, has given to Fernando Henrique Cardoso? What kind of a message does this send to Brazil and to the PT?

I don't know exactly what the relationship is between Carville and the White House. I don't know if he was an advisor to Clinton or if he still is an advisor to Clinton. If he still is an advisor to Clinton then I would consider it a grave situation because then a relationship has been established between two administrations with a secret partnership. This would not be good either politically or ethically, and would create a shadow on the relationship between the U.S. and Brazil. I would hope that President Clinton would resolve this situation quickly before it became anything more than a shadow.

Can you explain what the position of the PT is regarding the government's new economic plan, the *Plano Real*?

We have taken two approaches to discussing the *Real*. First, we tried to expose the *Plano Real* for what it is: an electoral-year program for the short-term. But we didn't have the power in the mass media to make our criticisms understood. So, little by little, we began to point out that, if elected president, Lula would provide stability to the new currency by searching for collective labor agreements and a policy of price and wage controls, though not necessarily price or wage freezes, that would include dialogue with important sectors of the business community.

In addition, we intend to remake the Brazilian state by reforming the tax system, ending tax evasion and passing a constitutional reform. Only then will we be able to initiate a consistent policy to control inflation.

Inflation has existed for 30 years in Brazil, with especially feverish moments and low moments as well. To confront inflation the next government will need credibility, above all else. A Cardoso government would have great difficulty achieving this credibility given the alliances it has made with the PFL (Liberal Front Party) and the PTB (Brazilian Labor Party), parties that have a predatory conception of the state. We think that the central problem of the next government will be its political nature.

Who will have the necessary credibility to bring stability? Who can do this? A great negotiator. A man who forged his political career negotiating between bosses and unions. A man who carries in his heart a strong social sensibility. You can't forget that behind whatever technical rationality, whatever brilliant economic formula, there has to be a guiding concern with the millions and millions of marginalized Brazilians who are outside the system.

Speaking of credibility, how would a future PT government deal with the mass media, institutions that have the power to create and change public opinion?

Obviously the media is an important part of the political process, one that must be negotiated. There will have to be a democratization of the means of communication. This doesn't mean that we want to close TV or radio stations. We have neither the means nor the laws to do so. But we do want to create alternative media sources for the population. The state is very powerful in Brazil, and it must comply with its function to inform the public.

38

The Need for International Solidarity:
An Interview with Aloisio Mercadante

Michael Shellenberger

A *loisio Mercadante is a Federal Deputy to the Congress for Rio de Janeiro and was the PT's vice-presidential candidate for the Fall 1994 elections. He is the party's most respected economist. He granted us this interview before he spoke at a campaign rally in São Paulo with Lula on September 11, 1994.*

As we enter the end of this century we are witnessing serious changes on the international scene. First, the end of international military bipolarity between the Soviet Union and the United States. At the same time we are seeing the formation of large economic trading blocs: the European Economic Community, NAFTA, and Japan with emergent economic powers in Asia. We in the Third World are outside of these blocs, excluded from the third industrial revolution. We must contest politically the closing of these economic blocs to the Third World. Above all else we must do away with the neoliberalism being imposed on our economies that will consolidate the system of social apartheid where millions of Brazilians are excluded from realizing their citizenship and from becoming producers and consumers.

For this reason we want to seek, without nationalism, a national project of sovereignty during this new scenario. In South Africa, Nelson Mandela represents an important alteration of international relations in his struggle against racial apartheid. Here in Latin

America, Lula and the PT represent the same perspective: struggling against social apartheid, resisting neoliberalism and consolidating a popular democratic project.

For the PT, international solidarity is fundamental. As a left party we represent a new political culture, one that needs the support of Greens, independents, socialists, social-democrats, communists and the progressive church. We need broad international solidarity to support future confrontations with the centers of power and the structural changes that must be made in Brazilian society such as agrarian reform and the distribution of national wealth, power and culture.

I want to ask for the support of solidarity activists and Brazilians living abroad to form international committees to support us, not only in electoral campaigns, but also in building a government that represents a larger vision of the poor in the southern hemisphere.

Above all else I want to ask for international support in resisting neoliberalism for a country that is capable of marking a new path of sustainable development with the environment, a different kind of production and consumption, and a fair distribution of the profit, wealth and power.

Conclusion

Michael Shellenberger
and Kevin Danaher

Will Brazil continue to squander its great resources on a neoliberal model that concentrates the country's wealth in the hands of a few? Will the Left be able to break the elite's grip on the electoral process? If the Left is elected to power in the future, how can progressive forces prevent capital flight from destabilizing the Brazilian economy?

The significance of these questions for those of us who don't live in Brazil was brought home to us during an interview with progressive activists in Jamaica. We asked them what they would do about Jamaica's foreign debt if they ever came to power. They replied that they would simply try to negotiate a better deal with the IMF and the World Bank. But wouldn't they be tempted to declare a moratorium on debt payments? we asked. They replied, "No, we're too small for such bold resistance; our economy could be crushed by the big lenders. But if a big debtor such as Brazil would lead the way and refuse to pay *its* debts, we could follow along behind them."

As the largest third world debtor, Brazil holds a special place in the eyes of many progressives and also in the eyes of many international bankers. A precedent set by Brazil—renegotiating a fair reduction in their foreign debt—would have a great impact in other parts of the world. A breakthrough in a big country such as Brazil would help embolden grassroots movements in the Third World and it would put elites on notice that their monopoly over investment decision-making will not be tolerated forever.

This is especially relevant for U.S. citizens, given the influence the United States has wielded over Brazil's political and economic direction. Washington's position as the largest power in the World Bank and the International Monetary Fund gives it an additional way to reinforce failed neoliberal policies in Brazil.

Some tensions exist between the U.S. government and the Brazilian government, mainly limited to economic matters such as the debt owed to U.S. banks and trade with U.S. corporations. Specifically, the U.S. government is seeking openings in Brazil for investment in pharmaceuticals and biotechnology. The U.S. is especially anxious for the Brazilian government to privatize its telecommunications, transportation, mining and oil industries. In recent years, the U.S. has pressured Brazil to tighten its patent laws with respect to U.S. products, especially computer software. Since Brazil rescheduled its private debt in 1994 and is opening up its economy, relations have improved.

As Foreign Minister and then Finance Minister, Fernando Henrique Cardoso was largely responsible for Brazil's debt negotiations with the Group of Seven (G-7), the International Monetary Fund (IMF) and private creditors that reduced Brazil's commercial debt by 35 percent. Cardoso's victory in the 1994 presidential elections sent a wave of relief through the halls of the World Bank, the IMF and the White House. Michel Camdessus, the Executive Director of the IMF, called Cardoso on election day to congratulate him on his victory. Cardoso's affection for neoliberal economic policies provide a basis for solidarity between U.S. and Brazilian elites.

But there is also a bottom-up version of international solidarity. One concrete example was the collaboration between the Environmental Defense Fund in Washington, DC and rubber tappers in Acre, Brazil. Prior to their alliance, Chico Mendes and the rubber tappers had tried unsuccessfully to get the Brazilian government to sponsor sustainable development rather than pillaging the Amazon to earn foreign exchange. In 1985, as part of its colonization of the Amazon, the Brazilian government sought money from the Inter-American Development Bank to pave the road BR-364 from

Porto Velho to Rio Branco, in the southwestern region of the Amazon.

Having seen the destruction in Rondônia after the paving of roads into the Amazon there, the rubber tappers wanted to prevent the same from happening in Acre. The Environmental Defense Fund flew Chico Mendes to Washington, where he successfully mobilized opposition to multilateral funding for the road-building project. U.S. congressional opposition to the funding sent a strong message to the Brazilian government. Government officials met with Mendes and the rubber-tappers and began to create extractive reserves that would help guarantee a more sustainable harvesting of products from the Amazon.

Unfortunately, such examples of grassroots international solidarity are rare. It is astonishing that there is not more of a Brazil solidarity movement in the United States. Brazil is a large and important country in the western hemisphere. Any plans by the business classes for a 'free market of the Americas' will demand Brazil's inclusion. There are somewhere between 160,000 (U.S. Census data) and more than 300,000 (*Veja* magazine) Brazilians residing in the United States. There is also a significant percentage of U.S. citizens who have a favorable attitude toward Brazil, whether because of its music, its dance, its soccer or its general aura.

Yet there is no national movement to lobby for better U.S. corporate and governmental policies toward Brazil. There have been efforts—such as the Brazil Network—to create a national movement in the U.S. to support more progressive policies toward Brazil. Yet these have usually foundered due to lack of financial and public support.

Since late 1993 some 100 progressive U.S. organizations have come together to build the "50 Years Is Enough" coalition, focusing public attention on the social and environmental costs of the neoliberal policies imposed by the World Bank and the International Monetary Fund. Brazil is certainly a prime candidate for attention by this growing coalition because few other countries have suffered as much under IMF/World Bank 'guidance.'

The members of the 50 Years Is Enough coalition understand

that effective international solidarity must include a broader base of support, including the labor movement, progressive businesses and many organizations that don't think of themselves as being affected by global economic issues. Whether or not we can build a movement broad enough to challenge elite rule—here and in Brazil—will depend on our ability to translate good ideas into effective political practice. We hope that this book makes a contribution to that effort.

Resources

The two best books on the Workers Party in English are Ken Silverstein and Emir Sader's, *Without Fear of Being Happy: Lula, the Workers' Party and Brazil* (Verso, 1991), one of the best introductions to Brazil generally; and Margaret Keck's *The Workers' Party and Democratization in Brazil* (Yale University Press, 1992), a good analysis of the São Paulo side of the PT's origins and militancy. Nancy Scheper-Hughes' *Death Without Weeping* (University of California Press, 1992) is easily one of the best ethnographies ever written on the violence of poverty in Brazil. An excellent overview of the history and politics of the Amazon is Susanna Hecht and Alexander Cockburn, *The Fate of the Forest* (Verso, 1990).

We recommend that everyone interested in Brazil become a member of the Brazil Action Solidarity Exchange (BASE) which organizes important grassroots solidarity work in the United States. Your $25 membership fee will bring you BASE's excellent monthly newsletter with articles on Brazilian politics, human rights issues, the grassroots movement and a calendar of Brazilian events. Based in the San Francisco Bay Area, BASE is a sister organization of Global Exchange. Your membership contribution is tax-deductible if made out to "BASE/Global Exchange." Send your check and address to BASE, 2017 Mission Street, Rm. 303, San Francisco, CA 94110.

A good source for current information about Brazil is the monthly *News From Brazil*. Every four weeks you get 60 pages of politics, culture, soccer news, events, announcements and plenty of advertisements for Brazilian restaurants and clubs throughout the U.S. And get this: a year's subscription costs just three dollars. Send your three dollars and address to: News From Brazil, P.O.

Box 42536, Los Angeles, CA 90050-0536

Relevant, analytical articles on Brazil and the rest of Latin America can be found in *Report on the Americas,* published by NACLA, the North American Congress on Latin America. If you can only read one magazine about Latin America, read NACLA. You can reach them at NACLA Report on the Americas, 475 Riverside Drive, Suite 454, New York, NY 10115, (212) 870-3146. Subscriptions are $27/year for individuals, $50/year for institutions.

Award-winning filmmaker Maria-Luisa Mendonça has produced the first documentary ever made in English about the Workers Party. Entitled "Without Fear of Being Happy," this fascinating video introduces the viewer to the Workers Party and social movements through archival footage and original interviews with activists, artists and candidates, including Benedita da Silva, Aloisio Mercadante and Betinho. You can order the 30-minute documentary from the nonprofit Brazil Information Committee, 2017 Mission Street, Rm. 303, San Francisco, CA 94110, $30 to individuals, $100 to institutions.

The Rainforest Action Network organizes some of the most imaginative activist campaigns to stop corporate pillage of the world's rainforests. To find out about their Brazil program, contact them at 450 Sansome Street, Suite 700, San Francisco, CA 94111, tel. (415) 398-4404.

For analysis of the global impact of neoliberalism, see Kevin Danaher's *50 Years is Enough: The Case Against the World Bank and the International Monetary Fund,* $14 from Global Exchange, 2017 Mission Street, Rm. 303, San Francisco, CA 94110.

The largest and best coalition (more than 100 groups) confronting the World Bank and the International Monetary Fund is the 50 Years Is Enough Coalition, 1025 Vermont Ave., NW, Suite 300, Washington, DC 20005 (202)879-3187. A direct way to help Brazilians and ourselves at the same time is to reform these institutions that are the main enforcers of the neoliberal dogma.

Contributors

Marshall Berman is the author of *All That is Solid Melts Into Air* and is on the editorial board of *Dissent*.

Beto Borges is the Brazil Program Coordinator of Rainforest Action Network, a San Francisco-based activist organization working to save the world's rainforests.

James Brooke is the Brazil Correspondent for the *New York Times*.

James Bruce, a veteran journalist living in São Paulo, writes regularly for the *Journal of Commerce* in New York.

Stephen G. Bunker, a sociologist, is the author of *Underdeveloping the Amazon* (University of Chicago Press, 1988).

John Burdick teaches anthropology at Fordham University and is the author of *Looking Good in Brazil: The Progressive Catholic Church in Urban Brazil's Religious Arena* (University of California Press, 1992).

Jon Christensen is a freelance writer, a Contributing Editor for *High Country News* and an Associate Editor for Pacific News Service.

Alexander Cockburn writes a bi-weekly column for *The Nation*, and co-edits *Counterpunch*, an excellent Washington newsletter.

Thais Corrall, a journalist and activist, founded "*Fala Mulher*," a women's radio program in Brazil.

Kevin Danaher is the director of the Public Education Department at Global Exchange, a nonprofit education and action center in San Francisco.

Gilberto Dimenstein is a reporter and columnist for the *Folha de São Paulo*. He is the author of *Brazil: War on Children* (Latin America Bureau, 1991).

Theotonio dos Santos is a visiting professor at Universidade Federal Fluminense-Niteroi Rio de Janeiro, and is the author of *The Political Economy of Brazil* (Westview Press).

Stanley A. Gacek is a labor attorney and Assistant Director of International Affairs for the United Food and Commercial Workers International Union (UFCW). He is also chair of the International Labor Law Committee of the District of Columbia Bar Association.

Daniel Hoffman is a freelance journalist and anthropology graduate student at the University of California, Berkeley.

Paul Jeffrey is a United Methodist missionary in Managua, Nicaragua.

Charles Johnson is a U.S. citizen living in Rio de Janeiro who works as a translator.

Margaret E. Keck is a professor of political science at Yale University and is the author of *The Worker's Party and Democratization in Brazil* (Yale University Press).

Marcus LaTour is a contributing author for the Rainforest Action Network in San Francisco.

Maryknoll NewsNotes is a monthly publication of the Maryknoll Peace and Justice Office; P.O. Box 29132, Washington, D.C. 20017.

Paulino Montejo is a contributor to ALAI (*Agencia Latinoamericana de Informacion*—Latin American Information Agency).

Multinational Monitor is a monthly magazine focusing on the social consequences of the world market; P.O. Box 19405, Washington, D.C. 20036.

New Internationalist is a monthly magazine devoted to the struggle for international social and economic justice: P.O. Box 1143, Lewiston, NY 14092.

The Pastoral Land Commission is a Catholic Church human rights and social justice organization in Brazil.

Linda Perny is the Senior Editor of *Audubon* magazine.

John Powers is a freelance journalist in California.

Carlos Ravelo is the Associate Editor of *News from Brazil*.

Ignacy Sachs is the director of studies at the *Ecole des Etudes en Sciences Sociales* in Paris where he currently heads the Research Center on Contemporary Brazil.

Nancy Scheper-Hughes is an anthropology professor at the University of California, Berkeley and the author of *Death Without Weeping: The Violence of Everyday Life in Brazil* (University of California Press, 1992).

Ken Serbin is a writer who frequently contributes to the *National Catholic Reporter*.

Michael Shellenberger is the Brazil Director for Global Exchange and a graduate student at the University of California, Santa Cruz.

Ken Silverstein is the editor of *Counterpunch*, a bi-weekly Washington D.C.-based newsletter.

Maria Clara Couto Soares is an economist with the Brazilian Institute for Social and Economic Affairs (IBASE).

Elizabeth Station is a writer and translator living in Rio de Janeiro.

James S. Torrens is an Associate Editor of *America*.

Index

A

abandonados 208
Abba 192, 193
ABCD region 235
abertura 209
Abrao, Colonel Francisco 115
Acre State Environmental Institute (IMAC)
    112
adjustment policies 8, 12, 13, 14
Afro-Brazilian Catholic 187
Afro-Brazilian Research Dance Company 175
Afro-Brazilian runaway slave colonies 186
agrarian reform 62, 96, 102, 109, 214
    226, 230
agricultural development 14, 26, 120
agricultural policy 15, 107, 121, 226
agriculture 24, 25, 29, 47, 102, 106,
    108, 119-122
agro-chemicals 14, 120
agro-industrial enterprises 116
agroforestry 108
aidético 199
AIDS 170, 197-202
alcohol abuse 14
Alexandre, Mauro Sergio 184
Alliance of the Peoples of the Forest 109
Alves, Darly 109
Alves, João 208
Amato, Mario 70
Almino, Afonso 234
Amazon 17, 19, 20, 22, 23, 24, 25,
    27, 31, 36, 116-119, 123-125,
    127, 130
    occupation of 166
Amazon rainforest 101, 102
Amazon Week II 109
Amazônia Campaign 128
Americas Watch 36, 38, 162
Amnesty Movement 234
Anti-Hunger Campaign 58
antiapartheid movements 186
aquaculture 108
Armed Forces 76, 82, 94, 97, 118
Arrupe, Pedro 190
Articulação 233, 238, 239
Atoba Group 169, 201
aviamento 22, 124
AZT 202

B

Bacha, Edmar 190
balance of payments 8, 11
banks, international 70, 72
Barbalho, Jader 29
Barbosa, Antônio 155
Barbosa, Julio 111
Barreiro, Alvaro 189

Barros, Marcus 207
Becone, Vilmar 120
Begala, Paul 73
Beretta 56
Berman, Marshall 84
biomass 104
biotechnology 11, 104
birth control 163
    coalition against 166
birth rate 163
black Catholics 186, 188
black consciousness movement 174, 175,
    178, 179, 180, 182, 185, 186, 247
black culture 187, 188
Black, William 75
Boff, Leonardo 214
Bolsonaro, Jair 97
Bonotto, Eloni 164, 167
Branco, Marshall Castelo 96
Brazil nuts 23, 28, 29, 30, 123, 124
Brazilian Central Bank 34
Brazilian Congress 155
Brazilian Constitution 107, 152
Brazilian Democratic Movement (MDB) 234
Brazilian Democratic Movement Party (PMDB)
    176
Brazilian fascist movement 77
Brazilian Indians 117, 118
Brazilian Institute for Geography and Statistics
    121, 152
Brazilian Institute of Socio-Economic Affairs
    (IBASE) 58, 265
Brazilian Inter-Disciplinary AIDS Association
    (ABIA) 198
Brazilian Labor Party (PTB) 254
Brazilian Social Democratic Party (PSDB) 73,
    77
Brazilian Society for Family Well-Being
    (BEMFAM) 165
British Common Law system 35
Brizola, Leonel 177
Budget Committees 34
budget cuts 158
Bunger Punta 56
bureaucratic inefficiency 158
Bush, George 210

C

caboclos 106, 136
Caesarian deliveries 164, 166
Caldas, Eduardo Jorge 73
Câmara, Dom Helder 58, 192
Candomble 202
capital investment 30
capitalism 249
    and "excess population" 156
capoeira 161, 175, 180

Carajás 14, 17, 19, 23, 25, 26, 28
Caravana da Cidadania 205
Cardoso, Fernando Henrique 70, 71,
    73, 93, 94, 218, 234, 250, 253
Cardoso, Hamilton 178
Carnival 169
Carvalho, Durval 47, 48
Carville, James 72, 253
Casaldáliga, Pedro 192
Castañeda, Jorge G. 214
Catholic 179
Catholic associations 234
Catholic base communities 238
Catholic Church 96, 109, 181, 186
cattle 117
cattle pasture 36, 126
cattle ranchers 116, 119, 124, 125, 126
cattle ranching 101, 119, 122-126
Center for Advanced Studies in Social Care
    138
Central Unica dos Trabalhadores (CUT) 47,
    48, 236, 240
Central Workers Union 164, 218
Centro de   Estudos Superiores, 189
chemical fertilizers 14
Chiapas 206, 251
child prostitution 245, 246
children 152
    and poverty 154
    artistic activities 161
    homeless 154
    rural 152
    working 152
children's cooperatives 161
children's prisons 159
children's rights 158
Chlopak, Leonard, Schecter & Assoc. 73
Chlopak, Robert 74
Christian Base Communities 190, 193-195
church activists
    intimidation of 162
church and birth control 163, 166
church leaders 159
Citicorp 71
    and Brazilian interest payments 72
Citizenship Caravan 205, 207
civil society 237
civil-rights 186
class cleansing 154
class divisions 249
Clinton, Bill 74, 251
coffee 37
Coimbra, Marcos 78
Collor de Mello, Fernando 48, 49, 62, 70, 75-
    83, 88, 120, 158, 210, 211,
    214, 215, 218, 224
Collor de Mello, Leda 78
Collor, Lindolfo 77
Collor, Pedro 80
colonial economy 20, 21
colonialism 103, 108, 157
colonists 107
colonization 21, 24, 25, 105, 107, 116
    124
Colosio, Luis Donaldo 56
commercial lending 16
Commission of Black Religious, Priests and

Seminarians 174, 187
Communist Party 247
Companhia do Vale do Rio Doce (CVRD) 17,
    18, 27, 28, 30
condoms 197, 198, 201
Congar, Yves 196
constitution 107, 158, 165
contraception 163, 165, 166
Convergencia Socialista 238
Cooper, Adrian 211
Cordeiro, Miriam 215
Correa, Maurício 93
Cost of Living Movement 234
coup, miltary 76, 93, 95, 96
Covas, Mario 77
criminality 122
Cruz Jr., Oswaldo 218

D

da Costa e Silva, Ubiratan 96, 200, 201
da Silva, Benedita 175, 244
da Silva, Luis Ignacio 177
da Silva, Luis Ignacio (Lula) 70, 72, 78, 81,
    205-207, 209-231, 234, 236, 237, 240,
    246, 253, 256
dams 14, 24, 105
Danaher, Kevin 1, 257, 263
Daniel, Herbert 199-203
Davi, Frei 174, 177, 179, 182
de Castro, Josué 58
de Gaulle, Charles 208
de Longchamps, Guy 80
de Macedo, Antonio Luis Batista 110
de Mello, Ana Luiza 78
de Souza, Antonio Maria 114
de Souza, Herbert "Betinho" 58-63, 152, 198,
    199
de Souza, Pedro Ramos 111
death squads 155, 169

debt 9-12, 19, 20, 24, 105, 106, 124, 252
debt peonage 124
debt rescheduling 71
deforestation 26, 37, 101, 105, 106,
    107, 116, 117, 119, 128
deforested land 107
delinquency 159
democracy 232, 241, 242, 253
democracy movement 215
Democratic Social Party 83
Democratic Worker's Party (PDT) 177
democratization
    of media 254
    of state industries 61, 62
Department for the "Protection of Nature" 119
depopulation 21
deregulation 16
developing countries 8, 14, 15, 19, 104
development 12, 13, 14, 15, 19, 25,
    29, 31, 103, 104, 105, 106, 107,
    108, 121, 122, 124, 126, 250
development policies 8, 18, 25, 107, 117,
diarrhea 133
dictatorship 48, 49, 76, 77, 81, 83, 95,
    116, 209, 210, 215, 216
Dignity Group 169

distribution of income 208, 230
do Nascimento, Walmer 158
domestic debt 9
domestic investments 16
domestic savings 16
Dorf, Julie 168
dos Santos, Renildo Jose 170
drug business 33-35, 80
drug lords 159
duty-free zone 106
dwarfs 157

E

ECA 159
Echea Project 117
ecodevelopment 104, 107, 108
ecological agriculture 120
ecology movement 103, 240
economic exploitation 21
economic miracle 157, 250
economic policies 48, 50, 60, 106
ecosystems 104
education 48, 50, 91, 122, 134, 216,
    226
Einstein, Albert 59
elections (1994) 70, 73
elites 60
embranquecimento 185
Emílio-Goeldi museum 114
empate 125
empowerment
    of street children 161
energy industry 252
environment 104, 117-119
environmental destruction 26, 121
environmental education 132, 133
environmental projects 14
environmental protection 104
environmentalists 30, 31, 109, 123, 126
Erundina, Luiza 221, 222
Estima, Luis Fernando 56, 57
European Community 117, 225, 228
exploitative labor 19
export-oriented industry 157
extractive enterprises 19
extractive exports 21, 23
extractive peoples' co-operatives 110
extractive reserves 19, 106, 107, 109,
    110, 112, 119, 123-125, 127, 128
extractivist movement 112

F

family disintegration 14
family planning 163, 165, 166
Farias, P.C. 34, 35, 75, 78, 79, 80, 83
farmers, small 117, 119, 120
Faus, José González 193
favelados 245
favelas 33, 85, 108
    artistic activities 161
Fearnside, Philip 128
feminist critiques 163, 164, 165, 166
Fernando 77, 79, 210
financial crisis
    and child labor 153

fiscal deficit 48
fishing 25, 118, 122
fishing factories 117
FLORAM Plan 107
forced labor 36, 37, 38
foreign capital 11, 12, 227, 228
foreign currency transactions 34
foreign debt 9, 11, 121, 158, 227, 252
foreign debt payments 8, 9
foreign investments 11, 14
foreign markets 19
foreign trade 14
forest conservation 124
forestry 102
Franco, Itamar 48, 81-83, 93-95, 224,
    225
free-market economy 11, 48, 50
free-market policies 217
Freyre, Gilberto 104
Fruition project 135
Fujimori 93

G

G-7 (major industrial countries) 15
Gacek, Stanley M. 39
Gandhi, Rajiv 104
gang rape 114, 115
Garcia, Marco Aurélio 249
garimpeiros 113, 204
Gavião people 29, 30
Gay and Lesbian Human Rights Commission
    168
gay culture 168, 169, 170
Gay Group of Bahia 169, 170
gay killings 170
gay rights movement 169, 170
Geisel, Ernesto 234
Genari, Onésimo 159
Genoíno, José 96, 229
Genro, Tarso 85
Gentry, Alwyn 126
Geography of Hunger, The 58
Gil, Gilberto 168
global warming 101, 103
gold mining 108
gold prospectors 18
gonorrhea 113, 202
Goulart, President João 76, 83, 96, 97
    249
grassroots councils
    and child welfare 159
grassroots movements 49, 109, 110, 118, 119,
    249
grassroots organizers 110
Great Mocorongo Health and Happiness Circus
    131
Greater Carajás Program (PGC) 26
Green Party 202
green revolution 120
Greenberg, Stan 73
greenhouse effect 101, 103
Gross Domestic Product 8-10, 47
Gross National Product 16, 25
Group Nzinga 175
Group of Unity and Black Consciousness 175
Grunwald, Eskew and Donilon 73

Grunwald, Mandy 73
guerrilla movements 96
gun market 56, 57
Gushiken, Luis 229

H

Harrad, David L. 169
Havel, Vaclav 205
Headcold Choir 135
health 132
Health and Happiness Project 131, 136
health care 48, 50, 122, 163, 166, 175
Higino, Ivair 126
HIV 197, 199
homeless children 154, 208
homosexuality 168, 169, 170, 171
housing 34, 48, 50, 122
human rights 110, 185
hunger and malnutrition 58, 117, 157
hydroelectric energy 25, 27

I

IBAMA—Brazil's environmental protection
    agency 110
Ifestel 56
IMF (see International Monetary Fund)
immigration 18
impeachment 75, 76, 81, 82, 210
import substitution 12
income concentration 12, 13
income distribution 166, 230
income tax 226
indebted labor 29
Indian agency (FUNAI) 29
Indians 117, 118
indigenous groups 30, 111
Indigenous Missionary Council 113, 187
indigenous people 20, 107, 110, 111, 118, 122
indigenous rights 26, 31
industrial base 108, 226
industrial capitalism 22
industrial development 12, 14, 19, 24-26, 47,
    224, 225
industrialized countries 16, 103, 104,
    105
inequality 61, 62, 72, 85, 157
inflation 8-10, 12, 48, 71, 88, 208, 253
    monetarist solution to 251
infrastructural projects 17
Institute of Advanced Studies 107
Institute of Economic Botany 126
Institute of Research on Negro Culture 178
Instituto Senghor in Porto Alegre 178
integralism 77
intellectual property rights 11
interest payments 72
    and social spending 158
interest rate 12, 16
internal debt 227
International Monetary Fund (IMF) 8-12, 15,
    71, 121, 191, 251
    and birth control 164
international solidarity 256
International Union for Conservation of Nature
    and 104

intimidation of church activists 162
investments
    international 248
    public 12
iron mines 23, 27
Itaparica dam 14

J

Jaminauá language 114
Japan 255
Japanese Overseas Economic Cooperation Fund
    (OECF) 14
Jeireissati, Tasso 81
Jobs Campaign 59
Johnson, Charles L. 130
Johnson, Lyndon B. 209
justicieros 156

K

Kampas 111
Kaxinawá Indians 110, 111
Kaxinawá, Sia 111
Kiddy Monitor program 133
Kotscho, Ricardo 215

L

labor law 47
labor movement 49
labor rights 48
Lacerda, Carlos 76, 77
land disputes 109
land reform 24, 29, 70, 107, 110, 120-122,
    125, 207, 215
land tenure 24
"laundered" money 33, 34
LDC Debt Report 71
Leadbetter, Philip 168
Lee, Brenda 200, 201
legislative elections 236
Legrands, H.M. 196
Lemos, Mary Ruth 160
Lenten fraternity campaign 188
Leonel, Benedito Onofre Bezerra 94
Leticia, Marisa 212
Liberal Front Party (PFL) 254
Liberation Theology 189-196, 214
lobbying reform 247
logging 101, 123, 126
Lopes, Roberto 95
lumber industry 18, 24, 25, 29

M

Macedo, Antonio 109-112
Macuxi tribe 207, 219
Mãe Maria Indian Reserve 29
Magalhães, Antonio Carlos 82, 218
Mailer, Norman 219
male prostitutes 169
Maluf, Paulo 83, 211, 216
Mandela, Nelson 255
Marabá 17, 23, 27-29
Marinho, Roberto 82, 218
market capitalism 206

marreteiros 114
Martinez, Mario Aburto 56
mass media 87, 155, 254
maternity leave 165
McDonald, Kate 74
Mendelsohn, Robert 126
Mendes, Chico 109, 110, 125, 126, 214
Mercadante, Aloisio 229, 255
Mercosur 228
Metal Workers' Union 87
Metalworkers Union 87, 213, 223
Methodist University 159
migrants 26, 28, 107, 116
migration 25, 27
military 24, 82, 93, 94, 95, 96, 97, 118, 209, 213
military budget 82
military coup (1964) 96, 249
military dictatorship 48, 81, 95, 116, 223, 234
military expense 94
Military Police
    violence against children 90
military regime 24, 26, 233, 235, 238
military rule 76, 232
military's land agency (GETAT) 29
Minas Gerais 61
mine 18, 19, 30
mineral 28, 105, 106
mineral deposits 17, 25
Mineral extraction 26
mineral extraction 26
minerals 17, 205
minerals deposits 25
minerals processing 26
miners 205
minimum wage 215
mining 24, 25, 26, 27, 29
mining company 18
Ministry of Health 163
"minors" and "children" 158
Missouri Botanical Garden 126
MNU 175, 176, 177, 178
modernity 190, 193
modernization 225
Moises 111
Montoro, Franco 176
morality campaign 76
more, reaching 137
Morelli, Mauro 174
morro 245
Mothers Clubs 134
Mott 169
Mott, Luiz 169
Moxafe region 113
mulatto 185
multilateral agencies 16
multilateral agencies' policies 10
murder
    of children 155
Murgel 56, 57
Murgel, Carlos Alberto 56

N

NAAC (Nippon Amazon Aluminum
    Company) 27

Nadal, Jerome 195
Nascimento, Milton 109, 187
National Conference of the Bishops of Brazil 186
National Congress 225
National Convention of Blacks for the Constitution 175
National Council of Churches (U.S.) 162
National Council of Rubber Tappers (CNS) 109, 123, 125
National Democratic Union 77
National Health Foundation 113
National Information Service 82
National Movement of Street Children 158
National Women's Rights Council 166
nationalization 87
natural resources 21, 24, 106, 121
nature reserve 103
negritude 185, 186
neoliberalism 13, 48, 49, 60, 70, 81, 206, 217, 250, 255
neoslavery 184
Neves, Tancredo 233
New Evangelization 192, 196
new evangelization 189
NGOs 14
Nicaraguan revolution 239
Niemeyer, Oscar 84
Nogueira, Zeca 199
nonviolent tactics 125
North American Free Trade Agreement (NAFTA) 228, 255
North-South gap 16

O

OECD countries 16
oligarchy 75, 76, 81, 82
Oliveira, Carlos Alberto 175
Oliveira, Luiz Fernando 186
Organization of American States (OAS) 229

P

Palácio do Planalto 95
Palmares National Park 176
Paracatu' 61
paramilitary 208
Paris Club 252
Parliamentary Inquiry Committee (CPI) 33
Partido dos Trabalhadores (see Workers Party)
Pastoral Agents 185, 186, 187
Pastoral Land Commission 37, 109, 116
patent law 227
PCBR (Revolutionary Brazilian Communist Party) 239
Pela VIDDA 199
Pellegrini, Dr. Marcos 113
Pentateuch 191
Pentecost 195, 196
pentecostalism 180
pesticides 14
Peters, Charles 126
Petrobras 62
petroleum industry 252
Petry, Andri 209-211
PIN (Program for National Integration) 25

Pinheiro, Wilson 126
Pires, Jose Maria 187
Plano Real 71, 72, 253
POLAMAZÔNIA 25
police 24, 38, 119, 184, 208
police discrimination 185
political prisoners 234
political repression 250
pollution
    from human waste 131
popular movements 246
populism 214
Portuguese colonists 21
poverty 13, 58, 60, 157, 164, 208,
    246, 251
poverty line 10, 226
Powers, John 204
presidential campaign
    outside interference in 71
press censorship 234
price controls 253
private investment 26
private property 206
privatization 11-13, 48, 70, 217, 227
    of state industries 252
Program for National Integration (PIN) 25
Project Borneo 128
Project Zumbi 176
property rights 104
prostitution 18, 28, 114, 175
protectionism 15, 105
public health 166, 226

Q

Quadros, Janio 76, 77, 96
Quercia, Orestes 81, 176
quilombos 186

R

racial democracy 176, 180
racial politics 175, 178
racial violence 186
racism 175, 178, 245
Rahner, Karl 193, 195
railroads 17, 18, 26, 27, 29, 30
rainforest 20, 101, 123, 124,
    126, 127, 128
Rainforest Action Network 262
rainforest products 127
Ramos, Pedro 109-112
ranchers 28
ranching 24, 25, 29
Raw materials 19
raw materials 19, 121
recession 10
recolonization 104
reforestation 107, 119
Religious Support Against AIDS (ARCA) 201
renewable resources 104
representative democracy 237
resource extraction 19, 24, 31
Rhodes, William 71
Rio Branco 114
Rio Cajari Extractive Reserve 112
Rio de Janeiro 86, 168, 198

road building 25, 124
Rodrigues, Gomercindo 110, 112
Romero, Oscar 192
Roraima 113
Rosa, Cherubin 94
Rossetto, Miguel 47
Rubber 22
rubber 22, 23, 123, 127
rubber barons 124
rubber tappers 23, 110, 112,
    117-119, 122-125, 127,
    128, 135
rural development 25, 132
rural violence 122
Ruralist Democratic Union 125

S

Saboya, Hélio 156
Sachs, Ignacy 103, 265
Sader, Emir 214
Salinas, President Carlos (Mexico) 251
samba 180, 181
sanitation 48
Santos, David Raimundo 186
Santos, Silvio 209
São Bernardo do Campo
    child welfare 159
São Lourenço 114
Sao Luis Shopworkers Union 165
São Luis Women's Union 164
São Paulo 86, 198
São Paulo's Center of Negro Culture and Art
    175
São Paulo's Council for Black Participation
    176
Sarney, José 81, 123, 233
Schechter, Dr. Mauro 198
Schirmer, Pedro 95
school drop-out rate 157
School of Forestry at Yale 126
Sclan, Shellie 84, 89
Seineldín, Mohamed Ali 95
self-help clinics 166
sensationalism
    in the media 155
seringalistas 22, 124
seringueiros 106, 107, 111, 124
Serpa, Ivan 94
Serra, Gilberto 94
Serra Pelada 28
sexual abuse 114
sexually transmitted diseases 165
shanty-towns (see *favelas*)
Shellenberger, Michael 1, 244, 249, 255, 265
Silverstein, Ken 64, 70, 214
slavery 21, 174, 247
Smith & Wesson 57
Soares, Jo 197
Social Democratic Party 216
social exclusion 250, 254
social groups 117
social injustice 190
social movements 235, 237, 240
social policy 60
social problems 121
social programs 117

social reform 122
social service infrastructure 18
socialism 206, 232, 233, 238, 240, 241, 249
soldiers
    attacks on women and children 114
    in the Amazon 113, 114
South Africa 255
Soviet Union 255
Station, Elizabeth 197, 265
Statute on Children and Adolescents (ECA)
    159
sterilization
    facts and figures 163
    female 163, 164, 165, 166, 167, 245
    male 164
    pressure from employers 165
street children 157
    as structural problem 160
    killing of 245
structural adjustment 10, 49
student movement 49
sugar cane 20, 37
Suplicy, Eduardo 240
supply-side economics 251
Support Group for the Prevention of AIDS
    (GAPA) 201
sustainable development 14, 16, 117
Swaminathan, Monkombu S. 104
syphilis 202

T

Tapajo 20, 21
Taurus International Manufacturing Inc. 56, 57
tax evasion 50, 226
tax reform 253
tax "safe-havens" 35
taxes 15, 214, 226
technology 12, 47, 104
telecommunications industry 252
telenovelas 88
television 167
Tenorio, Marcelo 168, 169
terms of trade 105
timber plantation 126
Timoteo, Agnaldo 177
Torrens, James S. 189, 265
torture 155
tourism 85
trade deficit 8
trade liberalization 11
trade surplus 9
trade unions 47-55, 209, 212, 213, 235
Transamazon Highway 116
transvestites 168, 169, 200
tropical rainforest 116
tubal ligation 163, 166

U

U.S. Federal Reserve system 71
U.S. Steel 17
U.S. Treasury Department 34
Umbanda 180, 181, 202
UNDP (United Nations Development Program)
    13, 16
unemployment 10, 13, 27, 225, 229, 246

Unicamp University 249
UNICEF 154
Unified Negro Movement (MNU) 175
United Nations 103, 109, 229, 245
    mission statement 61
United Nations Population Division 165
United States 2, 70-74, 255, 258, 259
United States Information Agency 84
Upper Jurua Extractive Reserve 111
urban violence 13
urbanization 106, 190

V

Vargas, Getulio 76, 77, 83, 96
Varig 199
Vatican 187
Veja 153, 209
Veloso, Caetano 168, 197
violence 58, 88, 89
    against children 154-162
    business-funded 155
violence, structural 246
Visconti, Francisco E. 95
von Balthasar, Hans Urs 195

W

wage controls 253
Walesa, Lech 205
Walters, General Vernon 70
Washington Consensus 10
Washington Consensus doctrine 11
wealth
    concentration of 72, 157, 251
White, Theodore 219
women's movement 247
Workers Party (PT) 70, 72, 78, 81, 82, 84,
    159, 177, 205, 206, 208, 211, 213-218,
    220, 221, 223, 224, 229-242, 245, 246,
    249, 255
    and black movement 247
    and women's movement 247
    structure of 246
World Bank 8-16, 25, 117, 130, 257-259, 262
world economy 16
world trade 16

Y

Yanomami Indians 113, 118, 204
Year 2000 Without Hunger 58

Z

Ze Pelintre 84
Zumbi 181

GLOBAL ⊙ EXCHANGE

Reality Tours

ENJOY adventure travel in some of the world's most controversial and beautiful places. On Global Exchange reality tours participants meet local people, appreciate other cultures, learn about the most pressing issues confronting the world today, while having a great time! Our experienced trip leaders will introduce you to some of the most exciting people and issues of the day.

Global Exchange organizes regular reality tours to the following destinations:

Cuba, Mexico, Honduras, Haiti, Senegal, Vietnam, Cambodia, South Africa, Puerto Rico, El Salvador, Brazil, Guatemala, Chile, Bolivia, Panama, Nicaragua, India, Washington, DC,
and more...

What is included in a Reality Tour?

Most of our seminar packages include round-trip airfare from Miami, Los Angeles, San Francisco or New York, double room accommodations, all transportation inside the country (including ground and air travel), two meals per day, translation of all programs, a qualified trip leader, seminar fees and reading materials. Global Exchange will also arrange personal meetings to suit your particular interests (as available).

Contact:
Global Exchange,
2017 Mission St. Rm. 303,
San Francisco, CA 94110
(415) 255-7296 or
(800) 497-1994

GLOBAL ⊙ EXCHANGE

JOIN US!

YES! I want to help Global Exchange build a strong internationalist movement. As a member I will receive:

☆ A free copy of *The Peace Corps and More: 120 Ways to Work, Study and Travel in the Third World*
☆ The quarterly newsletter *Global Exchanges* informing me of Global Exchange activities and trends in the internationalist movement
☆ Regular updates on the Global Exchange tour program
☆ Priority consideration on tours, often limited to 12-15 people
☆ 10% discount on Global Exchange crafts and educational materials

Name_____

Address_____

City_____State_____ Zip_____

Phone_____

❑ Enclosed is my tax-deductible membership donation of:

___$35 ___$50 ___$100

___ other ___$25 (low-income)

❑ Please send me more information about your Reality Tours

Send to:
Global Exchange, 2017 Mission St.
Rm. 303, San Francisco, CA 94110
(415) 255-7296

Please charge to my
❑ VISA
❑ MASTERCARD

Card #_____ - _____

_____ - _____

Expiration Date_____

Name on card_____